THE SUPERNATURAL

THE SUPERNATURAL

A Guide to Mysticism and the Occult

ANTHONY NORTH

BLANDFORD

A BLANDFORD BOOK
First published in the UK 1998
by Blandford, a Cassell imprint
Cassell plc
Wellington House, 125 Strand, London WC2R 0BB
Text copyright © 1998 Anthony North

Distributed in the United States by Sterling Publishing Co., Inc.,
387 Park Avenue South, New York, NY 10016–8810

A Cataloguing-in-Publication Data entry for this title is available from the British Library

ISBN 0–7137–2728–4

Design by Gwyn Lewis

Printed and bound in Great Britain by MPG Books Ltd, Bodmin, Cornwall

· CONTENTS ·

· INTRODUCTION ·

■ Many years ago I knew a mystical young man who could charm bees. Standing in a field, he could hold out his palm, and seconds later they would land in his hand. Delicately, he would stroke them.

Several people warned me of his weirdness. A placid young man, he could, however, curse those who upset him. Obviously, I dismissed this as superstition. Then, one day in February 1982, he cursed me. To this day, I cannot decide what he said to me, but a curse it undoubtedly was: two weeks later I passed out at the wheel of my car, nearly killing my wife and family. On that fateful day I also came down with what is now known as chronic fatigue syndrome, and I have suffered it in varying degrees from that day to this.

Is my condition the result of that young man's curse? Believers would no doubt say yes. My own logical mind rejects such a notion, but the implication still remains.

This is just one event of many in my life that eventually led me to undertake an investigation of the supernatural. Some of these events are far easier to understand than the young man's curse. Typical was the day my wife visited a fortune teller. Determined not to make it easy for her, my wife removed her wedding ring. Subsequently, a major part of the reading concerned my wife's deceit, both from the past and in the future . . . It is so very difficult to disguise where a ring has been worn after so many years.

Most people will openly declare their scepticism of the supernatural and, in the light of incidents such as my wife's visit to the fortune teller, this is understandable. But on many occasions I have spoken in detail to such sceptics, and when talking openly and in confidence their own scepticism is revealed to be a mask to hide their true thoughts from the scepticism of a wider public. Many researchers believe cover-ups are involved in areas of the paranormal – particularly in the strange world of UFOs – yet the real cover-up is not imposed by governments but concocted in the mind of the individual. Even major figures have had supernatural experiences, but have hidden the fact for years through fear of ridicule. Typical among these was the famed aviator, Charles Lindbergh.

His great adventure began when he was a US government airmail pilot. An excellent aviator with the tenacity of a future history maker, Charles Lindbergh began the walk on his road of destiny when he heard of the $25,000 prize offered by Raymond B. Orteig for the first non-stop flight from New York to Paris. Convincing a group of St Louis businessmen to back him, he had them build the 220-horsepower Ryan monoplane which became famous as *The Spirit of St Louis*. On the morning of 20 May 1927 Lindbergh departed from New York, and following a gruelling 33-hour solo flight, he landed at Le Bourget, Paris, on the night of 21 May.

Lindbergh returned a national hero. A ticker-tape welcome awaited him in New York – and rightly so. His heroic deed had opened up the Atlantic airway, and set the scene for the growth of transatlantic trade that would propel the United States to the forefront of multinational enterprise. A folk hero for material society, Lindbergh's place in history was guaranteed. Yet it wasn't until 26 years later, with the publication of his book *The Spirit of St Louis* (see Bibliography), that he told the full story of his epic flight and the fantastic experience that guaranteed his success.

Lindbergh's flight is depicted wonderfully in the film named after his aircraft. Taken through the historic journey by amiable Jimmy Stewart, we arrive at a brief scene where, overcome by fatigue, Lindbergh is on the point of collapse. But in typical Hollywood fashion, he is saved: the clouds disperse, and a ray of sunshine reflects from a pendant above his control panel and dazzles him, bringing him back to consciousness. Hollywood is marvellous at depicting such mythical moments, but in this instance there is only one word to describe the scene – and that word is understatement.

His moment of destiny close, Lindbergh was tired before he even set off on his flight, and by the ninth hour exhaustion had all but overtaken him. He struggled to stay awake, but the drone of the engines became mesmeric. However, rather than falling asleep, he began to feel detached from reality, as if in a state between wakefulness and sleep. He called this state an 'unearthly age of time', and he soon began to feel that he was not a single living thing but three separate entities – a fatigued body, a mind, and a growing driving force from within which he could only describe as spirit. He described the experience thus:

I'm on the borderline of life and a greater realm beyond, as though caught in the field of gravitation between two planets, acted on by forces I can't control, forces too weak to be measured by any means at my command, yet representing powers incomparably stronger than I've ever known . . .

His 'spirit' from within comforted him, told him that he didn't need sleep and that he could go on, for his body would be revitalized through relaxation. As for the possibility of death should he fall asleep, this was no longer a problem: 'Death no longer seemed the final end it used to be, but rather the entrance to a new and free existence which included all space, all time.' And while these feelings were going on within, an even more amazing experience was unfolding in the cockpit around him.

Suddenly the fuselage was filled with ghostly presences. Vague in outline, transparent, almost weightless, they passed in and out of the airframe, existing both inside and in the air around the aircraft. No matter where they were, Lindbergh could see them, for his skull had become 'one great eye', allowing unlimited vision even behind him. Yet these were not frightening but comforting presences which spoke to him in friendly voices. They talked about the flight, reassuring him and offering 'messages of importance unattainable in ordinary life'. Lindbergh described himself as 'almost one with these vapour-like forms behind me, less tangible than air, universal as ether'. And they were truly benevolent entities, for Lindbergh did not fall asleep, and did not die, but went on to achieve his dream.

How do we account for such experiences? Do we class these entities as supernatural spirits, observed because Lindbergh actually had approached heaven's door? Or do we discount the experience as an hallucination provided by a tired, fatigued mind? Regardless of which explanation you choose, you are, however, left with a clearly paranormal event which amounted to far more than just the experience itself. Whether these were some other-worldly entities or simply the delusions of his own mind, their guidance, their assurance and their benevolence invigorated Lindbergh and allowed him to complete his task. At a time when his body was finished, from some deep supernatural or psychological centre a power had risen to propel him to near superhuman abilities. Moreover, this paranormal event had not propelled only Lindbergh, for in his success the whole of mankind took an important step along its incessant road of technological evolution.

This is an important point to make. Human advancement is usually seen as the product of rational human endeavour. The mystical experiences of Buddha, of Moses, of Muhammad, even the abilities of Jesus, are regarded by material science as mythologies, used as a means of understanding for the people of their time – but such debunking does a disservice to the wider abilities of humanity, and the role the paranormal plays within it. Science would not have achieved the successes it has without characters such as Kepler and Newton, both of whom were mystics as well as scientists. And the road to rational thought itself began with the philosopher René Descartes, who began his road to reason with a series of inexplicable dreams.

Time and again scientists ridicule the paranormal, relegating it to the preserve of cranks, conmen or acute psychosis. The latest in this distinguished line of sceptics is Dr Richard Dawkins, who ridicules the whole of the paranormal and points to high-profile psychics as proof of the subject's stupidity. With some psychic superstars he may have a point, but to dismiss the entire subject out of hand is to abandon the spirit of scientific enquiry and revert to simple dogma. For in dismissing the subject we must assume, by implication, that Charles Lindbergh was either a liar or mad – yet neither can realistically be seen to be the case.

Paranormal events happen. Consider my own experiences of the night of 14 December 1996. That evening my family and I were watching television, my wife doing the ironing while she watched. Within the programme we were watching, the host staged an elaborate hoax upon psychic superstar Uri Geller, famed for psychically mending watches and bending spoons throughout the country during his television performances. During the hoax, a stoodge came up to Geller and advised him that during one such episode he had broken the stoodge's clock. A few moments later Geller realized that something was wrong with the whole scenario and that the lady with whom he was having dinner was lying to him. You could see this growing realization on his face, and as the knowledge dawned my wife's iron suddenly burnt out, badly scorching the ironing board. Amazed by this, she phoned her mother to tell her what had happened: her mother had just checked the entire house because she could smell burning and had seen a haze of smoke, yet nothing in the house was on fire.

Being familiar with the idea that paranormal events can come in clusters – a subject we will discuss later (see page 193) – I took out my National Lottery ticket and told my wife that when the draw came on the television she should hold the ticket and concentrate on the numbers in the hope that events would conspire to cause further coincidence. In light-hearted fashion, she agreed, but just before the draw our baby daughter woke up and my wife went upstairs to bring her down, leaving me with the lottery ticket. The first five numbers were drawn before she came back downstairs. I had none of them. Quickly, I thrust the ticket into her hand. The sixth number was 34, which I had. The bonus number was 44, which I also had. Jokingly, I lamented her failure to make me a millionaire.

Scientists dismiss such episodes as pure coincidence, with no meaning to them at all. They could well be right, but can offer no proof of this assumption other than the word – 'coincidence' – which is no explanation at all, simply the upholding of a belief system. I am not prepared to explain such events by a simple denial; rather, I go in search of possible mechanisms to explain them. However, such mechanisms do not have to be supernatural. Indeed, some apparently inexplicable experiences do not even have to be paranormal, as I found out one night when I saw an angel.

It was windy that night – not so windy as to be a gale, but significantly more than a simple breeze. I was late going to bed, so when I eventually went up to the bedroom I was tired and ready for sleep. However, before I was able to get into bed a gust of wind blew up against the window and I peered out to check how bad it was.

It was then that I saw my angel in the garden next door. About 1 foot (30 cm) off the ground was a cluster of golden lights. Brilliant and sparkling, they held a beauty all of their own and the sight of them was mesmeric. For a moment I believed in the divine, and as I watched this 'supernatural' entity a peacefulness came over me. Eventually – I don't know how long I watched my angel, for time was an irrelevance – I went to bed, and had one of the best night's sleep I had ever had.

At no time during the experience did I question the angel's existence, but the following morning I went out to see if anything of a more down to earth nature could have caused the phenomenon. At the time, the neighbours were carrying out some alterations, and there was a pile of bricks in the front garden at the point where my angel had appeared. Caught between two bricks was an empty crisp packet, ripped open and exposing its reflective inside. In an experiment on the following windy night, I again observed my beautiful, golden angel – a reflection of an orange street light upon an empty packet of crisps.

Such an episode could easily have been seen as some form of divine or paranormal intervention upon life. Indeed, even to my trained mind the image was appealing and went on to cleanse and calm my mind, evidenced by my good night's sleep. But the trained mind eventually clicks into gear, and quite rightly produced caution concerning this particular event.

I learned such caution many years ago. During the 1980s there were a number of inexplicable disappearances of large flocks of homing pigeons over the sea. The paranormal research community went into full gear, offering explanations from bursts of solar energy confusing the pigeons to UFO abductions.

Then one day I got into conversation with a pigeon fancier. I told him of these disappearances, and some of the explanations offered. He smirked and advised me of the confusion pigeons experience over water when they see their reflection on the surface. It usually causes them to fly so close to the water that many pigeons can be lost if a sudden wave comes along, dragging them into the sea.

I do not know if this is the explanation for all those lost pigeons, but I do know that it is possible, and equally that no paranormal researcher suggested it. Paranormal events do happen, but perhaps not as often as is thought. Simpler explanations can occasionally be offered, and even when real paranormality breaks out it is still valid to offer the simplest explanation possible.

This book is about such paranormal experiences as these – but this statement needs to be qualified. The word 'paranormal' is usually taken to mean an experience that is beyond normal. This is distinctly different to 'supernatural', which is seen as the influence of forces beyond the natural world – forces from some mystical 'other world'. Personally, I am uneasy about either meaning. Consider the following.

Professor Arthur Ellison – one of the few modern scientists who has dared to move into psychical research – once carried out a fascinating experiment. During a lecture he had rigged a bowl of flowers next to him to rise into the air and slowly descend again. During this 'event', he carried on as if nothing was happening. At the end of the lecture, when it was time for questions, a few individuals bravely commented that they had seen the flowers levitate.

These individuals can be classed as thinking they had seen a 'paranormal' experience; an event that was 'beyond normal'. However, it then became clear that others had had a more defined experience, for some had seen 'spirit hands' lift the flowers. To them, the experience had been 'supernatural', in that 'otherworldly' forces had intervened in the physical world. However, there was also a third experience involved – for the rationalists in the audience had not seen the event at all. The rising of flowers into the air by no apparent means was alien to their world view, and their psychology was such that the event had not even been recognized.

The event was, of course, fraudulent, but none of the experiencers knew that at the time. However, this experiment demonstrates perfectly that an unusual event can be seen in different ways, depending upon the world view of the experiencer. Whether paranormal, or supernatural, or not happening at all, the value of the event belongs to the mind of the individual rather than to the event itself. And this brings me to the central theme of this book.

In the following pages, events are not as important as the perception of such events. We all exist in the same world, but we all have different ways of relating to it. With such a psychology, 'labels' such as paranormal or supernatural bear more importance to perception than to the actual reality. In a real sense, we see what we want to see. Yet what processes are involved when we 'see' such events?

Vital to the world view of every individual is the 'culture' to which he or she belongs. Culture is the definer of the outside world – the filter through which we interact with reality. So omnipotent is its hold that if floating flowers do not enter a particular world view, then the experience is cancelled out of reality. Hence, this book is not so much about the paranormal or the supernatural as the culture through which we relate to such phenomena. And in approaching phenomena from this cultural perspective – in arguing that a cultural force exists above the idiosyncrasies of the individual – this book is also an analysis of God.

· SYMPATHY OF SOULS ·

Moral Ghosts

■ In the final year of his reign, the Egyptian Pharaoh Akhnaton quarrelled with his daughter. In revenge, he had his priests rape and murder her. Cutting off her right hand, they buried her secretly in the Valley of the Kings. This was a particularly sadistic act, for in being buried without her hand, her body was not intact and she could not go to paradise.

Over 3,000 years later, the occultist Count Louis Hamon visited the city of Luxor. The year was 1890, and the count used his occult powers to cure a prominent Egyptian of malaria. Healed, the Egyptian insisted upon giving the count the mummified hand of a long-dead princess. Hamon's wife thought the gift revolting, so upon returning home the count locked it away in a safe – and there it remained until 1922, when his wife opened the safe and was amazed to discover that the hand was no longer shrivelled, but softened with new flesh.

Together, the count and his wife decided to give the hand a proper funeral. Hamon laid it in the fireplace and began to read a passage from the Egyptian *Book of the Dead*. As he did so, the house shook from a crash of thunder and a sudden wind blew the door open, revealing the apparition of a beautiful Egyptian princess, her right arm ending in an ugly stump. The princess walked across the room and bent over the fireplace. A moment later, she disappeared, taking the mummified hand with her.

This tale represents the very stuff of the supernatural. It has all the hallmarks of a classic ghost story, designed to titillate, appal and terrify the superstitious – an effect made ominously worse as the tale is said to be true. However, as with most ghost stories of antiquity, while a shred of truth may well exist, the bulk of the story can be discounted as embellishment and myth-making.

A similar analysis can hopefully be made of events following the sinking of

14

the yacht *Pierrot* in the Atlantic in July 1884. Only four men survived the event: Captain Edwin Rutt, mate Josh Dudley, and seamen Dick Tomlin and Will Hoon. Adrift in a dinghy, it was to be 25 days before they were picked up by the *Gellert*. Or at least, three of them were, for Tomlin had been partially eaten after being killed following the drawing of lots.

Such cannibalism has been reverted to both before and since, and although the surviving trio were initially sentenced to death for murder, this was later commuted to six months' imprisonment. Dudley eventually found work as a drayman, but one day, as he drove his horses down a foggy London street, they bolted, sending him flying to the cobblestones and shattering his head. Witnesses later said that they had seen a ghostly figure in the fog swathed in bloodstained bandages; a figure that had obviously spooked the horses.

Vengeful ghosts were, of course, all the rage in nineteenth-century England, but the ghost of Dick Tomlin was a particularly busy one. Soon Captain Rutt heard of the fate of Dudley and went in search of Will Hoon to warn him. He found him in a drunken stupor in a bar in London's Soho. Hoon ended up in a charity hospital and eventually died during a particularly harrowing screaming fit, aided – according to witnesses – by another patient dressed in bandages, who held him down before vanishing into thin air.

By this time Rutt was in a state of terror. He went to the police, gibbering about a ghost who was out to get him. The police didn't believe him, but considering his agitated state, they decided to allow him to spend the night in a cell. At three o'clock the following morning the police rushed to the cell following a particularly blood-curdling scream. They found Rutt's corpse, eyes staring in terror, a shred of bloodstained bandage held tightly in his hand.

Again, the rational mind can easily discount most of this story. But also again, we can see a distinct psychology at work within the tale, with guilt leading to alcoholism and mental instability, and the embellishments adding a form of cultural taboo to cannibalism. In the story's telling, a severe moral message is highlighted.

This is a point that is often forgotten in relation to ghosts. Throughout history, the supernatural has played an important moral role in society. In the deep past, such a moralizing form went on to birth mythologies, and it was through such mythologies that a culture identified itself. Sadly, such mythologies are no longer given any importance, modern society preferring to find answers only in rationalism, and as a result tales such as that of the ghost of Dick Tomlin are said to be the inventions of crazy people or fraudsters. In our materialist culture, they clearly are, but to a more believing society the moral of the tale was of greatest importance, the actual truth of the matter taking second place to this vital social role.

Sometimes, the moral imperative was not for society as such, but was born from the guilt of an unfulfilled promise. One such embellished tale grew from events surrounding Burton Agnes Hall, a Jacobean country house near Driffield in Yorkshire. Built by three spinster sisters in the seventeenth century, shortly after its completion one of the sisters, Anne, was robbed and badly beaten. She died shortly afterwards, but before dying she made her sisters promise that after her death they would chop off her head and place it within the walls of her beloved home.

The sisters were horrified at the idea and lied to their sister simply to comfort her before she died. She was therefore not decapitated but buried intact. However, a week after her burial doors began to slam throughout the house. By the third week the ghostly happenings had increased, and the sisters regularly heard people running through the echoing corridors.

Frightened, they contacted the vicar. They told him of Anne's dying wish, and the vicar had her body exhumed. Anne's head had become detached from her body, and decomposition was so advanced that it was now a bare skull. The sisters took the skull to the house and the hauntings ceased. Now known as Awd Nance, the skull has been temporarily removed from the hall by the current occupants. It is said that every time this is done, the hauntings begin once more.

Again, we have an apparently ridiculous story, but in a macabre way the tale can be seen as reinforcing family values and advising of the consequences of dishonesty. However, the moral imperative is not the only theme of the ghost story: heartbreak surrounding love is also a popular theme. Typical is the most persistent ghost of a woman dressed in brown who has been said to haunt Raynham Hall near Fakenham in Norfolk since the early eighteenth century.

The woman is said to be Dorothy Walpole, sister of British Prime Minister Sir Robert Walpole. Dorothy lived in Raynham Hall with her father, who was made guardian of 13-year-old Charles Townshend. Dorothy and Charles grew up together and eventually fell in love, but when they wanted to get married, Dorothy's father refused them. Charles eventually married a baron's daughter and, distraught, Dorothy left the hall and went to London and then Paris, scandalizing society by setting up house with a known womanizer.

In 1711 Charles's wife died and Dorothy headed back to Raynham Hall. Knowing nothing of Dorothy's recent escapades, he married her at last. But he soon began to hear the tales of her exploits in Paris, and in disgust he imprisoned her in her rooms. And there she remained for the next ten years until her death. However, within days her ghost was seen by servants, and from that day to this the ghost of Dorothy Walpole has periodically haunted the hall, finding the building's oak staircase particularly attractive.

The first famous haunting, however, had to wait until 1786, when King George III was said to be staying at the hall. Waking during the night, he saw the brown-clad lady standing by his bed. Following this incident, the Townshends began a nightly vigil. They only had to wait a few nights before the lady was again observed walking down a corridor. One of the witnesses moved forward to confront her and she walked straight through him, leaving him chilled to the bone.

Another famous haunting occurred one night around Christmas 1835. Colonel Loftus, a relation of the Townshends, was staying at the hall when he saw the lady. He described her as wearing her normal brown attire, but the apparition had taken on a more sinister nature: she had no eyes, just black hollows where they should have been.

Several years later, the author Captain Frederick Marryat stayed at Raynham Hall. A sceptic, he had ridiculed the stories of such hauntings. Because of this, he purposely stayed in a room which had a portrait of Dorothy Walpole hanging on the wall. Late that night Marryat and other guests observed her. As they ran into a room, Dorothy followed them, grinning wickedly as she stood in the doorway. Sceptic Marryat was driven to such terror that he fired a shot at her, presumably a sceptic no more.

However, perhaps Dorothy's most famous haunting took place in 1936. Two photographers had been commissioned by the then Lady Townshend to take pictures of the hall. Dutifully, they set up their camera to take a shot of the oak staircase. Suddenly, a vapour-like shape began to take form on the stairs. One of the photographers saw the shape and told the other to expose the plate. In the flash the shape disappeared, but the developed plate showed the vague outline of a woman, dressed in bridal veil and gown.

The brown lady of Raynham Hall is different to the moral ghost story in a number of ways, not least the apparition's persistence – she has been seen for over two centuries and even posed for a photograph. It would appear that there is a greater element of reality involved here.

Ghost investigator Andrew Green would say that such 'ghosts' are electro-magnetic energy between 380 and 440 millimicrons in the infra-red section of the light spectrum. Gaining long-overdue fame in 1996 after spending a night looking for a ghost in the Royal Albert Hall accompanied by a posse of reporters, Green's interest in ghosts began in 1944, when he was 16 years old.

At this time Green's father – an ex-policeman – was a rehousing officer, part of whose responsibilities it was to find empty buildings in which to store furniture from bombed-out houses. Number 16 Montpelier Road, Ealing, London, had been empty since 1934. The building had an infamous reputation: a murder had been committed there, and there had been 20 suicides associated with an adjacent 65-feet-high (20m) tower. Rumours abounded that the place was haunted.

Green's father went to check out the viability of the building as storage space, and as it was supposedly haunted, he asked young Andrew if he wanted to see the place. Andrew eagerly went with him. However, once installed at the top of the tower, he had the strangest sensation and felt the urge to climb over the parapet. Had his father not seen this strange action and hauled him back, Andrew Green is quite convinced that he would have been suicide number 21.

Outside the house once more, Green got out his camera and took a photograph to show his friends. When it was developed, he was surprised to see the image of a small girl's face peering above some curtains from a first-floor window. Investigation showed that three of the suicides were children, and after sending the film to both Kodak and Ilford, Green was satisfied that it had not been tampered with. Surprisingly, Kodak informed Green that it was not unusual to get a photograph of an image that couldn't actually be seen, especially if Verichrome had been used, which it had. Such a photographic emulsion could record images between 380 and 440 millimicrons in the infra-red.

Does this mean that ghosts actually do exist? Green would say no – they are heat images generated by someone thinking of their loved one. When a person dies, someone who loved the deceased would obviously think about the death, including the scene where it occurred. Such thoughts place a heat image of the deceased upon the location. Occasionally when another heat source is present at the location, such as a visiting person, the 'ghostly' heat source regenerates and the visitor sees the image, or ghost.

Such an explanation has not, of course, been scientifically validated. But then again, no scientist has seriously bothered to check out its viability. However, as well as offering a tentative explanation of how a ghostly image can appear on a photograph, Green's experience in Ealing is interesting because of the urge he felt to throw himself off the tower.

Similar experiences had been felt by researcher Tom Lethbridge and his wife, Mina. Lethbridge had spent most of his life as Keeper of Anglo-Saxon Antiquities at Cambridge, but in 1957 he retired to Hole House, a Tudor mansion on the south coast of Devon. His next-door neighbour was an elderly woman who professed to be witch. His interest in psychical research began one night when his wife woke up with the eerie feeling that there was someone in the bedroom. The next morning the 'witch' informed them that she had visited their bedroom while engaged in astral travel.

Three years later the witch died in suspicious circumstances. Shortly after this, while passing the witch's cottage Lethbridge experienced a deep sense of depression. Walking around the cottage, he discovered that this feeling seemed to be more a property of the environment than of his own mind, for he could literally walk into and out of the area of depression. This reminded him of an experience he had had as a teenager, when he was out walking with his mother near Wokingham. Suddenly they had both experienced a feeling of gloom and depression and had hurried away. A few days later the body of a suicide was discovered at the exact spot.

There are obvious similarities here to Green's experience on top of the tower in Ealing, as if something in the environment is willing the person to action. Indeed, Lethbridge's continued research on the subject showed amazing parallels. About a year after the death of the witch, Tom and Mina Lethbridge drove to Ladram Bay to collect seaweed. As Lethbridge stepped on to the beach he again experienced a feeling of depression. Mina soon felt it too and decided that there was something frightful there. Most interestingly of all, on a subsequent visit the following weekend Mina walked to the top of the cliff. She felt the depression again and had the oddest feeling that something was urging her to jump off.

Lethbridge went on to associate these fields of depression with magnetic fields produced by water. Calling them 'ghouls', he became convinced that the same fields could produce ghosts. Basically, the feeling of depression was caused by the high emotion of a tragic event at the particular location, creating the magnetic field.

Most logically minded people would scoff at such ideas. However, a grain of acceptability comes from the work of Michael Persinger, a professor of psychology and neuroscience at Laurentian University in Sudbury, Ontario. Persinger is particularly interested in the effects of low-level electromagnetic stimulation of areas of the brain.

Using what he calls his 'heaven and hell' chamber, he seats subjects in a room and places apparatus similar to a bizarre motorcycle helmet on their heads. The 'helmet' places solenoids on the head, and he goes on to direct pulses into the amygdala and hippocampus, which are involved with interpreting information from the senses and memory respectively. Shaking up the neural networks in this way, Persinger believes that the invasion of electromagnetic energy affects levels of melatonin in the brain, the end result being the sudden experience of imagery and deep feelings, which have been extreme. Subjects have experienced everything from visions of ghosts, gods, aliens and devils, to feelings of abject terror, possession by demons and ecstatic mystical experiences.

The brain is, intriguingly, often bombarded by unusual pulses of electromagnetic radiation, suggesting that the environment can cause ghostly encounters.

Typically, such experiences can be caused by the close proximity of power cables, earthquake activity and the build-up of electromagnetic activity prior to thunderstorms. It therefore appears that the mythology of the good old thunderstorm associated with hauntings is not a fallacy. Similarly, although earthquake shudders may be relatively rare in many areas, we constantly experience earth movement, especially in specific localized areas. As for high-voltage power cables, few people these days are not living in close proximity to them. The mind and our environment are involved in a close interplay with one another, and there is now little doubt that strange experiences can be triggered by such a relationship. However, such experiences can equally well be triggered by other factors.

Contrary to popular mythology, we are all natural hallucinators. An hallucination, while most commonly associated with mental instabilities such as schizophrenia, can nevertheless be induced in us all. The reality we all experience is caused by the constant bombardment of sensory images; the mind is predisposed to analyse these images and produce the sense experiences we all take for granted. However, this clear interpretation of reality is totally dependent upon receiving these constant images. Should sensory images cease, or, alternatively, our ability to process information from the images wane, the mind is then predisposed to seek out interpretations of reality based more on our inner fantasies than on an exact external reality.

This is the process through which hypnosis is believed to work. By tampering with our interpretations of reality, the hypnotist can produce in the hypnotized person an hallucination. However, such an hallucinatory state can equally come into being for no other reason than tiredness, which can affect a person's ability to process outside stimuli from sensory experience. It is for this reason that most ghostly experiences occur when we are near sleep, or when we are woken up in the middle of the night. Similarly, prolonged driving or driving when tired can also cause – and is infamous for – ghostly experiences.

All this theorizing suggests that ghosts are our very close bedfellows. However, rather than being of supernatural cause, they can be better understood as psychological manifestations of a tired mind or one bombarded by electromagnetic radiation. But while such an explanation can be used to understand the mechanics of the experience, it fails to explain the phenomenon of ghosts in their entirety, as evidenced by the appearance of the ghosts of Bluebell Hill.

Ghosts and ESP

■ Bluebell Hill is a fairly steep incline on the A229 in Kent. As with most stretches of road, it has had its share of accidents, but none was more tragic than the crash between a Ford Cortina and a Jaguar one night in November 1965. The occupants of the Jaguar survived, as did one of the four girls in the Ford Cortina, but sadly Judith Lingham, Patricia Ferguson and Suzanne Brown died. All in their early twenties, even more tragic was the fact that Suzanne was to have been married the following day.

Since then there have been many authenticated sightings of ghosts on Bluebell Hill. For instance, in 1968 a local paper received some 90 telephone calls from people claiming to have seen ghostly images on the hill, mainly in November, the anniversary of the crash. Sean Taylor, who has investigated the case, knows of 18 definite sightings, some of them particularly nerve-racking.

Consider two cases from 1975. In the first, a taxi driver picked up a distressed girl on the hill. The driver took her to the house at which she said she lived. Later, he returned to check that she was all right: there was no girl there. Ten years earlier, however, a girl *had* lived there – it was Judith Lingham's home. Later that same year, another driver rushed into a police station saying he had run into a girl on the hill. He had left his coat over the body at the side of the road. When the police arrived at the scene, there was no body to be found.

Even as late as 1992, the sightings were continuing to happen. One night a coach driver was driving home from work in his car. Suddenly a girl stepped out in front of him and disappeared under his bonnet. He jumped out of the car and was shocked to find no one there. The police later said the driver was greatly agitated by the experience. Taylor later showed the driver photographs of the girls – he recognized Patricia Ferguson immediately.

The first point to note about the ghosts of Bluebell Hill is that they are free from mythological embellishment. While ghost stories were rife up to the nineteenth century, as the twentieth century has progressed they have become less and less acceptable to the general population. Hence, while the experiencer of a ghost was likely to be believed in times past, they are more likely to be ridiculed today, and there is therefore no conceivable reason for people to make up such stories. Rather, there are incentives for them to shut up about them. So, whether such cases assault our sensibilities or not, it has to be accepted that the events really happened, as described. But what, exactly, *did* happen?

The theories of Andrew Green and Tom Lethbridge break down under such circumstances. At best, such theories allow the sighting of a re-enactment of a tragic event, as if a tape recording has been left within the environment. In no way do such theories allow for a ghost to get into a car, or be knocked over by one. The way in which such ghosts seem to interact with the experiencer adds a new dimension to the experience.

The 'tape-recording' theory of ghosts – that they are re-enactments of tragic events – has been suggested by many researchers in various forms, and for decades has been regarded as the most viable explanation of such sightings. Within the theory, the environment is the central factor in the experience. But there is a *more* viable explanation. My own view is that if the theory is reversed, it can be seen to make more sense. To do this, we must place the mind of the experiencer as the central factor within the experience.

In such a theory we must see the environment as a form of trigger. The future experiencer moves into the environment where the tragedy occurred. For the sighting to manifest, the person must be in a state of mind conducive to hallucination; that is tired, or something in the environment must exist to allow electromagnetic bombardment of the brain. And it is here, I argue, that information is received in the experiencer's mind to add form to the hallucination that occurs. In other words, some form of extra-sensory perception (ESP) occurs, with the environment jolting the unconscious mind and allowing the experiencer to intuit the tragic event that occurred.

Such an idea allows for all the intriguing idiosyncrasies of the ghostly experience. Most obviously, it allows the experiencer to hallucinate a valid and identifiable event, to the extent that they can recognize the ghost from a photograph or drive the apparition to its former home. Further, it allows for interaction between the ghost and the experiencer: the experience is not a re-enactment as such, but an interplay directed by the unconscious mind of the experiencer in a similar fashion to the way in which we can interplay in dreams. And finally, in a lesser experience, we can simply intuit the mood of the experience, allowing for Andrew Green to want to jump off a tower in Ealing, and for Tom Lethbridge to be 'possessed' by depression at certain tragic locations.

The sceptic will, of course, point out that where the theory fails is that it is dependent upon the mind of the experiencer picking up information by extrasensory means – something that is not proved to happen. This is quite true. But in relegating the experience to nothing more than a form of hallucinated clairvoyant ability, we simplify the requirement of explanation within the field of the paranormal. Indeed, such a form of extra-sensory perception has already been widely accepted as the basis for the existence of another form of ghost, a form known as the 'crisis apparition'.

Typical was the case of nineteenth-century physician Dr S. Weir Mitchell. Following a hard day's work in snow-covered Philadelphia, he sat down and dozed off. Suddenly there was a knock at the door. Answering it, he found a thin girl in a shawl, saying that her mother was desperately ill and needed help. Dr Mitchell followed the girl through a blizzard to her mother's house, where he found a woman suffering from pneumonia. Making her comfortable, he told her about her brave daughter, which was a great surprise to the woman. Her daughter was dead.

In this experience we can see the doctor gaining unconscious knowledge by extra-sensory means that a woman close by was exceptionally ill. To spur the doctor into action, the unconscious provided an hallucinatory image he would react to. However, the usual form of the crisis apparition is more subtle.

Take the case of a young woman working in her kitchen during World War I. Suddenly the door opened and in walked her brother, his army uniform covered in mud. She was surprised to see him, for he was supposed in have been fighting in Flanders. 'Put the kettle on, Maud,' he said, 'I'm dead tired.' He sat down and his sister went to do as he asked. When she turned round, her brother had disappeared. In fact, he had never been there. At the moment he had appeared to his sister, he had been killed in Flanders.

Both these experiences have common parallels within the arena of extra-sensory perception, the only difference being that the received information does not take an hallucinatory form. Typical is the story of midwife Gladys Wright, who was unable to visit her patients in Norfolk one day in December 1952 because of bad weather. One patient, Joyce Goodwin, wasn't due to give birth for over a week, but Gladys couldn't get her image out of her mind. Even when she went to bed that night the image continued to trouble her. Indeed, it was so strong that in the end Gladys got up and drove the 4 miles (6.5 km) across snow-covered roads to Joyce's house. Joyce had gone into labour early, her son being born at five o'clock the following morning.

Joicey Hurth, from Wisconsin, had an extra-sensory experience in 1955. Her daughter set off for the cinema one afternoon, leaving Joicey to wash the dishes. Suddenly a chill came over her and she dropped a dish, saying, 'Please don't let her get killed.' She ran to the phone and rang the cinema, telling them of an accident she had seen in her head. The accident had, in fact, only just happened. Joicey's daughter had run in front of a car. Luckily, she was not seriously hurt.

Trainee army officer John Dawes was puzzled one night when he woke up and told his wife that in a dream his mother had been trying to give him the combination of her safe. The following morning his brother rang with bad news. His mother had died the previous night. Just before dying, she had tried to mouth the combination of her safe.

Such experiences are so common, so well documented and so similar in nature that only the most ardent sceptics will draw the conclusion that nothing extra-sensory is happening. Such sceptics will use all forms of delusion to ignore the evidence; the experiencer is a liar, or mad, or both; the experiencer is deluded; or the researcher who compiles the evidence is a fraud, or simply a crackpot. The reason for such an assault is that modern science says that such supernatural, or paranormal, events cannot happen. They break the laws of nature. Yet in reality this is not the case: they simply show cracks in the theories that have so far been offered to explain nature. It is man's process of knowledge appraisal that is under assault, not the world in which we live.

That world is a far stranger one than we think. But whereas the sceptics may be wrong in their intransigence, the believers are also possibly wrong in their susceptibility to the supernatural. As I have tried to show, ghosts are not super-natural visitations from the afterlife, but most likely nothing more than an hallu-cinated form created by the receiving of extra-sensory information. If this source can be proved to exist, then ghosts will also have fallen to the continuing accu-mulation of knowledge. And whereas the sceptics may maintain their scepticism, it seems that higher authorities have been dabbling in such powers for decades.

ESP and Culture

■ It is a peculiarity of the English lan-guage that the first three letters of espionage are ESP, which are famed for meaning extra-sensory perception. And it seems that as well as conventional spying methods, intelligence agencies have been using psychics to augment their work for quite a long time.

The first known instance of ESPionage is chronicled in the Bible. In the Old Testament, the prophet Elisha is said to have used his psychic abilities to assist Israel and save it from defeat. However, it wasn't until the advent of the Cold War that such abilities were said to have really taken off. Indeed, it was in the Soviet Union that psychics were first employed.

Since 1845 Russian researchers had been interested in the possibility of con-trolling minds from a distance. In that year, a hypnotist called Andrei Ivanovitch Pashkov had perfected what he called telepathic hypnosis, when he claimed to have hypnotized a woman from 300 miles (480 km) away. At his command, she would fall asleep. By 1954, the Soviet Union's psychics were said to have perfected such techniques and turned them into weapons.

In that year, a Soviet assassin called Dr Nikolai E. Khokhlov defected to the West, bringing with him information that the KGB were perfecting 'psychotronic' weaponry. Early research into such abilities had been carried out in Leningrad, following experiments with Russian psychic Nina Kulagina, who was said to have stopped frogs' hearts beating with the power of her mind. However, by the end of the year it was said that the KGB could destroy missiles, blind radar and disrupt computers by psychic means. It was even claimed that in one experiment psychotronic weaponry had successfully broken a man's back.

Leaks continued to come out of the Soviet Union as the years went on. Particularly worrying was the claim that psychics were in a position to read minds prior to the taking of crucial decisions about such matters as the use of nuclear weapons. Whether fact or disinformation, it seems that the American authorities decided it was time for them to get in on the act.

One early 'unofficial' test occurred in 1971, when astronaut Edgar Mitchell aboard Apollo 14 attempted telepathic contact from space with four psychics. Mitchell concentrated on a sequence of 25 random numbers, attempting to transmit those on which he was concentrating. Chance would dictate any one psychic getting 40 right out of the 200 sequences he attempted. One psychic is said to have guessed right on 51 sequences.

Such a success was only moderate, and as the American authorities began their ESPionage projects, they knew that psychics would not only have to do better, but that they would have to devise a repeatable ability which had real intelligence usage. During the early 1970s, physicists Russell Targ and Harold Puthof at the Stanford Research Institute in California were already perfecting a form of extra-sensory perception called 'remote viewing'. In their early tests, a person would go to a location unknown to the psychic, and the psychic would then be asked to describe or draw the location. However, as their abilities increased, the psychics would simply be given map coordinates and asked if they meant anything to them.

One particular 'remote viewer' used by Targ and Puthof was retired police commissioner Pat Price. When, in 1972, the team was offered a $50,000 grant to find a valid repeatable experiment that might have intelligence applications, Price is said to have performed exceedingly well. Given one map coordinate, he went on to describe the location, the building that stood there, the layout of the inside of the building, details of the equipment in each room, the names on some of the desks, and apparently certain code names on files in a filing cabinet.

Unbeknown to Price at the time, he had just infiltrated a top-secret National

Security Agency communications centre near Washington. From then until his death in 1975, Price became a vital component in Project Scanate – or Scanning by Coordinate – a project which over the following couple of decades would be variously known as Star Gate, Grill Flame, Sun Streak and Centre Lane, and would use up at least $25 million of tax payers' money. Indeed, a 1978 survey showed that of 14 parapsychology units in the United States, five had been approached concerning such government research.

Central to the ESPionage projects in the United States was Fort Meade in Maryland. Here the intelligence community set up a remote-viewing station manned by psychics. As well as using natural psychics – the well-known psychic, Ingo Swann, was one who lent a hand – the intelligence community recruited from the US Army. From 400 personnel whose profiles seemed promising, 14 were chosen to become psychic spies. Among them were army intelligence officer Joe McMoneagle and Major Ed Dames. McMoneagle worked as a psychic spy from 1977 to 1984, and Ed Dames eventually left the army to set up his own psychic spying company. One of his recent projects was an attempt to find the missing murder weapon in the O.J. Simpson case.

Among the supposedly successful projects attempted were finding the location of a crashed Soviet bomber in Africa, discovering secret tunnels between North and South Korea and locating terrorist training camps in the Middle East. To carry out their work, the psychic spies would empty their minds and attempt to induce a meditative state. Once achieved, they would think of their mission and then write down or sketch images that came to them. As well as the above routine work, they claimed a high degree of success during some major incidents.

In 1979, for instance, the psychic spies were used to locate American hostages during the Iranian hostage crisis. Given a photograph of a particular hostage, they would attempt to describe the condition and location of incarceration. In 1986, they were used to locate psychically Colonel Gadaffi of Libya prior to the American air strike. One psychic is said to have located him exactly. During the Gulf War, it is believed that psychic spies were put on to the problem of locating Scud missiles in the Iraqi desert. At times their success was measured statistically at around 50 per cent – a figure way above chance result.

Of course, much of the information we have on American ESPionage could be embellished to the same extent as many of the more spurious ghost stories narrated earlier. Intelligence matters are as much about disinformation as valid information. But it cannot be denied that the US government *did* involve itself in psychic research over a number of decades, and such a project would not have gone on for so long if the abilities had repeatedly proved to be non-existent.

And the simple fact that the idea was entertained at all shows evidence of the validity of extra-sensory abilities. And the latest evidence of such abilities is coming from a study of psychic pets.

The literature concerning psychic abilities in animals is both vast and convincing. Just three anecdotes are enough to demonstrate their uncanny powers of location. For instance, before going off to fight in the trenches of World War I, Kevin O'Keefe moved his wife and pet dog Prince from Ireland to stay with relatives in London. Because of this move, he managed to visit them for a weekend before returning to France. Prince was particularly agitated when his master left him once more, so much so that he disappeared. Mrs O'Keefe wrote to her husband telling him of the disappearance, but before the letter was received Prince had somehow made his way to the south coast, hitched a lift across the English Channel, travelled 60 miles (96 km) to the front and located his master out of the half-million troops that were stationed there.

Even more remarkable were the adventures of Joker, a cocker spaniel, during World War II. His master, army Captain Stanley Raye, was posted from his native California to the South Pacific. Two weeks later Joker disappeared. Making his way down to Oakland, he sneaked aboard a transport ship, where he was 'adopted' by a major. At every port at which the ship stopped, Joker would disembark, check out the port, and then return to ship. Finally, at one port he literally ran down the gangplank, ignoring all commands to return, and didn't stop running until he pulled up at the feet of his master, Captain Raye.

Cats also have a remarkable power of extra-sensory perception. When Mr and Mrs Charles Smith moved from Florida to their new home in California, they decided to save their cat, Tom, from the trauma of moving by leaving him with the new home owner, Mr Hanson. However, by the time the Smiths arrived in California, a letter was waiting for them advising that Tom had disappeared. Two years later, Tom – skinny, bloody and exhausted – leapt into Mr Smith's arms, his journey obviously having been more traumatic than expected.

Many zoologists attempt to explain such abilities as nothing more than heightened senses, such as smell. If this is to be accepted, then we have to believe that Prince could sniff out his master above the stench of burning and cordite of Flanders; that Joker could sniff out his master from all the smells of a foreign port; and that the Smith's trail was still sniffable even when two years old. Such a possibility is highly unlikely, and fails to explain such locating powers.

Maverick biologist Rupert Sheldrake has recently involved himself in tests to discover the prevalence of psychic abilities in pets. Starting in 1995, some 410 households in Greater Manchester were contacted at random to see if owners suspected that their pets knew when they would be coming home. About 120 dog owners were convinced that their pet did know. To test out the validity of such claims, pets were caught on video as their owners were about to leave work and return home. It seems that 46 per cent of dogs and 14 per cent of cats appeared to be aware of their returning master, the pets rousing themselves to peer out of the window, sometimes as much as an hour before the return.

The obvious star of the survey was a mongrel terrier called Jaytee, owned by Pam Smart from Ramsbottom, Lancashire. Jaytee was a perfect dog to test, for Ms Smart's homecoming varied from day to day, so prompters couldn't explain Jaytee's actions by his somehow knowing what time it was. Out of 153 tests, Jaytee seemed to be aware of his owner's homecoming in 80 per cent of cases. Failures also seemed to correspond with sickness or distraction due to a nearby bitch being on heat.

Of course, such tests are not conclusive. Indeed, no absolutely conclusive test has yet been devised to demonstrate the existence of paranormal powers. This could mean that such powers do not exist, and any evidence we do come upon could be more to do with human credulity, delusion and wish fulfilment. Alternatively, paranormal powers do exist, but they are so subtle that absolute proof will evade us.

There is, however, another possibility: that paranormal powers are not some separate ability divorced from our normal, everyday ones, but the province of a deeper psychological and sociological understanding of ourselves and the societies in which we live.

Let us tackle these psychological and sociological aspects separately. Taking the psychological first, it is becoming clear that ghosts are not some super natural visitation from the afterlife. Rather, they appear to be images created by our own minds. We live in a world of impulses; we exist in an ethereal sea of interaction with forces outside our selves. Reality and reason are based on our correct interpretation of such impulses, and it is the continual task of the mind to grasp definites from this clutter of stimuli.

However, there are times when this constant bombardment of stimuli wanes. What does the mind do? Close down? No. The mind is constantly active. It has no 'off' button, so can never switch off, as our dreams clearly testify. Hence, when those stimuli wane or, through tiredness, our interpretation becomes faulty, the mind continues to produce a picture of reality. But at such times, the picture it produces is reliant more upon its inner fantasies than the exact reality 'outside'.

Sometimes this interaction between the reality outside and the fantasies within can become almost permanent. When this happens, we class the sufferer as insane. We label them schizophrenic, for their inner fantasies become uppermost in their life, and they suffer acute delusions and hallucinations. But this is simply a state that we can all find ourselves in temporarily. With the 'sane' person, this imbalance between reality and fantasy can produce an event which, for the sake of labelling, we call paranormal, and a ghostly encounter can occur. But in reality it is simply a brief psychological imbalance between the world within our mind and the physical world outside. It is not supernatural. In a way, it is not even paranormal. Rather, it is a brief moment of decalibration, a hiccup in our perception of reality analogous to that brief atmospheric clutter that can turn our television picture fuzzy.

This is the essence of paranormality. But if this is the case, how is it that we do not experience such ghostly hiccups more often? If it is simply a moment of decalibration, surely we can expect to experience it often?

Well, maybe we do. When our taxi driver picked up his ghost (see page 21), he was unable to distinguish it from a proper person. Had he not gone back to check that she was all right, he would not have had a ghostly experience, but simply picked up a rather distraught girl. Perhaps if he had touched her in some way, and his hand had gone through her, he would have realized that he was seeing a ghost. But ask yourself: when you are tired, or there is high electromagnetic activity in the atmosphere, do *you* go up and touch everyone you see? Perhaps if you did, you might find you see ghosts more often than you think. Perhaps we appreciate what we often see as ghosts only when we touch, or doubt, or have some other reason to suspect.

Some researchers, such as paranormal investigator and UFOlogist Jenny Randles, have offered intriguing possibilities as to the prevalence of 'real' people who are not real at all. Towards the end of the 1980s and beginning of the 1990s there was a spate of scandals concerning the authorities' mania towards suspected cases of child sex abuse. Beginning with the fiasco in Cleveland, northern England, it developed into the American-led satanic sex abuse scandal. Such scandals created a terror of social workers within society. For a time they became demonized, and rather than being seen as helpful towards families, they were feared.

During this period, the police began to receive hundreds of telephone calls from worried mothers who had been visited by social workers. Exhibiting ridiculous behaviour, and offering equally ridiculous reasons, they advised that they were taking the mothers' children into care. The prevalence of such cases caused immense media speculation, with identikit pictures of some of these 'social workers' appearing in the papers. It was soon realized that they were bogus, and the idea grew that they were child abductors, out to steal children either for themselves or for sale.

If this was so, they were remarkably incompetent, for only one mother was taken in. The child in question simply walked around with the 'social workers' for about half an hour and was then returned home. Bearing in mind such incompetence, it was thought that they would soon be caught, but not one of these hundreds of bogus social workers was apprehended. Why? Could it be that our general concern about social workers produced our fears in a social, cultural hallucinated form?

This intriguing possibility leads us on to the sociological aspect of the supposed paranormal. We like to think of ourselves as individuals, totally separate from other people and our society – but how true is this appreciation of our selves? I am who I am because of the experiences I have had, yet the vast majority of those experiences have been social. They have involved interaction with others: hence, the actions of others are as much a part of me as the 'I' in my head. For instance, the most important part of me is the love I have for my wife and children, but they are not a psychological part of me. They are outside of me, yet their power over my actions consumes me, for the most important things I do are regulated by my feelings for them.

In a real sense, our supposed individuality is a delusion. We cannot experience, we cannot love, we cannot even hate without something outside of us infecting us and prompting us to thought or action – and this outside stimulus is omnipotent. For instance, I am a writer, but what I write is dependent upon the actions of others and the experiences and sensations I have had because of them. Further, my success as a writer is totally dependent upon the reader, for without the reader there would be no reason for the writer, and it is the appreciation of my abilities by the reader that will decide my success. My success or failure is therefore not dependent only upon my abilities, but upon the reader's appreciation of those abilities.

As a writer, I contribute not only to society, but also to that overlord of society, culture. My place in society is decided by that culture. I class myself as being as intelligent as many researchers within the world of science; further, I class my work as being as important as science – yet culture defines me as existing in a world of the weird. Regardless of the fact that (hopefully) I write logically and with reason, culture dictates my place in society, and that place is within the world of nutters and cranks. I am, to all intents and purposes, a pseudoscholar, a false academic.

Culture can thus be defined as a form of overall arbiter of society, bulging with society's fears, hopes, delusions and idiosyncrasies. That culture has been created by the actions of individuals, yet in their communal actions an overall entity – a god, if you like – becomes apparent. Culture is the result of a knitting together of all our actions, and in the process, it becomes something more than the sum of its parts: it becomes a connectedness of everything we are individually, defining what we are, who we are, and what it is acceptable for us to do.

One aspect of this deity we call culture is an understanding of morality. In defining our actions, the higher culture also defines our moral responsibilities. For millennia, such responsibilities have been devised poetically, for symbols and allegory seem to connect with conscience to a far greater degree than reasonable argument. Hence, culture controls best through mythology and that marvellous facility of storytelling.

Connecting this to the paranormal, we can see how culture infects experience to produce a moral tale from a supposed supernatural event, or to create hallucinated social workers to snatch our children. Such hallucinations and delusions become no longer personal experiences, but the province of the higher culture defining what we are. These experiences become a form of social contagion, picking out individuals for experience in a similar way to a virus picking out certain people to catch a cold. And it seems that the mind of the individual is far more receptive to this invasive culture than we might at first realize.

There is a psychological phenomenon known as cryptomnesia. To understand this phenomenon, we have to understand the mind. Basically, the mind is seen in two forms: the conscious and the unconscious. The conscious mind is the part we use on a daily basis; it is essentially the 'I' inside my head. Through it, I exist in the dual world of reason and emotion. My thoughts are distinct and obvious, because the conscious mind allows me to concentrate. Without this ability to concentrate, my thoughts would not be distinct but chaotic, constantly moving from subject to subject and prohibiting any attention to detail.

However, the conscious mind is also the receiver of information. Constantly bombarded by outside stimuli, information is forever getting into my head. However, due to concentration, I define which bits of information are useful and which are not. For instance, as I walk down a busy street my eyes can see everything in it, but most of this information is of no use to me. Hence, the conscious mind acts as a filter, sieving out of attention those bits of information I do not need. To take an example, when crossing the road I need to pay attention to the cars passing by. If I also focus on the contents of the shop window on the other side of the road, my attention on the passing cars would wane and I would most likely end up underneath one of them.

Where does the information concerning the contents of the shop go? Do my eyes switch off to the point that I don't see the shop? No. The information is still received, but goes through the conscious mind into the unconscious, almost without being noticed. Within the unconscious, every bit of information concerning the shop window is received. It has gone directly to the unconscious, which can be seen as a repository of information not required at a particular time. By thinking about something, we can retrieve this information, which we call memory.

However, the shop I saw but didn't see consciously was a computer shop. Later that day I enter into a conversation regarding computers, and this prompts a memory of having seen a particular computer that day. But can I remember where I saw it? No, I cannot. The information is there, the information was received, but it wasn't received consciously. This is cryptomnesia, and the mechanism holds great importance for the paranormal.

Let us go back to the ghosts on Bluebell Hill (see page 21). How could our tired driver actually have seen the ghost to such an extent that he could recognize her from a picture? It was a terrible crash, and as with all terrible crashes it would have been reported in the newspapers. What we must consider is the possibility that years ago our tired driver had read that report and seen those photographs. He wasn't that interested in the crash at the time, so the information passed virtually straight through to the unconscious, which is what happens most of the time when we read a newspaper. Then, years later, our driver is tired and the environment he is driving through prompts the retrieval of information from the unconscious. He didn't know it was there, but every experience we have ever had, everything we've ever read, every sight we've ever seen, every noise we've ever heard, is there. Cryptomnesia can be seen to answer every aspect of the hallucinated ghosts of Bluebell Hill, and in answering them we are dealing with the paranormal as not so much distinctly different to normal life, but simply a form of heightening of normal psychological abilities.

Such mechanisms can be extended to an even wider unconscious repository through which cryptomnesia can work, and this can offer tantalizing mechanisms to allow for extra-sensory perception. Let us go back to seeing ourselves as individuals. We have already dealt with the psychological aspect, but what about our physicality? Is that individual? We assume so. Our bodies are quite literally a distinct watery bag of flesh held up by a frame of bone. This body is unconnected to any other body, thus showing our distinct separateness from others. However, if we look at our bodies through a microscope, a different world emerges. Rather than being a distinct individual, we become a grouping of thousands of different bugs, bacteria and creepy-crawlies. Our actual make-up consists of millions of distinct and individual cells which somehow work together to produce a biological system called a life form, but how they group together is totally unknown.

This cellular construction is also far more 'socially interactive' than our bodies suggest. It exists in a sea of cells and bacteria *outside* our individual bodies; it reacts with bacteria in the air about us, and these bacteria invade our bodies on a regular basis, giving us a cold or a stomach bug. Our body, it seems, is more than our individuality – and this world becomes even stranger and more interactive when we go even smaller.

At our fundamental level of existence, our cells disappear and are shown to be made up of electromagnetic vibrations. This is the world of atoms and particles, and they are totally reactive with all other atoms and particles in the universe. The blueprint of reality begins at this level, and for the blueprint to begin here, information must also begin here – information that goes on to react with our cellular level and upwards to our normal bodily level. How this happens we do not know, but happen it must or we would not exist. At this level, all reality is totally interactive with everything else, so could it be that at such a subtle level of reality all information is also interactive?

At present this is a speculative possibility only, but if such a reality really does exist, then it answers extra-sensory perception – for it is arguably the case that our deep unconscious could contain knowledge of everything. Our higher culture, it seems, echoes the idiosyncrasies of this electromagnetic reality, and the supernatural becomes not only better defined as psychological, but involves a marriage between consciousness and physics. It suggests a world where our actions are not so much individual, but a product of an interconnected world of overall destiny, guided by culture and experienced through universal stardust. Which brings us back to our opening case, and the defining experience of Charles Lindbergh (see pages 8–9).

A possibility: culture controls society, yet society is a congregation of individuals. A supposed individual action, such as Lindbergh's successful crossing of the Atlantic, can be seen as advancing society, and thus becoming part of culture – but Lindbergh's success, it seems, was dependent upon an hallucinatory experience which drove him on. Was it an individual experience, or was it a product of a wider interconnectedness? Could it be that Lindbergh's experience was not personal at all, but part of a wider mechanism where interactive culture 'knew' that advancement was about to happen, and helped society along to achieve it? If my theorizing so far provides indications that this could, indeed, be the case, then we are not talking of the paranormal as a simple idiosyncrasy but as a distinct higher mechanism within the universe, forwarding our actions through moments of destiny. In a way, we are talking of the intervention in normal, human reality by God. This is a possibility we will come across again and again within the pages of this book

▪ MINDS POSSESSED ▪

The Future Now

▪ When it came, it was horrific. An intense, slithering blackness, destroying all in its wake, its final destination a school. This it enveloped, smashing it, smothering it, leaving many a broken heart behind.

Truly, 21 October 1966 was a different kind of day, for that blackness was a sea of coal waste, avalanching down a mountainside to fall upon the local school at Aberfan in Wales. It was a costly day in human lives: 28 adults and 116 children perished, making it the greatest disaster to befall Wales in modern times. But while the tragedy should never be eroded in our minds, there was another aspect to this disaster that has entered the literature of the paranormal.

Up to two weeks before the disaster, many in Aberfan were unconsciously aware that the disaster was coming. At least 200 people had premonitions of that coming day, some 60 of which were later authenticated. Some were merely feelings – an unconscious, undefined knowing – while others were more intense. Typical was a girl who dreamed that when she went to school there was nothing there, 'just a big black hole'. Her parents dismissed this as simply a normal dream and packed her off to school, where sadly she died. Others had impressions of gasping and choking, while still others had visions of billowing black clouds, and of children running and screaming.

Unfortunately, there was no authority to go to in order to tell of these disquieting premonitions so the signals went unheeded, the facts of the visions coming only after the event. This has led many to dismiss them as fabrications, or the delusions of over-zealous researchers. Neither point is realistic. Grieving parents do not invent the incredulous – they merely grieve; and researchers are not so callous as to invent from such misery. Something paranormal *did* happen in the days leading up to the disaster at Aberfan, and when sceptics decry the paranormal as the world of cranks or fraudsters, I want them to show their total conviction by moving away from lambasting psychic superstars and voice their scepticism of the events that happen to normal people and brand them as insane or liars.

The classical answer to the events at Aberfan is that the visions were caused by a glimpse of the future. However, while I do not deny that the visions occurred, I feel a far simpler explanation can account for their manifestation. Indeed, we need only ask a simple question: could a sea of coal waste have simply slithered down a mountain without prior movement as the mass began to dislodge? This is doubtful. It is far more likely that stresses and strains had been building up for days before the actual slide. Some of these movements may have been observable, but many of them would have been so slight as to be unnoticeable, at least to the conscious mind. But, as was pointed out earlier (see pages 31–32), the unconscious mind is far more observing than we might at first realize.

Typical is our growing understanding of subliminal messages. A frame in a film is shown so briefly that we cannot identify each individual frame consciously, yet we are now aware that the unconscious does register its image. It has been said that if a single frame within a film depicts an advertisement for a product, the viewer is unconsciously persuaded to buy the product. This claim is a gross exaggeration of the facts – we are apparently not that suggestible – but unconscious knowledge of the product is, nevertheless, received.

This information is vital for understanding the premonitions at Aberfan, for it suggests that the subliminal movements of the coal waste *prior* to the disaster could also have been unconsciously known. Hence, a sudden sense of foreboding, a knowledge of impending doom, could easily have surfaced from the unconscious. Further, in the dream state we know that unconscious imagery invades the conscious mind, and so too at Aberfan with the unconscious knowledge of subliminal movements providing an obvious outcome within a dream.

Paranormal literature is bulging with incidents of premonition that could be better explained in this way. Typical is the case of Lisa, a golden retriever that lived in the British Embassy in Peking in 1976. Early one morning she woke up the entire staff with her continuous barking. She appeared greatly agitated, and passed on her agitation to the staff, who for some reason decided to leave the building. Moments later the whole area was devastated by a massive earthquake. As with the fall of coal waste at Aberfan, an earthquake is preceded by subliminal rumblings, movements so slight that they are not appreciated by the conscious mind – and, due to a remarkable coincidental medical examination in

1989, we now have evidence of such rumblings being registered by the brain.

At 10.28 a.m. one morning in December 1989 an earthquake hit the town of Newcastle, 100 miles (160 km) north of Sydney in Australia. Measuring 5.5 on the Richter scale, it killed 12 people and injured hundreds. Exactly 28 minutes earlier – at 10 o'clock – two radiographers had begun a computer-aided tomography scan of a psychiatric patient. At 10.11 a.m. a series of unusual streaks appeared on the scan, as if the patient's brain was involved in some unique activity. Seventeen minutes later the earthquake struck. It is not absolutely proved that this brain activity was due to the coming earthquake, but the idea is most attractive. If the earthquake was responsible for the activity, two options are open to us. First, the patient could have unconsciously sensed earth movements at a subliminal level. If this option is correct, the unconscious mind is more accurate than seismology, for seismologists did not detect a tremor at this time. Or second, the brain was reacting to the electromagnetic activity that often precedes earthquakes.

The above incident does, of course, have immense value for research into earthquake prediction, but because it is quite clearly an incident that could prove an area of paranormality, science is loath to move in this direction. However, such a suggested ability, combined with the idea that the mind can intuit the course of a future event by unconscious knowledge of a subliminal prompter in the present, has great implications for the idea that the future exists.

Premonitions have always been troublesome for the logical paranormal researcher. Every indication gleaned from our accumulated knowledge suggests that the future cannot exist before it happens, and the above ideas indicate that in this sense at least science is correct: premonitions may not be a definite glimpse of the future, but an unconscious appraisal of a probable future. In a real sense, stimuli exist in the present to give prior knowledge of a possible event, and in this way a clearly inexplicable paranormal event is inexplicable no more. Rather, it defers to psychology, becoming nothing more than a new understanding of our power to observe the world around us.

In this sense, the information that provides the premonition can be seen as extra-sensory, but not in any way supernatural. In the normal world, we rely on the five senses to provide the information through which we interact with reality. As we saw earlier, this allows for concentration and attention to detail (see page 31), which are essential for ordered living. But in the slightly more fantastic world of paranormality, we can also view the senses as filters designed to assist our non-appraisal of the total information within reality. In this way, our five senses are also gaolers, locking out of normal perception a wider interactive world whose existence it then becomes easy for us to deny. For if we do not experience such a world, then that world does not exist. Except, of course, we *do* experience it – but only in the sense of the paranormal.

Psychic Acting

■ There are times when the outside world is said to invade the individual mind to such an extent that the individual mind disappears. Such an invasion is classed as possession. From January to April 1949, a 14-year-old boy from Washington DC exhibited 'possession' to such an extent that when the story finally broke it was used by William Peter Blatty as the basis for his novel *The Exorcist*, which later became one of the great horror films.

Robbie Mannheim – the name is a pseudonym, his real identity being a closely kept secret – began exhibiting signs of possession after his Aunt Harriet died. Before her death, Robbie and his aunt had tried to contact spirits of the dead with a Ouija board. Consequently, following her death Robbie tried to contact her. Soon after, strange noises were heard in the house and Robbie began to lose control of himself, swearing incessantly. Next, a number of cuts began to appear on his body and he was taken to a doctor. The doctor diagnosed him as perfectly healthy.

However, Robbie's behaviour became worse, and it wasn't long before his parents began to believe that he was possessed by the devil. They called in a priest and a number of exorcisms were attempted, but each time the boy's behaviour seemed to get worse. At one stage he attacked a priest with a loose bedspring – the priest required nearly 100 stitches in his arm.

The 'possessions' usually occurred at night. Robbie would thrash about, spit and swear. The cuts continued to appear, and at one stage words began to appear on his body in blood, including the word 'hell'. By this time, a number of priests were involved in the exorcisms, and finally, on Easter Monday 1949, Robbie ceased his thrashing about, opened his eyes and said: 'He's gone.'

Most possessions are neither as severe nor as violent as this. Indeed, they are not considered as possessions in the same sense, but rather as cases of reincarnation. Typical was Nicola Peart from Keighley in West Yorkshire. When she was two her mother bought her a dog. Deciding to call it Muff, Nicola announced that this was the name of the dog she had had before. Kathleen, her mother, thought this strange, for Nicola hadn't had a dog before, but then the strangeness increased when Nicola asked why she was a little girl this time. When her mother quizzed her about such comments, Nicola said that her other mummy was called Elsie Benson and they had lived in a grey stone terraced house in Haworth, a couple of miles from where she presently lived. She had two younger sisters and her father always had a dirty face, for he worked on a railway engine. She had died when she was knocked over by a train after walking on the railway line with her dog, Muff.

Intrigued by her daughter's story, Kathleen took her for a walk across the moors to Haworth. Nicola showed her mother the house she had lived in as a little boy. Later, Kathleen checked the parish records and was shocked to discover that a boy called John Henry Benson had been born there in 1875. His father had been a railwayman. A check of the census records of 1881 gave the additional information that by then the only children living at the house were two young girls. Presumably, by then young John was dead.

Jonathan Pike caused equal consternation at the age of three when he suddenly began talking about his wife, Angela. Jonathan and his parents had just moved from Hull on Humberside to Southend in Essex, and one day, while riding on a bus, Jonathan pointed to a house and commented that that was where he used to live with Angela. Later, he pointed out the garage where he used to work, and further advised that he had had a son and daughter.

The situation became even worse on another trip when Jonathan suddenly burst into tears after passing a crossroads. This was apparently the place where his daughter had been killed by a car. Jonathan's case of supposed reincarnation became public knowledge, and it soon transpired that a long-serving policeman from Southend remembered the tragedy of a little girl being knocked down and killed at that very crossroads.

In recent years a new dimension has been added to the reincarnation debate – the phenomenon of past life regression. Here, a subject will be hypnotized by a therapist and taken back 'beyond birth'. In such a session thousands of people have recalled past lives, including a number of well-publicized cases involving stars. Typical was Glenn Ford, who in 1978 was regressed to previous lives as a Colorado cowboy and then a Scottish piano teacher. Sylvester Stallone believes he has had at least four past lives. In one such life he was a French aristocrat beheaded by the guillotine, and in another he was a boxer, killed by a knock-out blow in the 1930s.

One answer to such cases is that cryptomnesia is involved, researchers arguing that the knowledge is not of past lives but of unconscious memories retrieved under hypnosis of stories previously read or heard. For instance, in 1977 a woman called Jan was regressed on British television. She 'became' Joan Waterhouse, a witch from Chelmsford who just managed to escape the death sentence in 1566. However, the date Jan gave was 1556. This error was tracked down to an error in the printing of a Victorian pamphlet on the trial.

One of the earliest cases of known cryptomnesia happened in 1874, when the medium William Stainton Moses was 'possessed' by the spirits of two young boys who had died in India. However, six days prior to the seance in which contact was made, *The Times* had published an obituary of the boys. All the information from the 'possession' seems to have come from this source.

Most sceptics are happy to accept cryptomnesia as an explanation – cases solved. However, this is not quite so easy to do, for while cryptomnesia almost certainly plays a part in such 'reincarnations', the occasional piece of evidence can upset the 'neatness' of the idea. Consider the case of journalist Ray Bryant, regressed to the past life of an Essex farm labourer from the nineteenth century by hypnotist Joe Keeton. It seems that on 22 April 1884, Essex experienced quite a violent earthquake. Keeton found out about this and wondered what would happen if Bryant were 'taken back' to this day. If cryptomnesia alone were responsible for such regressions, it would be unlikely for the subject to have had knowledge of the quake. Keeton took Bryant back: Bryant became terrified and spoke of the house shaking and plates falling off shelves.

Does this suggest that such 'possessions' are real? American schoolmaster Max Freedom Long decided they were. Arriving in Hawaii in 1917, he carried out an intensive study of the native Huna religion, particularly the way in which a 'spirit' seemed to be able to take over certain members of the population. According to the Huna religion, man is not a single co-ordinated individual. Rather, he has three separate and distinct 'selves': the low self, middle self and high self. Long identified the low self as analogous to the unconscious mind. The middle self, he argued, was the normal, conscious mind, but the high self was a form of superconscious which, as well as having extra-sensory powers, could, at times of trance, take over the individual, becoming a form of higher spirit.

Canadian psychiatrist Dr Adam Crabtree would not go this far. In the course of his work he has come across many cases suggestive of 'spirit' possession, but rather than patients coming to him with the spirits intact, they can be better seen as being 'created' within therapy.

One such case was that of Sarah Worthington, who was directed to Crabtree after experiencing bouts of depression and urges towards suicide. Crabtree asked her if she ever heard voices in her head. She said that she had, and she was then asked to relax and try to recall these 'inner conversations'. Suddenly she tensed and her whole persona changed. Whereas Sarah was under-confident, she now appeared confident, and when she spoke her voice was very different. Suspecting that some other 'entity' was now in control of Sarah, Crabtree asked her who she was. She identified herself as Sarah Jackson, Sarah Worthington's grandmother. She was there to help Sarah. However, it soon became apparent to Crabtree that the grandmother required help too, and by concentrating on the grandmother's problems, Sarah's problems also seemed to lessen, thus providing successful therapy.

Was the 'grandmother' a spirit? This is unlikely, for Crabtree purposely used a form of psychodrama, urging his patients to enact scenes which had emotional impact for them. During such enactment, the patient often took on the form of another personality involved in the drama, and Crabtree understood that by analysing such 'personalities' he could treat the patient through the back door. In easing the 'personality', he was actually easing the mind of the patient, suggesting that the 'personality' was not some outside entity but a psychologically created fantasy.

The ability to 'create' apparently outside entities is far more common than we think. One profession in particular – the acting profession – provides thousands of examples of such fantasized 'personalities'. In a real sense, a good character actor (or actress) does not just act the part, but 'becomes' the acted personality. He (or she) doesn't just read his lines and act as directed: the good actor studies the character intensely; he explores the character's emotions; he practises his idiosyncrasies by rote; he devises specific mannerisms; and the end result is that, when the actor walks out on to the stage, it isn't him, but a psychologically created entity.

Sometimes, this fantasized entity can become so 'real' that it threatens to 'take over' the actor. A case in point was identified in a letter written by Peter Sellers to Britt Ekland shortly after their marriage in 1964, and auctioned as part of Miss Ekland's property at Christie's in 1996. At the time, Sellers was filming in Hollywood, and the character he was playing was creating havoc with his mind. He wrote: 'When I finish at the end of the day's shooting, I try to forget him and his moods. But . . . he nearly always follows me home and lingers slyly in the back of my mind.'

In both Sarah Worthington and Peter Sellers, we can see evidence of a form of fragmentation of the mind resulting in a fantasized 'personality'. Rather than 'spirit' possession, we can see this as a wholly psychological phenomenon. Indeed, the annals of psychiatry are littered with similar cases, known as 'multiple personality'.

As with the therapy devised by Dr Adam Crabtree, many cases of multiple personality have been discredited as nothing more than the patient attempting to please the therapist by providing fantasized 'entities' – but perhaps this is an essential element of what is going on in such 'possessions'. For instance, we can see Robbie Mannheim's possession in a similar, fantasized way. To begin with, he simply swore a lot, as is often the case with rebellious adolescents. He only became 'demonic' when the possibility of being possessed by the devil was suggested, and as priests became involved in 'exorcizing' him, he simply went on with the fantasy being suggested to him. Hence, the 'possession' was a very real element provided by suggestion and inner fantasy. In other words, Robbie Mannheim was being a good boy in behaving exactly as was expected of him, and in doing so was approaching a state bordering on multiple personality, with an 'entity' taking him over.

Sometimes multiple personality can exist outside the consulting room. For instance, in 1977 a young man called Billy Milligan was arrested and charged on four counts of rape. Known as the 'Campus Rapist', he had carried out his assaults at Ohio State University. However, during interviews he appeared so confused that he was referred for psychiatric assessment. During his assessment he was shown to possess over 20 different and distinct personalities. Indeed, he was so severely handicapped by them that the case against him was withdrawn and he was committed to psychiatric care. But where did these personalities come from?

It seems that in order to cope with life, Milligan had compartmentalized each of his inner emotions and fantasized a specific personality around each. As such, a particular situation would bring 'out' a particular personality. Some of his personalities were loving, others were angry, others were logical. The 'rapist' turned out to be a fantasized frustrated lesbian called Regan with a desire to be wanted by women.

To the rational mind this, of course, seems ridiculous and far-fetched. The mind of the individual is seen as 'whole', and the only time the person can fantasize in such a way is when chemical imbalance causes schizophrenia. However, this is not the case, and the brain itself is no longer seen as a co-ordinated whole.

At the top of the brain are two huge walnut-shaped masses known as the left and right cerebral hemispheres, connected to each other by a highway of nerves known as the corpus callosum. During experimental treatment to cure epilepsy, the corpus callosum can be cut, thus restricting the electrical storm of epilepsy to one side of the brain. However, it has been shown that such treatment demonstrates a distinct difference in the purpose of the two hemispheres.

Known today as the split-brain concept, this shows that the left hemisphere seems to be responsible for logical appraisal, while the right controls emotion and insight. In the well-balanced individual the two hemispheres work together to produce what we know as the sane person. However, at times a particular hemisphere can become dominant. For instance, when we are flooded with emotion, the right hemisphere is dominant. When we are involved in a logical task, as is often the case in work, the left hemisphere tends to be in charge. However, at times these co-ordinated functions can seem to conflict. A typical example is when we are doing something we know to be wrong. It is then that we hear that little voice at the back of the mind which we refer to as our conscience. At other times we may be undecided as to a course of action. In our Freudian way, we say we are 'in two minds', with an inner argument going on between the logical course of action and the emotional. In such cases, unless we are extremely strong-willed the emotional side will invariably win.

This 'normal' psychological and physiological phenomenon tells us that our emotional side can become distinct and overpower our logical mind – and of course, fantasies are very much a product of emotion. Hence, it is not difficult to envisage the possibility of fantasies rising from the right cerebral hemisphere and apparently taking over the mind, as if some outside 'entity' has invaded individual consciousness.

Such 'possessions', although fantasized, are nevertheless real, at least to the individual. Hence, the emotional right side of the brain can be seen to become demonic, a spirit, or even a fantasized previous reincarnation. The possessions may be very different, but they are all based in personal, or suggested, emotional fantasies. Except, that is, for occasional annoying inconsistencies, such as Ray Bryant's knowledge of an earthquake on 22 April 1884.

Subliminal Influence

■ The idea that 'possessions' are nothing more than inner fantasies producing fragmented personalities within the individual's mind provides a definite basis for replacing spirits, demons and reincarnated past lives with a simple, and explainable, psychological phenomenon. Adding my ideas concerning premonition to the equation, we can also see that subliminal outside influences can affect the fantasy, in a similar way to my earlier suggestion that an environment can have a bearing upon an hallucinated ghost.

By following this methodology, an important point becomes apparent. Ghosts, premonitions and possessions can all be seen as different variations of the same basic phenomenon – the hidden depths of the human mind. Rather than seeing such phenomena as supernatural – that is, part of the world of spirits, demons and the afterlife – they can better be seen as psychological. In this way the paranormal is no longer as inexplicable as we imagine, but answerable to simple laws and mechanisms that often impinge into normal life. We do not need to extend this model too far in order to explain Ray Bryant's knowledge of the earthquake – we simply have to bring a form of extra-sensory perception akin to telepathy into the equation. For one thing is clear: while Ray Bryant didn't know of that earthquake, hypnotist Joe Keeton did.

This is an important point to make. With Robbie Mannheim (see page 37) we saw how the most likely explanation for his 'demonic' possession was not so much his own fantasy, but that of those around him. Such an idea is simply a variation on the idea of the environment as prompter for paranormal activity. The only difference is that instead of the individual being an expression of an environment, he becomes an expression of a 'community'.

Such an idea offers a clear indication that the mind of one individual can affect subliminally the mind of another, and we thus approach a form of extra-sensory perception. Such an invasive mind ability could actually be far more common than we think, especially when we bring into the argument an all-pervading cultural bias towards a particular idiosyncrasy.

In the previous section, we saw how our fears concerning social workers could have caused a form of cultural hallucination, with hallucinated social workers calling at homes in order to try to snatch children (see page 29–30). This was an outcome of a previous cultural fear that child sex abuse was rampant. Whether this is actually the case or not is irrelevant to the argument: all that is needed is a fear. And such a fear need not just express itself in my suggested cultural hallucination of child snatchers.

As with ideas concerning satanic child abuse, another social phenomenon on the subject began in the United States in the mid-1980s, spreading to Britain by the early 1990s. Promulgated by a large number of self-help books, the idea was put forward that the repression of early sex abuse can be so complete that the sufferer can totally forget that such abuse happened at all. Helped along by writers such as Ellen Bass and Laura Davies, the psychoanalytical community clung to this idea as an answer to most psychological disorders. Are you depressed? Then maybe this is due to forgotten memories of sex abuse by your father. Are you anxious? Ditto. Do you have trouble relating to men? Double ditto.

As a result of the suggestion, therapists soon began uncovering repressed memories of the most horrific forms of sexual abuse in their patients, eventually suggesting that the recommended course of action was to tell the father that the memories were now remembered, and cut themselves off from him. Throughout America, and eventually in Britain, hundreds of families were destroyed. Perhaps the best-known case is that of American executive Gary

Ramona. Following therapy, his 23-year-old daughter, Holly, accused him of abusing her and cut herself off from him. As a result, Ramona's marriage broke up and he lost his highly paid job.

To give some idea of the prevalence of the problem, the British Psychological Society carried out a survey among chartered psychologists. They came out with the impressive result that nine out of ten psychologists thought that the memories recovered during therapy were 'essentially accurate'. Such evidence appears complete, but is this really the case? For instance, while the media widely reported the impressive finding of the British Psychological Society, few made it clear that the result came from the 27 per cent of psychologists who replied. It can be assumed that the majority of the remaining 73 per cent didn't think the survey worth answering. As for Gary Ramona, he successfully sued the therapists involved, being awarded $500,000 after it was decided the therapists themselves had put the idea in his daughter's mind.

Such facts are, of course, no comfort to members of the British False Memory Society, set up by accused parents in 1993 to counter allegations. The society knows of over 500 families in Britain alone that have been torn apart by such allegations.

To test whether such memories are real or false, Drs Harrison Pope and James Hudson surveyed the findings of therapists. Both are psychiatrists at Harvard University, and their results appeared in *Psychological Medicine* in 1995. They argued that out of a possible one million sex abuse survivors in America, well-documented evidence of repressed memory should be easy to find. They proposed three criteria for a proved case of repression. First, the abuse must actually have happened. Second, repression had to be distinguished from concealment, pretending or lying. Third, the form of amnesia involved must be separated from simply forgetting.

To the layman, such criteria may seem harsh, but in the world of psychologists these are valid criteria. In other words, to prove repressed memories of childhood sex abuse as a definite phenomenon, these criteria must be applied. And when they were applied, Drs Pope and Hudson were astonished to discover that from all the literature and case studies published, not one case could be proved!

Whether repressed memories of childhood sex abuse actually exist can here be seen as a social debate, for there is not a shred of evidence for its existence within a scientific approach. Since Gary Ramona, other successful lawsuits have been brought, and many others are under way. In the light of this evidence, it seems most likely that such repressions do not exist, and the phenomenon is caused by a marriage of the ideas concerning prevalence of abuse with the current social requirement to degrade families and the place of the father within them. But if this is so, how do we explain the extraordinary claims of otherwise sane young women?

Elizabeth Loftus is a psychologist from Seattle. She recently attempted to plant a false memory in her subjects. Obviously, the trauma involved in the false memory could not be severe, for if successful, it could lead to invented psychological problems. Hence, she tried to implant the memory of being lost in a shopping mall as a child. Her therapy was so successful in some of her attempts that she was unable to erase it following the test.

As well as demonstrating the prevalence of possible paranormal phenomena within society, we can see that such false memories are remarkably similar to past life regressions and other forms of possession. They are not the result of the individual's mind, but an invasion of thoughts from outside, and while this does not prove the existence of extra-sensory perception – for instance, the memories can be 'suggested' in other subliminal ways – it does show that such suggestion can seem to bypass normal consciousness and become implanted into the unconscious. Indeed, it could even be argued that the invasion bypasses the senses and enters the mind directly. However, there are cases that do strongly suggest the existence of extra-sensory perception.

One of the most remarkable on record was witnessed by biologist and paranormal researcher Lyall Watson. He was spending several weeks with a remote tribe and its female shaman in the Philippines, when one day a ten-year-old boy was brought to her. Apparently, some three years previously the boy's mother had been killed and horribly disfigured by a truck while walking down a road, holding the boy's right hand.

When the boy appeared before the shaman Watson was horrified, for while the left side of the boy's body was normal, the right side resembled that of a hideously disfigured dwarf. On the left side his hair was healthy, on the right it was lifeless. The left eye was clear, while the right appeared squinted. On the left side his teeth were normal, but on the right they resembled fangs. On the left, his skin was healthy, while on the right he was covered in sores. With such disfigurements the boy shuffled painfully about, and when he spoke it was in a snarl and in a language that none of the tribe could understand.

For three days the shaman tried various potions and invocations, attempting to shift what she regarded as an evil spirit, but without success. Then, on the fourth night, as the boy, Watson and members of the tribe sat in a circle, the shaman joined them, hurled something into the fire and began to shout angrily at the boy. The shouting carried on for some time, the boy screaming and writhing about on the ground. Eventually he threw himself down and lay still, part of his body in the fire. The shaman came forward and carried him to her hut.

By the following morning the boy had already begun to recover, and by the end of the week he was back to being a normal ten-year-old boy. However, to Watson the most fascinating element of the whole 'possession' was the 'strange' language the boy occasionally snarled in. While the tribe did not understand it, Watson did – for the boy growled the occasional phrase of clear Zulu, a language Watson had learned when he was the boy's age.

What we are clearly dealing with here is an acute psychiatric disorder, caused by horrendous trauma and manifesting in dissociation of the personality combined with extreme, but not inexplicable, psychosomatic disorder. However, it is the way in which the disorders manifested that is fascinating. To the boy's culture, psychiatric disorder was not psychological but involved supernatural possession. Hence, the disorders followed a cultural pattern rather than being simply a product of individual psychology. Similarly, cure eventually came as was expected by the culture to which he belonged. Once he was convinced that an 'evil spirit' had been exorcized, the boy's psychological disorders lessened and eventually disappeared. At the time of the cure, Lyall Watson had become a clear element of the society through which the boy's culture worked, and this is the crux of the matter. Culture had invaded the boy's mind, and in his joining the society, elements of Watson had also invaded the boy's mind, allowing an element of Watson to manifest in the 'possession'. Hence, the boy spoke Zulu.

Of course, the sceptic will easily discount this case as either deception by the shaman – she knew Watson was researching her, so provided suitable evidence – or sloppy observation and embellishment by Watson. Indeed, in recording the case in his book *Beyond Supernature* (see Bibliography), Lyall Watson makes it clear that he does not put the case forward as evidence, well aware of the charges sceptics will advance in defence of their world view. However, a lesser, though nonetheless similar, form of possession is becoming quite popular within western culture.

First carried out on 20 January 1994 by the Vineyard Christian Fellowship at Toronto Airport, the Toronto Blessing is becoming all the rage amongts various charismatic movements. Gathering believers together, an orchestrator induces a form of violent trance in the individuals, accompanied by mass ceremony. Carrying out a similar function to tribal shamans, the orchestrator then induces a range of disturbing psychological phenomena: the trance subjects will fall over, shake violently and utter a whole host of animal noises. During such trances, healing is claimed to take place and the subjects often speak in strange languages that they do not otherwise know.

Known as xenoglossy, speaking in foreign tongues is quite common in such states, and is often identified during past life regression. Sometimes cryptomnesia can be applied to the phenomenon, but in many cases experiencers come from cultures that could not have had unconscious knowledge of such languages. In such cases, it is attractive to suggest that some form of extra-sensory perception could be involved.

Further evidence of extra-sensory perception being the product of cultural phenomena comes from the Ouija board. This device should really be called the 'yes yes' board, for the name is made up from the French and German for 'yes': '*oui*' and '*ja*'. Some claim that the messages received on the board come from spirits, but the most likely answer is that the board amplifies our reception of unconscious thoughts. The messages that come out are therefore from the unconscious, which is all very well as long as only one person is using it. When more than one do so, it can still be argued that the messages are from the unconscious, but the way in which the pointer is manipulated suggests that the various unconscious minds of the users have become communal, forming a kind of superconscious.

If such a superconscious can, indeed, be created by the coming together of a 'community' in this way, then the only possible answer to the phenomenon is that some form of thought transference akin to extra-sensory perception is involved, subtly manipulating not only the individual mind but also body function, as seen in the Filippino boy and the shakings involved in the Toronto Blessing.

Mind and Culture

■ We cannot prove the existence of extra-sensory perception: we can only offer evidence and theory suggestive of the fact. Sceptics use this to decry and ignore its existence, but what they leave out of the equation is the fact that such scientific concepts as evolution through natural selection and 'Big Bang' theory cannot be proved positively either. As with extra-sensory perception, their validity is based purely on accumulated evidence and theory suggestive of the fact.

If this is the case, why is the idea of extra-sensory perception treated with such contempt by science? The reason is that paranormal abilities do not fit our current world view. In other words, such powers face an overwhelming cultural bias. This in itself can, of course, be seen as a similar form of cultural suggestibility to those areas we have already discussed.

For instance, the idea of repressed memories of childhood sex abuse caused 'evidence' to accumulate from supposed sufferers. In other words, cultural biases had affected a 'community', causing a process akin to, but obviously more subtle than, possession. Hence, it could be argued that in trying to gain the acceptance of extra-sensory perception, we are not fighting science *per se*, but the cultural bias against such powers provided by the suggestion by science that such powers are impossible. Stated simply, this implies that it is a form of mind invasion through extra-sensory means that is preventing such an ability from being accepted. In this sense, scientists can be seen as not far removed from magicians and mystics. Indeed, mystics provide further evidence that the mind is not just extra-sensory, but totally adaptive to input from culture, if not from the totality of experience within the universe.

The role of the mystic has been much degraded. History has been the process of great social religions, such as Christianity, eventually giving way to sciences and reason. But archaeology and anthropology tell us that prior to the growth of such historical movements, cultural life was based on mysticism and ritual orchestrated by mystics. One of the last great survivals of this kind of system was the tribal culture of the Amerindians, which found its last great flurry in what became known as the Ghost Dance.

As with all human social systems, mystical movements are adaptable to changing times and evolve to meet the changing requirements of the people. The Ghost Dance satisfied this need admirably. Beginning in the mid-nineteenth century, it consisted of a shuffling circle dance with slow chanting. Within the dance, dancers would eventually experience mystical visions and hallucinate the dead. The dance would go on for four or five days, by the end of which the dancers were exhausted and thoroughly entranced, and it usually ended in their falling unconscious. Such dances had existed throughout Amerindian history, but at this time the purpose of this particular dance echoed the fears and needs of the entire Indian nation, moulding many different tribes together into a single want – and that want was essentially Messianic and Apocalyptic.

By the 1850s, white oppression of the Amerindians was well under way. We have all seen the early Hollywood films of the Indian wars, where Amerindians were portrayed as wild savages. We now know this to be a total lie. The 'bad guys' were really the white empire builders, intent on stealing Amerindian land, destroying their tribal culture, and indulging in one of the nastiest periods of genocide and apartheid in history. The Amerindians were quite literally involved in a struggle for survival. This led to the idea that some great mystical intervention would come, bring about the destruction of the white man, and return the land to how it was, including the resurrection of the Amerindian dead. The dance grew as an expression of this need by honouring the dead, in preparation for a coming new world.

By 1869, the mystic Wodzuwob, from Nevada, began to see the Ghost Dance as the vehicle for salvation and survival. His son, Wowoka, expanded his father's ideas. In a vision he saw that soon a flood would cover the Earth and destroy everything, including the white man. By dancing the Ghost Dance, however, the flood would pass under his people. As the waters receded, the Earth would revert to a more paradisaical state with only plants and animals. Into this world the Amerindian would return, the living and the dead existing in harmony, free from suffering for ever. Amerindians had to earn the right to this new world, however. To enter it, they had to learn how to live honestly and in harmony. This was particularly achievable by avoiding the ways of the white man, including his alcohol, to which by this time many Amerindians were addicted.

Perhaps the most important element of Wowoka's vision was its non-violence. He specifically opposed violence against the white man. It was not needed: the dance was the way to salvation. Such ideas became particularly evident in the Sioux, who took to the dance in a big way in the summer of 1890. However, by November of that year the white man had begun to see the dance as hostile and banned it on all Sioux reservations. The Sioux ignored this ban and continued to dance, as did many other tribes, and this defiance caused troops to be sent into several reservations. Scuffles broke out and several people were killed. However, a large group of Amerindians who had offered no resistance were sent to make camp at Wounded Knee Creek. Soldiers went among the Amerindians to collect all remaining weapons. Suddenly a shot was fired, and the soldiers immediately opened up with guns and cannon. Three hundred Amerindian men, women and children were massacred. The Ghost Dance, and any hope of freedom, disappeared.

This period of tribal Amerindian culture is vital to an understanding of the paranormal. We can see how mystics can somehow be overcome, or possessed, by a vision. Such a vision is seen not as a personal requirement, but as a form of social adaptation, bringing about a new phase of culture. The vision goes on to be expressed communally, where it is virtually re-enacted within ritual.

Such ritual brings out elements of the paranormal *en masse*, with a whole society sharing hallucinations of the dead and being 'possessed' within a trance-like state. But more than this, such dances seem to tap into a superconscious mind, as if the mind of each Amerindian had become interlinked. Put simply, the sheer power of the overall culture being expressed had subsumed individuality, leading to the possession as an expression of the culture itself. In this state, the requirements of destiny were satisfied, with the ritual going on to become a form of magical invocation that the Amerindians thought could actually change reality to their way of thinking.

In a social context, this gives the paranormal importance. The intuitive reader will see parallels between the requirements of the Ghost Dance and the beginnings of our western civilization, for following a number of expulsions and invasions, the ancient Hebrews also saw their world falling apart and birthed the most famous Messianic tradition the world has ever known. This was eventually formulated, outside the Hebrew peoples, in Jesus Christ, thus laying the foundations of Christianity and the world we live in today. As with the Ghost Dance, this earlier period of history was very much an expression of mysticism and feats of paranormal power.

Whether the paranormal actually exists or not is irrelevant to the argument being applied here. A *belief* in the paranormal is all that is required for a society to see the paranormal in action. The people see it because it is an expression of the culture they belong to, and within that culture a society finds meaning.

Today, the paranormal is generally scoffed at. Possessions are seen as forms of madness and delusion. I find it interesting that in such a world, meaning is also degraded. Today, without a paranormal culture, we are meaningless beings, living in a meaningless universe, slowly moving towards fragmentation in all social spheres. Science can decry the paranormal as much as it likes, but the above shows that culture is more than science, and culture requires meaning. Only the paranormal can satisfy such meaning, for without it we lose our sense of wonder and of the awesome power of nature, to which we belong. Perhaps the most important role of meaning within culture is that in finding meaning we also realize our direction, and through direction we find purpose.

The most famous of the Ghost Dance mystics showed this requirement in action, and it was through paranormality that cultural direction expressed itself. Nicholas Black Elk was born into the Sioux in 1863. When he was four years old he began to hear voices in his head. A year later he had a vision where two men came to him from the clouds and walked in circles around him before disappearing.

At the age of nine he had his 'great vision'. Falling ill, he slipped into a coma for 12 days. During this time the two men came out of the clouds again and took him up into the heavens. Here he met the 'grandfathers', or 'powers of the world'. The grandfathers showed Black Elk the universe and invested him with powers of healing. Then they showed him the 'sacred hoop' of his people, which can best be described as their spiritual unity, or oneness. The grandfathers told him that troubled times were coming, and the sacred hoop would be broken.

Towards the end of the vision he stood on the highest mountain and saw the hoop of the world. He expressed his feelings of this vision in 1932 in *Black Elk Speaks*:

> And while I stood there I saw more than I can tell and I understood more than I saw; for I was seeing in a sacred manner the shapes of all things in the spirit, and the shape of all shapes as they must live together like one being.

As the vision ended he saw the sacred hoop mend itself, and the sacred hoops of all people joined together in a huge circle.

When he was 18 years old, Black Elk had become a changed individual, acting like a withdrawn and old man. He found he had paranormal powers and he began turning his vision into ritual, convinced that through ritual the sacred hoop of his people would be repaired. Convinced that by experiencing the world of the white man he could learn how truly to bring about his vision, he joined Buffalo Bill Cody's Wild West Show in 1886 and toured the world for three years. Upon his return, he saw the Ghost Dance and knew that this was the ultimate expression of the sacred hoop. He performed and became a leader of the dance, where he experienced many possessions and trances.

Following the massacre at Wounded Knee Creek, Black Elk was sent to the Pine Ridge Reservation in South Dakota, where he lived to become an old man, devastated that he had failed his people by not repairing the sacred hoop through reviving their oneness and spirituality. In 1930, American writer and researcher John G. Neihardt sought out Black Elk for his first-hand account of the Ghost Dance Messianic days. This led to renewed interest in Black Elk, and by his death in 1950 he had regenerated Amerindian consciousness of their culture – the sacred hoop beginning to repair. If he had lived to see the dawn of the environmental movement and how important Amerindian ideas of nature would become, he may well have died knowing that his task on Earth was approaching completion.

Black Elk was undoubtedly a mystic, but he also tells us what a mystic is. His mind was not possessed by personal thoughts, but invaded by the cultural expressions of his time. In a real sense, his inner mind became a repository for cultural and social expression.

■ Through this chapter we have seen how possessions of all kinds can be regarded in a similar way. Robbie Mannheim became possessed in a way directed by the Roman Catholic culture to which he belonged. Lyall Watson's Filipino boy was similarly possessed by culture. In past life regression and the memories that are created in false memory syndrome, we can again see the possession in societal terms as opposed to personal. For in coming together, the patient and the therapist have formed a 'community'.

Possession can here be seen as culture; and in being possessed, we can usually find an element of meaning and direction. As Adam Crabtree realized, in treating the 'possession', you cure the problem. In a wider sense, this is what Black Elk attempted to do for his people. He took his vision and impregnated it upon culture in the form of ritual, and through ritual the individual was possessed, found meaning, and realized his future direction. The paranormal thus becomes a cultural form of therapy, and a means through which destiny can be achieved. In its being an expression of culture we can see, in a philosophical sense at least, how possession taps a form of consciousness – a soul, if you like – that is much greater than the individual.

· TRIBAL PSYCHISM ·

Cave Art

■ A simple deduction can be made from the theorizing in this book so far. Culture can be seen as the 'soul' of society. Through culture we define our place in society, our place in the cosmos, the meaning that gives us our identity, and receive an indication of the direction we must follow.

Most cultures throughout the world follow a similar line of evolution. Due to our past supernatural and superstitious ways, all societies seemed to express culture first through mythology. Such mythologies eventually birthed the great religious movements that gave us our place, identity, meaning and direction. To interact with our culture, society devised several forms of cultural expression through which meaning was ascertained. We call this endeavour art – the painting, sculpture, music and literature that define how we see the world. However, if we trace our cultural inheritance further back than history and the great religious movements, we can see that before all of these factors, there was the paranormal.

Our first cultural expressions can be seen in perhaps the most enigmatic art forms ever created by human hand. Today, when an artist paints, his finished work is put on display for all to see, but in the deep past this seems not to have been the case. Rather, the first artists seemed to live in a secret world of darkness, removed from society, carrying out their art with such dedication as to astound contemporary man.

Evidence of their work has been found in many locations. Near the town of Les Eyzies in the Dordogne lies the cave of Lascaux. Venturing into this deep cave has been described as entering a magical world, the walls covered with artistic representations of horses, bulls and deer. Made with rudimentary equipment and paints, they transfix the viewer, for it is easy to imagine them no longer as paintings but as animated creatures, magically coming alive.

The cave of Tuc d'Audoubert in the Ariège region of France is even more fascinating. Following a narrow, winding tunnel, you must travel for over a mile into the deepest gloom, your flashlight transforming reality from the normal world outside into something more primeval. Eventually you will enter a chamber and stop, uttering a gasp. Before you are two eerie clay sculptures of bison and, as with the art of Lascaux, it is easy to see them move.

The ceiling of the cave of Altamira in northern Spain is spectacular. Entering a chamber and shining your flashlight at the ceiling discloses a spectacular array of art, including some two dozen bison in a circle, a couple of horses, a wolf, three deer and three boars. Painted in bright yellows, reds and blacks, the images were thought for a while after their discovery in 1879 to be so perfect that they must be recent and fraudulent. However, learned opinion has changed, and they are now widely regarded as genuine.

Other figures can be found in other caves. Sometimes the host of animal representations is accompanied by strange stick men, as if enacting ritual. In other caves, such as Trois Frères in south-western France, images depict combinations of animal–human forms. In every case the images come alive, as if they are more than just simple art forms.

Cave art preceded the agricultural revolution of 10,000 years ago. A product of hunter-gatherer societies that migrated with the great herds, some scholars date their beginnings to 35,000 years ago, while most accept that the period of cave art dates back at least 18,000 years, finally coming to an end just before the beginnings of the agricultural revolution. During this period artists did not simply find a cave, paint their pictures, and leave. Rather, evidence suggests that they continually returned and changed their images, sometimes painting over them – and continued to do so for centuries, as if events required a new representation. In this way, the art was dynamic, and changed in line with a changing world.

What was this art for? One interpretation that was accepted for a time was that the caves were filled with simple, idle doodles, a form of stone age graffiti, with no purpose at all. This 'art for art's sake' interpretation was thrown out with the growing understanding of the animal–human combinations, known as chimeras. These are not mere representations, but well thought-out images.

Central to the understanding of cave art is the idea of animism and spirits. All primitive, tribal cultures see nature as a living, spiritual form. Rivers and mountains and trees are not merely the sum total of their physicality, but are invested with a more ethereal presence. They can come alive and exist with consciousness. Such concepts are known to have infiltrated ideas concerning animals, for these, too, were more than they appeared. Rather than being simply animals, they were invested with spirits – guiding entities that held powers far more awesome than the jaws of the predator.

This primeval view of the world has led many scholars to see cave art as the domain of hunting magic. It is known that hunting cults existed in primitive cultures; hence, it is thought that the cave art is not a representation of the animal as such, but of its spirit. In this view, before the hunt the cult members used a form of sympathetic magic to assist in the coming chase, perhaps subduing or entrapping the animal spirit. Here, the chimeras themselves are seen as representative of humans 'becoming' the animal being hunted.

A variation on the hunting theme is to see cave art as a form of telepathic aid, with the hunting cult enacting ritual in the cave in order to 'locate' the animal to be hunted, or even to 'charm' it to go to the hunters. In this instance, the chimera can be seen as a form of Pied Piper, with the head of the cult dressing in animal skins and then 'projecting' himself out-of-the-body to lead the beast to the required location.

Of course, all this is supposition, but the idea that ritual was, indeed, enacted in such caves is advanced by our growing knowledge of the *position* of animal representations within the cave. For instance, the French archaeologists Iégor Reznikoff and Michel Dauvois carried out the most unusual survey of a number of such caves. They went into them and walked around, singing. Covering three octaves, they went on to draw resonance maps of the caves, and discovered that the areas of highest resonance were the most likely places to find the art.

For a time the hunting magic theory held sway, but today, while we know that some form of hunting magic must have gone on, we also know that the picture is much wider than this. For instance, while the artists' most common representations were of horses and bison, analysis of animal remains around the living sites of people of the time shows that their main diet was reindeer and ptarmigan. If hunting was the only reason for such art, we would expect the images to represent the animal being hunted, but this is not the case.

Researcher David Lewis-Williams offered an intriguing, and remarkably logical, theory to account for cave art in issue 29 of *Current Anthropology* in 1988. One of the most puzzling aspects of the representations is the prevalence of geometric designs accompanying the art, including dots, chevrons, rectangles and zigzags. Lewis-Williams has pointed out that such images – known as entoptic images – are often seen in the early stages of altered states of consciousness, such as trances. These images eventually give way to actual hallucinated representations. Such a view gives a wholly new reason for cave art, for rather than being simple animal representations, the inclusion of geometric design suggests that the images were a way of making permanent the hallucinated 'animal spirits' observed by ancient tribal adepts during trance.

An overall picture is beginning to emerge. Rather than being simple representations, we can see cave art as being just one part of a much more complicated form of ceremony and ritual enacted in the cave, involving some form of music or chanting and trance-like states. During such ritual, hallucinated forms appear. These 'spirits' are then 'captured' upon the walls and ceilings of the caves, thus bringing the supernatural world into the physical – and we continue to represent the supernatural in such terms even today, for supernatural forms still decorate our churches. In looking specifically at the cave art, we have missed the point: it isn't the cave art that is of primary importance, but the cave itself. In enacting ritual in such caves, mankind had devised the first form of temple, birthed the first form of representative religion – and done so by virtue of paranormal forms, hallucinated through trance.

By highlighting this logical idea, we can place the values of religion upon these stone age caves. Rather than seeing the images as simple artistic forms, we can see the cave-temple as the centre of culture. Seeing the caves as a form of church, we can argue that whoever carried out such rituals did so for the people of some stone age parish. Within the cave, those people found meaning and direction. Society was ordered by the representations of the temple, and thus by the paranormality of their hallucinated form. Within the hallucination was found a world view of reality and the cosmos. In other words, these 'mothers of culture' can be seen as a spiritual microcosm of the world: but then why bury them deep in caves, inaccessible to most of the population that held them to be of such importance?

Through various anthropological studies we know that the earliest religions revolved around the idea that the Earth was a deity. Known as Mother Earth, this feminine principle was often represented as the Goddess. Central to such religious forms was the idea of rebirth, with nature going through its yearly cycle of death and regeneration. Hence, the concept of birth was vital to such early religions.

Such an explanation can be attached to the hallucinated forms in the stone age caves, for as each image is revealed we can see it as being 'birthed', or created for the first time, or regenerated anew. And with birth therefore being so important to this early religious form, where is the most logical place to create the first temples? Life begins deep inside the female form, and in birth that life leaves the darkness of the inside of the woman, and, after coming down a tunnel, breaks into light. Remembering that the Earth was seen as a feminine deity, could it be that the caves represented the womb, deep inside the body of the female? And if so, wouldn't those who had just been 'reborn' through ritual come out into the light from a deep, dark tunnel?

The suggestion here is that the cave-temple allowed for a ritual rebirth steeped in an already existent culture. The cave-temple was a microcosm of that culture and, its people being hunter-gatherers who moved around dependent upon the migrating herds, we can see the cave-temple ritual as being a regeneration of the cultural inheritance of the tribe as it moved from location to location, regenerating itself anew to guarantee the benevolence of the 'spirits' that occupied the region and thus guaranteeing the people's safety, meaning and direction. Such an idea can be enhanced by studying the adept who is most likely to have carried out the hallucinated trance – the shaman.

The Shaman

■ The film is set in deepest Africa. The hero is the great white hunter – tall, muscular and handsome. He knows the jungle as well as any native; he lives it, breathes it. By his side is the glamorous woman – still looking glamorous after all the trekking, still walking fine even after the great white hunter has chopped off her high heels. But when the going gets tough, she'll scream and shout and go into hysterics – just to make the great white hunter look good.

Now they hear the drums. An air of expectancy descends, and before they know it they are surrounded by an African tribe and bundled off to the village. Tied up in the middle of a circle of tribesmen, a sudden, blood-curdling scream announces the arrival of a demented lunatic, horns stuck on his head, beads dangling from his neck. He carries a strange rattle, jumps about the circle and pulls manic faces; his eyes are deep and staring, an obvious mania shining through from within. Dancing around the tied-up great white hunter and damsel, he begins to shout curses, and their fate is clear. The pot is approaching the boil.

Thus has the westerner developed the starkest stereotype of the most intriguing profession mankind has ever devised. Fundamental to tribal society, this is the shaman – and the above movie depiction could not be further from the truth. Variously known as the witch doctor, medicine man and a thousand other localized labels, anthropologists have found him, or occasionally her, in tribal societies throughout the world. From Haiti to the Philippines, from Siberia to South Africa, he appears in almost exact form.

Where the word 'shaman' came from is a point of debate. The original term seems to be have been *saman*, which exists in both Tungusic societies of Siberia and Central Asia, and can also be found in the Sanskrit. Here, it is thought to mean 'song', but while this can be allied to the magical chanting and music involved in shamanic ritual, it fails to explain his remarkable powers. In his classic book *Shamanism* (see Bibliography), Professor Mircea Eliade wrote that the shaman practised 'one of the archaic techniques of ecstasy – at once mysticism, magic and "religion" in the broadest sense of the term'. However, this is thought to be too narrow an explanation of his function.

Shamans provided a host of services for their tribe. As well as practising spiritual healing and divination, they were thought to be able to find plentiful game for hunting, control the weather, identify criminals among the tribe and contact and communicate with the spirits of the dead and higher spiritual deities. Shamans were also essential to the ceremony and culture of the tribe. Perfecting ritual dance and storytelling, they oversaw the entire culture in which the tribe lived, defining their place in the world through ceremony and allegorical storytelling. While the shaman rarely held political status – this was the preserve of the chief – he was an expression of the 'soul' of the community, a bridgehead between the physical tribe and the other-worldly entities they worshipped, often using such entities to offer direction for the future.

Essential to these tasks was the shaman's ability to achieve a trance state at will. During such trances he would be possessed by a dead or higher spirit, and through the shaman, the spirit would speak. At other times, the shaman would not be possessed, but would leave his body and enter the astral plane, where he would walk in another, higher world, receiving messages of benefit to the tribe. Such skills we can now see as being psychological rather than supernatural in nature. And as in cases of possession (see Minds Possessed), we can see that in his trances the shaman actually connected with the 'communality' of the tribe, or its superconscious.

The shaman was also an orchestrator of higher ritual, in a similar way to the orchestrators of the Toronto Blessing (see pages 46–7). A natural hysteric, in his dances and chants he induced a form of controlled hysteria within the tribe. Through this practice, hallucinations can appear to take place *en masse*, thus confirming to the tribe the existence of the supernatural. But more than this, in the ecstatic dances of tribal religion, the shaman cleansed the tribe of frustrations. Anyone who has been to a pop concert or rave will have seen this form of tribal cleansing in action. By approaching an hysterical state in the company of others, our well-being is boosted and problems and frustrations seem to dissolve before us, the end result being a person who is enriched and psychologically cleansed, as if their batteries had been topped up. We can see here that the shaman was the first form of psychoanalyst, and also how such tribal practices could be of great value to us today, in a world where material living leads to psychological problems of epidemic proportions among the population.

The more sceptical researcher would, however, be of the opinion that the abilities of the shaman were not 'special', in terms of his talents being a 'gift', but rather that he was simply a schizophrenic. After all, both shamanism and schizophrenia involve hallucinations and the hearing of voices. In an exact, clinical sense, this may be true – the shaman could well have been schizophrenic. But this is to ignore the culture to which the shaman belonged, and is also where our earlier film depiction gets it wrong.

We have seen how hallucinations are caused by a dislocation of the mind from the sensory stimuli about us (see page 20). Further, we have seen how the hearing of voices in the head can be a product of the right cerebral hemisphere being out of phase with the left side of the brain (see pages 41–42). The right brain is emotional, and cutting ourselves off from outside stimuli involves going into the personal mind and accessing the unconscious. This, too, can be seen as a descent into a more emotional side of us.

Here, we can see that hallucinations and inner voices are both the product of a more emotional stimulus than the logical world in which we are supposed to live. In the modern world, we still feed this emotional side of us in a variety of ways. We have already seen this in action in the case of raves, but we also read novels, listen to music or play with our video games. But as well as being activities to stimulate our emotions, these are also the vehicles through which we connect with culture.

In this sense, we can see the shaman infecting the tribe with a more omnipotent form of emotion, and thus cultural inheritance. So even if he was a schizophrenic, we can see him as having cultural value. The society to which he belonged realized that he had a place, and utilized his 'abilities' for the good of the tribe. If, in the modern world, we want to ease psychological problems, we could perhaps learn from tribal societies. Instead of seeing the schizophrenic as 'mad' and dosing him up with drugs, why not use and channel his hallucinations and voices to benefit us all? In so doing, we may discover that he is less insane than we think: it may be us who are mad in living without the psychological release he could induce.

We can see here how tribal societies confirmed the existence of the supernatural through a form of controlled and channelled 'madness', orchestrated by a schizophrenic who eased psychological problems and brought forward the collective hopes and wishes of the tribal superconscious through trance. In a real sense, the messages he would have received during trance echo the role of the Ouija board (see page 47). Through his voices and hallucinations, the shaman expressed the soul of the tribe.

This idea of the shaman being a controlled schizophrenic is reinforced by the way in which a shaman was picked. Shamanic abilities were usually identified in childhood. Often the 'gift' was hereditary, just as schizophrenia can sometimes be seen as hereditary, but most often the future shaman was picked spontaneously by the tribe's supernatural deities. The way in which this happened again echoes the onset of schizophrenia. Typically, the child would begin to act eratically, progressing towards hysterical collapse, and would eventually hear voices. Because of the cultural inheritance through which he had lived, the voices would, of course, echo the supernatural deities the tribe believed in, and when the hallucinations appeared they, too, would be as expected. Hence, even in this early stage, the growing schizophrenia was controlled, and from then on the tribe would separate the child and train him in the controlled abilities he increasingly manifested.

So what, essentially, was a shaman? We have seen how the stereotype depicts him as simply a mad individual infecting the tribe with his madness. At the other end of the scale, believers in classical shamanic abilities see him as a truly gifted individual who gains insights from an existent world of the supernatural. But the most likely answer can be found in a marriage of psychology and sociology.

By seeing the shaman as a controlled schizophrenic, we cast him as neither mad nor gifted in an easily understood way. He is not gifted because he is mentally ill, but neither is he mad, for his 'madness' is controlled and is of value to his society. Indeed, in expressing his shamanic abilities, he isn't even an individual in a way we can understand. In entering the trance state, he becomes a repository of the thoughts of his society; he becomes a communal being, a mouthpiece for a collective soul, and an expression in the physical world of a higher, cultural mind.

The Genesis of Religion

■ No one knows how ancient shamanic abilities are, but we do know that such abilities were being expressed and practised 20,000 years ago. Until he was replaced in our consciousness by the prostitute, the shaman was regarded as practising the world's oldest profession – and we can now see why. Until the shaman came into existence, culture could not be defined, and without a defined culture, organized society could not come into being. We can therefore see the shaman as the first form of cultural expression, and that expression was essentially paranormal.

As he is at least 20,000 years old, we can also see the shaman as the man behind cave art, extending a purely psychological cultural expression to make its mark on the physical world. In being represented in the physical world, the spirits – the first ones being animal spirits – then became that much more real and easy to define.

We call this practice 'symbolism', and perhaps the most baffling symbol that tribal societies left to tease us today was the spiral maze. The pattern of the maze may vary, but the basic design is of a spiralling, circular configuration, sometimes including a form of path or tunnel leading from the bottom to the centre. Such a design comes from deep antiquity, pre-dating structures such as Stonehenge, and is clearly identifiable in cultures which indulged in cave art.

Sometimes carved on rocks, sometimes gouged out of the earth, the symbol is universal. It is prolific in Europe, has been found in both North and South America, and can also be found in abundance in some areas of Asia. Such is its enigmatic quality that some extraordinary theories have been developed to account for it. Writer Geoffrey Ashe proposed that it was symbolic of a centre from which occult knowledge spread outward. Other theories centre around the spiral maze being suggestive of an awareness of geomagnetic forces within the Earth. Dowser Guy Underwood claimed to detect such a spiralling magnetic force in the 1960s, and since then several researchers have claimed to detect it.

One obvious answer to the symbol is that it represents the deep cave, where art and ritual were performed. The tunnel and the spiral configuration can be seen as the narrow entrance to the cave, leading to a chamber at its centre. A further theory suggests that the symbol represents a form of heightened consciousness. For instance, today we play games in mazes; building them with walls or hedges, we get a 'buzz' by becoming lost in them and trying to find our way out. Such a practice can be seen psychologically as the safe frill, where a process of danger and disorientation leads to heightened consciousness. However, whereas the maze we design today can clearly be seen to originate in the design, there is no evidence from prehistory that mazes were built with walls before about 3000 BC. Evidence suggests that prior to this the designs were always simply carved in rocks or gouged out of the earth. No 'games' were played in these representations.

Early research into spiral mazes found an intriguing connection with the ancient Greek mythology of Troy, for the way in which many of the symbols are named actually includes the word 'Troy'. There is a turf maze at Troy Farm in Oxfordshire, for example, while another turf maze in North Yorkshire is known as the 'City of Troy'. However, it now seems that this association is incorrect. In Latin, the word *troare* means 'to turn', as does the Celtic *tro*; hence, the supposed association with Troy simply means turning, or possibly dizziness.

Other researchers see the spiral maze as symbolic of the afterlife, or of death and rebirth. We know that man has been fascinated by death for at least 50,000 years, when Neanderthal man began to bury his dead ceremonially. The tunnel and spiralling effect have been identified in the 'near death experience', where the experiencer goes down a tunnel and enters a form of 'heaven' before waking up once more. However, the near death experience is thought of as a recent phenomenon, identified because of our technological abilities to save people who would otherwise die. It is thus doubtful that prehistoric man would have experienced the phenomenon and been revived to recount it. However, a possible, and allied, answer to the spiral maze can be offered by recent research into the near death experience at the University Clinic Rudolf Vichow in Berlin.

Here, Dr Thomas Lempert induced prolonged faints in some of his healthy students. Usually a faint lasts for a second or two, but he maintained it for up to 22 seconds. Reporting the results in *The Lancet* in September 1994, he stated that many of the students had experiences that cannot be separated from the near death experience, including hallucinations, out-of-body experiences, visions of 'heaven' and feelings of joy and absolute peace. These students appeared to experience components of the afterlife, and their experiences can tell us a great deal about our prehistoric ancestors.

It is known that by the time the historical record came into being, man's fascination with death and rebirth was well entrenched in the psyche. We have also seen how hallucinations can cause beliefs in spirits, and how shamanic ritual involved deep trance, ecstasy and hysteria. The eventual outcome of such ritual practices would be a deep faint, where, it seems, the hallucinations again appear. But the important question to be asked is this: to a primitive people, would such a deep faint be seen as similar to death? Such a possibility is attractive – and in coming out of the faint, the experiencer can be seen as magically cheating death. Thus, in shamanic ritual we can see the possibility of the shaman having power over life and death, and inducing death and rebirth.

With such an idea, we can see the spiral maze as symbolic of this ritual, in that we have the insinuation of a tunnel, dizziness (this always comes before the faint) and the suggestion of occult knowledge of the afterlife at the centre of the spiral. In addition, we can also see this death/rebirth as a common phenomenon, universal among tribal peoples, thus explaining the symbol's universality. Indeed, we can even extend the symbol to represent the cave ritual. We have already seen how the most likely purpose of the cave was 'rebirth', with a 'coming out' of the cave being analogous to the birth of a child. We can now see the 'going into' the cave as symbolic of death, with a fainting ritual being performed inside.

With such a theory we can see a real starting point for religion, for the death/rebirth aspect is vital to many religious forms, the most famous being remembered at Easter with the resurrection of Jesus Christ. But perhaps most importantly, it tells us how ideas of an 'afterlife' first appeared: could it be that the visions seen during the prolonged faint were not seen as *analogous* to the afterlife, but as the afterlife itself? If so, we can see the afterlife not as an existent state, but as a psychologically produced symbolic landscape.

Standing Stones

■ Cave art disappeared from the archaeological record some 10,000 years ago. Why was this? Did tribal society suddenly leave its supernatural culture behind? This is, of course, one explanation, but the most obvious is that, rather than society leaving it behind, it became more refined. And we can say this because 10,000 years ago mankind began to evolve society away from the hunter-gatherer lifestyle that people had lived for millennia.

The reason for this change was essentially geological, for 10,000 years ago the last ice age came to an end and the great glacial formations retreated to within the Arctic Circle. This led to a more stable climate, in which a variety of plants prospered. Slowly, people learned how to use these plants to supplement their diet, and it wasn't long before they began cultivating them. In doing so, they left their hunter-gatherer ways for the agricultural revolution, which, among other things, meant they no longer had to be nomadic, following their food source, the herd. Rather, communities became static, building a permanent home near their crops. And this inevitably led to a more permanent form of supernatural cultural symbolism, aided by the new form of endeavour known as building.

Evidence of this new cultural outpouring can be found throughout northwest Europe, in over 1,000 variations of standing stones known as megaliths, the most famous of these being at Stonehenge on Salisbury Plain, Wiltshire. The construction at Stonehenge consists of a horseshoe arrangement of standing sandstones and bluestones, surrounded by a circle of sarsens (or standing stones) topped by horizontal stone lintels – hence the name Stonehenge, which means 'hanging stones'. Many of these stones weigh up to 26 tonnes and some – the bluestones – came from the Preseli Mountains in South Wales. One legend has it that Merlin magically transported the bluestones, but more realistically, they were dragged overland and floated across water in a transport operation that would have taken decades.

Construction at Stonehenge went on for many thousands of years, the stones showing signs of being readapted many times. Carbon dating of bones and other artefacts buried in holes at the site fix its ceremonial importance to 8000 BC. We can thus see the site gaining importance immediately upon the glaciers receding and the caves falling out of use. However, the bulk of the present Stonehenge is believed to have been built in three major stages between 3500 BC and 1100 BC, with its present shape in existence by about 2000 BC. As to previous construction, we have no idea, but the carbon dating of the holes suggests a previous construction most probably did exist.

The sheer engineering difficulties and time taken for construction clearly tell us that whatever Stonehenge was for, it was central to the culture of the people. It provides us with the first signs of epic monumental building, and we can only imagine the fanaticism involved in its construction. Clearly, whatever the motive for such megaliths, it was above any form of individuality or contemporary social endeavour, for many generations would have been involved in its design and construction. The transportation of the bluestones is testament to this, for the people who began to move them would have been long dead before their descendants completed the journey.

What *was* Stonehenge for? The most commonly accepted theory was first hinted at by clergyman Dr William Stukeley in 1740. He noted that the axis of the structure was aligned to the north-eastern sky when the sun rose at dawn on the summer solstice of 21 June. This observation was confirmed at the turn of the twentieth century by British astronomer Sir Norman Lockyear.

In the 1930s, Scottish engineer Alexander Thom decided to test this idea by carrying out on-site surveys of megaliths. Over the following 40 years he surveyed over 600 sites throughout north-west Europe. He showed that in practically every case the constructions were aligned to astronomical positions of the sun, moon and stars, suggesting not only astronomical abilities, but also an understanding of geometry.

In 1965, astronomer Gerald S. Hawkins began his own computer analysis of Stonehenge. He discovered that every stone within the construction provided sightlines for the rising and setting sun on key dates, and concluded that Stonehenge was a prehistoric observatory.

The observatory idea is further enhanced by study of other ancient structures, such as the deep 'tomb' at Newgrange in Ireland. Here, a thin shaft is perfectly aligned to allow the midwinter sun to shine into the tomb. However, the observatory function, while clearly a part of the purpose of megaliths, overshadows other ideas concerning them. In marvelling at the sheer engineering prowess of the builders, we mask the possibility of more 'supernatural' and 'cultural' functions. Indeed, I myself am not particularly impressed by the supposed brilliant calculations involved in astrological alignment. We must not downgrade the ability of the good old eyeball to see where the sun rises and mark a point that it shines on. This simple observation, combined with decades of trial and error and sheer fanaticism, is all that is needed eventually to get the alignment right.

A further idea concerning megaliths such as Stonehenge has developed into what have become known as 'Earth mysteries'. If such mysteries have a starting point, then it is arguably the publication of Alfred Watkins's *The Old Straight Track* in 1925 (see Bibliography). Watkins noted that many ancient sites such as megaliths and old churches could be joined together by straight lines. Calling them 'ley lines', he argued that they constituted an ancient network of trade routes. Where two lines intersected, you would usually find a major monument. By the 1960s, however, ley lines had developed into a far more esoteric concept, with writers such as John Michell arguing that they were channels for mystical Earth energies. Prehistoric people were more in tune with such energies and built monuments to represent, or even channel, these powers.

In 1977, the Dragon Project was formed by researcher Paul Devereux to study such mysteries using the expertise of scientists, psychics, dowsers and folklorists. At some sites – particularly the Rollright Stones near Oxford – energy anomalies were recorded, but this success was not generally achieved. Even the results at the Rollright Stones can be put down to various other factors, and cannot be seen as proof of existent Earth energies.

Sceptics of 'Earth mysteries' point out that ley lines are not so much a fact as a fallacy: look at any Ordnance Survey map and it is easy to find a number of ancient sites and draw a straight line connecting them. Earth mysteries are therefore more a mystery of human gullibility. On the other hand, there is evidence of 'straight tracks' within European mythology. Known variously as 'ghost roads' or 'corpse ways', they were particular routes for funeral processions, taking their dead to cemeteries.

The 'ancient observatory' and 'Earth energies' theories represent the two extremes surrounding megaliths such as Stonehenge, but could it be that the two positions can be combined to provide a more balanced idea of what Stonehenge actually was?

There is, of course, more to Stonehenge than the above theories. For instance, as noted earlier, ancient holes at the site included bones. Many of these have been identified as cremated human bones, suggesting ceremonial funerals were also carried out at the site. This indicates that death was of importance to the builders. Indeed, these holes are the oldest element of the site, suggesting 'death' to be fundamental to it. We have also seen how death was combined with rebirth, the stone age caves showing evidence of the ceremonial death and rebirth of nomadic society as it went from site to site. And there are indications in the evolution of early religious forms that death/rebirth continued to be vital to early cultures.

The first known religions were 'fertility' cults, and they appeared in line with the agricultural revolution. The importance of animal spirits involved with hunter-gatherer cultures was waning, and was replaced with a more distinct Mother Earth, or Goddess. Finding her primacy in the fertility of the Earth itself, she guaranteed the success of a society's crops.

In order to grow crops successfully, primitive societies required knowledge of the seasons; for instance, they had to know when to sow seed and when to harvest the crop. Ceremonially, the death/rebirth aspect of culture developed to represent the changing seasons, with nature appearing to 'die' during the winter and to be 'reborn' in the spring. To guarantee the accuracy of this seasonal change, the early farmers realized that indications were offered by the celestial bodies in the sky, such as the sun; and to represent this new awareness, the 'temple' was now required to be open to the sky.

We can now see how and why Stonehenge developed into an observatory, measuring the course of the sun and showing the early farmers when the time had come to sow seed and harvest the crop. But this observatory aspect was indistinguishable from the ceremonial requirement of honouring Mother Earth: the two aspects were one and the same. The most important seasonal 'moments' were, of course, the four solstices, and to this day pagan religions hold these moments as primarily ceremonial occasions. Thus we can see an extension of the death/rebirth rituals being carried out in line with agricultural requirements.

A further aspect of Stonehenge is that it is basically an enclosure of stone. In this respect it echoes the enclosed qualities of the stone age cave, with the addition that it is open to the deities of the sky. It is thus attractive to argue that shamanic hallucinatory practices continued to be carried out within the stones on the 'special' seasonal days. Remembering that a temple has a 'parish', we can envisage the possibility of ritual processions leading to the stones.

With this information, we can imagine the cultural expressions of the time. Information arrives in a village that the megalith indicates the solstice is coming. The village shaman immediately begins his ceremonies, perhaps placing magical properties in the seed to be planted. To honour the Goddess, the ceremony continues as each village in the area sends its emissaries to the temple. These emissaries are already approaching hysteria, and as they proceed by the shortest route they will already be experiencing hallucinations, the paths they take being thought of as ghost roads, or even 'spirit' paths. Once at the temple, the collective hysteria from all the emissaries explodes into a mass hallucinatory ritual, echoing the hallucinations previously carried out in the cave.

As well as demonstrating the 'observatory' aspect of Stonehenge, this scenario can also address the idea of Earth mysteries. To those ancient peoples, the 'spirits' they would see were fundamentally linked to the Earth; they were part of the Earth, and were seen as coming from the Earth. Such an idea would leave a deep cultural heritage within us, and perhaps it is this heritage that is being tapped today when we associate such phenomena with being a part of the Earth. Paul Devereux is coming to a similar conclusion himself. He sees ley lines more as trails along which people were 'drawn' towards a spiritual centre. The mysteries themselves, he surmises, can be seen as a product of our 'collective' consciousness, as if part of my suggested superconscious.

We can enhance this idea. As we have seen, the most likely explanation of cave art is that the cave was a representation of the womb. In this respect, the cave became a ceremonial representation indistinguishable from the real thing. Within the cave, the hallucinations were equally seen as 'real' because the interior of the cave was not a physical existence, but a spiritual realm. This may seem a ridiculous concept today, but the idea has survived the passing of time and still exists today. When a Christian walks into a church, he does not walk into a building, but a spiritual representation of the 'body of Christ'. The Christian church as a whole is similarly seen as existing within the 'spirit' of Christ – a concept known as the 'mystical body of Christ'. The Christian therefore exists in both the physical world and the spirit world at the same time: it is quite possible that the worshippers of Stonehenge had similar ideas. They were not just farmers planting seed; they were spiritual beings existing within the spirit world of their gods, and the two worlds – the physical and spiritual – were indistinguishable.

Stonehenge was a burial ground, an observatory and a temple, but these distinct functions are modern inventions of a culture for which specialization is commonplace. The worshippers of Stonehenge knew of no such distinction, and Stonehenge carried out all these functions as one. As with the idea of the shaman being the cultural centre of society (see page 60), the agricultural revolution led to an extension of this ideal, with Stonehenge replacing the shaman but being essentially the same thing. And again as with the shaman, it led to the cultural expression of spirits and a close affinity with the paranormal.

Druids

■ Agricultural society was different to hunter-gatherer society in several respects. First of all, it led to a more permanent form of living, in that the people began to remain static as opposed to being wanderers. And second, it led to the need to specialize, for in hunter-gatherer societies you required a chief, a shaman, hunters and gatherers, but as agricultural society came into being you also needed farmers, builders, merchants and guards to protect the crops.

This urge towards permanence can be seen in Stonehenge. Shamans may at one time have been the spiritual and cultural centre of society, but shamans died and needed replacing. Megaliths such as Stonehenge did not die, and thus allowed permanence. But did this mean that shamans fell out of fashion? This could not be further from the truth.

Early history was one of invasion and conquest. While we may see this as despicable today, the practice is useful to the historian in that it highlights areas of culture that would otherwise have disappeared. We know that the agricultural revolution eventually led to the city-state, such as Babylon or Athens, but the progression from basic agrarian society to the city in such cultures is shrouded in mythology. However, due to the early invasions, we can occasionally see an advanced culture invading a more primitive one. When this happens, important stages of societal development are freeze-framed in the historical record. The last example of this was the white man's conquest of the Amerindians. At first, the history being freeze-framed is distorted by the victor – in this way, the Amerindians were seen as savages – but as time passes this stage of societal development becomes open to more balanced analysis.

Such a freeze-framed culture can be identified with the Roman invasion of ancient Britain. With the Celtic peoples, the Romans 'took over' a society which was experiencing the transition between basic agrarian culture and city-state. Stonehenge had already fallen into disuse around 1000 BC, and Celtic society had moved forward from isolated village communities to a more co-operative society akin to kingdoms, with a well-advanced form of market economy. Arguably, if the Celts had been left alone, they would have eventually realized the city.

In such a freeze-framed society, we can identify the shaman. We know him as the Druid. Thought to be well established by the sixth century BC, we know him as a form of shaman who indulged in sacrificial ceremonies, particularly around oak trees. Belonging to a pre-literate society, he indulged in oral traditions and consequently left little in the historical record himself.

One early mention of the Druids comes from the Roman writer Tacitus. He speaks of hysterical Druid women running about and shouting curses in AD 60 as Roman soldiers invaded the Isle of Mona, now known as Anglesey. We can discount this picture of Druid barbarians in the same way as we can discount the white man's view of Amerindians, or the film stereotype of the African tribal shaman. We can do this not only because the victor invariably portrays the vanquished in a bad light, but because of growing archaeological and anthropological evidence of a distinct Druid culture.

Elements of shamanic practices can still be seen in the Druids, in that they orchestrated ecstatic ceremony, had prophetic dreams and read the future from the entrails of animals. The drinking of blood following sacrifice and burning of sacrificial people in man-shaped wickerwork cages can also be identified. But alongside this we can also identify the shaman going on to specialize in specific talents, for the Druids can be better identified as forming the professional middle class, developing into philosophers, early scientists, jurists, musicians and poets; and with their growing knowledge of herbs, we can also identify in them the first known form of medical practitioner.

Evidence of Druid-style societal development can just be seen in other cultures such as that of the ancient Greeks. Most people are aware that the earliest great scientist was Pythagoras. Thought to have been born in about 540 BC at Samos, he was the first to see nature as answerable to numbers, thus laying the foundations of mathematics. However, his main deduction concerned the numerical ratios which determined musical intervals and he was actually more concerned with music than with science.

Pythagoras is also believed to have formed a religious society at Croton, aimed at liberating the soul from the corruption of the body. In this we can see him more as a mystical, shaman-type individual than a distinct scientist. Indeed, some commentators maintain that Pythagoras did not exist as an individual: rather, the talents attributed to him are really the product of a Druid-like order known as the cult of the Pythagoreans.

In both Druids and Pythagoras we can see aspects of the transition from agrarian to city culture, with shamanic-type individuals advancing their ceremonies and skills towards vital professional aspects of progress and culture. In this respect, Einstein can be seen as a continuation of the important role of the shaman, in directing and defining what a culture must be. Indeed, most of the main advances in practices such as science have involved intuition from some deep centre of the mind – Einstein is said to have begun his understanding of relativity theory following a dream in which he rode on the end of a beam of light – and, as with the shaman, such intuitive scientists continue to show signs of mental instability (Einstein and his ilk were well known for their eccentricities).

It seems that the paranormal centre of culture expressed by the shaman is still with us, marrying the world of the physical to that of the spirit. And in understanding the growing agricultural requirement for permanence in early agrarian societies, we can go on to see how the physical/spirit aspect of culture redefined itself in the mystical professions of architect and builder.

Glastonbury

■ In my younger days, I was a relatively uneducated soul. I had left school at 15, and had little interest in culture or any other area of academe. My quest to understand the human condition had not yet begun. Nowadays, when I look back on my life, I search for prompters to show how my journey of discovery began, and one of those occurred on a warm, lazy Sunday in the early 1980s.

My wife and I were touring rural Norfolk. Coming to what we considered a pleasant, picturesque village, we decided to stop and look around. Getting out of the car, we were immediately taken aback by a sudden feeling of peacefulness. The village was practically deserted but, unlike with most villages, the silence was quite overwhelming. As we began to walk around, the feeling of tranquillity intensified. Our personas lifted and we felt as if we could walk on air. The peacefulness was not simple or ill defined, but omnipotent. You could feel it in the air, and it was accompanied by a deep sense of joy and goodness.

When we first arrived in the village, its name meant nothing to us, but our continued walk identified a hint of importance. Arriving at the heart of the village, we began to recognize the Catholic symbolism, and soon the tones of church music met our ears. Later, we saw a hospice, and then a shrine. The village was Walsingham, a place blessed by supernatural visitation and the site of many a pilgrimage.

Walsingham was more than just a physical thing: it held a supernatural aura that infected us the moment we left the car. Today, it reminds me of the idea of emotions being felt at particular locations where much emotion has been expended. Earlier, I showed how this often involved a form of field of depression, as felt by Andrew Green and Tom Lethbridge (see pages 17–19). This emotion was different – joyful – but essentially the same thing. I felt the emotions of the past; but in a more psychological sense, I felt the pull of culture, and that culture invaded my mind by means that can only be called extra-sensory.

This infiltration of culture can work in many areas of the paranormal. It can provide the expectancy that heralds a ghostly visitation in a house you know to be haunted. Related to sites such as Stonehenge, we can imagine the constant outpouring of emotion there to live down the centuries, causing hallucinations and feelings today in those who visit and are attuned.

Most countries with unbroken cultures that reach into the deep past can boast of locations such as Walsingham and England is no exception, its most famous centre of mysticism being Glastonbury. One of the oldest and most sacred sites in Britain, it can be found in Somerset, not far from the Bristol Channel. In the town, New Age shops and therapists vie for space with Christian institutions, competing for mystical pre-eminence within an area steeped in mythology for both. Glastonbury is believed to stand on a powerful intersection of ley lines, one of which goes on to include Stonehenge itself.

Outside the town is a huge terraced rock over 500 feet (150 m) high, with the remains of an old church on top. This is Glastonbury Tor, at the bottom of which is a well known as the Chalice Well. Close by is an abbey, and in its ruins you will find the Glastonbury Thorn. Each year, Christians, pagans and New Agers flock to this mystical place to pay homage, and at times strange lights have been seen hovering above the Tor.

It is not known who first occupied the site, but archaeological evidence suggests the place had achieved importance by the fourth century BC. The Druids are the most likely people to have declared Glastonbury sacred, but as it gained in importance it became impregnated with cultural expression, handed down to us today through mythology.

One of the earliest myths suggests that the Tor was the home of the mythical Gwynn ap Nudd, the lord of Annwn. Today we know him through continuing folklore as the Fairy King. Christian mythology first came to Glastonbury in the first century AD, when Joseph of Arimathea is said to have brought Jesus to the site when still a boy. Later, after the Crucifixion, Joseph returned to build the first Christian church below the Tor. He brought with him the chalice that Jesus used at the Last Supper and threw it into the Chalice Well, and the waters are still thought to have magical healing properties.

Joseph of Arimathea is also thought to be behind the legend of the Glastonbury Thorn. This magical bush, which never fails to bloom year after year, was his staff, which took root when he leant on it. Such a legend led to the building of the abbey here, first founded in the fifth century. The site has been rebuilt many times, the last in the fourteenth century, finally being destroyed by Henry VIII during the Reformation. Legend says that the original abbey was built by St Patrick, who is thought to have been buried at the site.

However, without doubt the most persistent myths with their roots in Glastonbury concern King Arthur. Up to the sixteenth century, Glastonbury surrounded by watery marshlands. In this respect, the site used to be thought of as a virtual island. But it was no ordinary island, for according to myth it was the Isle of Avalon. It was here, that the mythology of Arthur, of Camelot, and its association with the Holy Grail arose. Indeed, in 1190 monks are said to have found the buried remains of a man in the abbey grounds. With them was an inscription: 'Here lies the renowned Arthur in the Isle of Avalon'.

Of course, none of these myths can be proved, and they are most probably all untrue – at least, in an exact sense. But in the sense of cultural symbolism, every one of them can be seen to hold a definite grain of truth, for above all else, Glastonbury is the story of Britain up to the close of the Dark Ages. The place tells the tale of the arrival of Christianity shortly after Christ's crucifixion, and the spiritual and political battle it fought to become established by suppressing paganism.

In this sense, we can first see Glastonbury as a pagan spiritual and cultural centre. It was not a mere tribal centre, however: we have seen how the Druids came into being as tribes began to co-operate, forming kingdoms, and as a result tribal centres such as Stonehenge and other megaliths would not have been grand enough. Hence, we can see Glastonbury Tor becoming a form of 'national' temple and point of cultural expression.

Into this pagan kingdom comes a new cultural expression in Christianity, symbolized by Joseph of Arimathea. By placing the chalice in the well, he converts an already sacred well into a Christian well, and in planting his staff, he takes ritual away from the sacred Druid oak tree. With both the well and the thorn, the symbolism invests them with magical properties, but these are part of a greater magic than the earlier pagan magic, showing clearly its power over the previous Fairy King.

Into this spiritual and political turmoil comes the mythical King Arthur. At first he is a pagan king, gaining his power from the magical sword Excalibur, given to him by a Goddess figure through the magical powers of the Druid-like Merlin. But here, the purity of the Holy Grail becomes his quest, and in his search for it he moves away from paganism to embrace Christianity. The political conquest is complete, and the spiritual conquest comes when he throws the magical sword back to the Goddess, his magician, Merlin, eventually being imprisoned by the greater magic of Christianity.

The myths of Glastonbury tell the history of the Christianization of Britain, and the story is so completely placed here because Glastonbury was the spiritual heart of the kingdom being Christianized. In being its heart, it was its culture – but what led to the importance of Glastonbury in the first place?

A possible answer was given by illustrator Katherine Maltwood in 1929. Surveying the natural formations in the area around Glastonbury, she came to the astonishing conclusion that the natural lie of the land expressed the symbolism of the 12 signs of the Zodiac. Whether this is true or not is irrelevant. The question that must be asked is: if Katherine Maltwood could see this pattern, could the Druids have seen it also? And if we decide the answer is yes, then we can see that Glastonbury was not a mere physical site, but an expression of the universe above our heads. In other words, it was a microcosm of reality, a place where the ancients could walk in the physical and the spiritual at the same time.

We have seen that such a practice has been important since the days of cave art (see page 67), and while we can see Christianity as attempting to destroy paganism, this requirement to walk within the spiritual is still practised today in the idea of the 'mystical body of Christ'. A similar requirement can be seen in the abbey that was eventually built at Glastonbury, for at the turn of the twentieth century it was excavated by Frederick Bligh Bond, who came to the conclusion that the abbey was constructed with the use of practices that have become known as 'sacred geometry'.

Sacred Geometry and the Pyramids

■ We have seen how the spiral maze was nothing more than a symbol etched in stone or cut from the ground, and was symbolic both of the prehistoric cave and of death and rebirth (see page 62). However, as civilization advanced, the concept of the maze, or labyrinth, took on a new purpose, being built with walls and a more symmetrical shape.

The most famous example of this new design was known as the Cretan labyrinth and it had a vital mythology all its own, for within the labyrinth lived the mythological Minotaur, a mysterious, bull-headed monster. According to legend, the labyrinth was built by Daedalus, and the tyrannical King Minos of Crete used to send captives into the labyrinth to be killed by the Minotaur.

One person to be sent into the labyrinth was the Athenian Theseus, but Minos's daughter, Ariadne, fell in love with him. She gave him a length of string and a sword. Using the string, Theseus left a trail to allow him to escape the labyrinth, which he did after slaying the Minotaur. Theseus went on to be king of Athens.

The labyrinth upon which this myth is based is said to form part of the palace complex found at Knossos on the island of Crete. As with most myths, a great deal of symbolic truth can be found in the story. For instance, it is widely believed that the Cretans who built Knossos later went on to form one of the foundations of classical ancient Greece. Such an earlier civilization would presumably have had an earlier form of religion, akin to the 'animal spirit' deities of the hunter-gatherers. Such deities eventually gave way to the more familiar god-kings, and superhumans such as Hercules and, of course, Theseus. Hence, we can see the Cretan labyrinth myth as a simple story of a human-type god replacing an animal god, which had its lair in the depths of a symbolic cave. However, central to the myth was the labyrinth itself, which had now become symmetrical, built by an architect who took on divine status. As with Stonehenge, divine cultural representations had moved from natural structures to manufactured, so could it be that as man's technology advanced he continued to represent the two worlds of the physical and the spiritual in building form?

According to the Greek historian Herodotus, the labyrinth myth actually finds its roots in Egypt, which he visited in the fifth century BC. Here he encountered mythological tales of huge labyrinths, many of which could be found underground. Indeed, ancient Egypt is the perfect place to study in order to understand that vital social phase of history between the beginnings of agriculture and the formation of the distinct city-state, for the ancient Egyptians remained in this phase for some 3,000 years, thus providing the grandest and most unrivalled cultural expressions of these early religions in building form.

The greatest of these expressions were, of course, the pyramids, of which some 80 remain today. One of the oldest is the pyramid at Saqqara, built around 2650 BC. Some 200 feet (60 m) high, it is said to have been built by Imhotep, who, legend tells us, was the first man to build in stone. The existence of Stonehenge tells us that this is wrong, for Stonehenge is older, but the fact that Imhotep was also revered as an astrologer and sage, and went on to become the god of medicine, shows clearly that he was an extension of the shamanic form. This early pyramid does not take on the classical four-sided conical shape of later ones, but rather is stepped, giving evidence of an evolving form to the pyramid. However, by the time of the building of the greatest pyramid – the pyramid of Giza – the classical form was in use.

The Great Pyramid of Giza is said to have been built by the Pharaoh Khufu, or Cheops in Greek, around 2500 BC. One of three pyramids at Giza, some 10 miles (16 km) west of Cairo, it is the only survivor of the Seven Wonders of the World, and almost definitely the oldest. Thought to have been finished at one time with limestone with a cap of gold, it covers 13 acres, has a base of some 750 square feet (70 sq m) and is 450 feet (140 m) high.

These are mere figures, and many analogies have been used to express its greatness. For instance, you could group together four large cathedrals on the site; the stone used in its construction amounts to more than all the stone used for every church in Britain; and you could build a wall 10 feet (3 m) high and 3 feet (1 m) thick around the whole of France with the materials used.

Many of the stones used were perfectly shaped and weighed from 2 to 15 tonnes each. Some 2,300,000 such blocks were used, and it is said that it required 100,000 labourers working over a 20-year period to complete it. Once finished, its mathematical alignments were said to be almost exact, with the four sides pointing to the four points of the compass. The sides of the pyramid are said to be as exact as a couple of feet to each other, and its height in relation to its base is said to prove that the builders understood the value of pi (π).

This supposed mathematical excellence, however, only adds to the mythology of the pyramid, for all the builders really needed to know was how to measure a straight line, plus rudimentary formulae for calculating volumes and weights. Similar rudimentary mathematics went on to be used to construct the far more technical cathedrals of medieval Europe. So, super-intelligent mathematicians were not required for the pyramids. What was required – and it is here that ancient Egyptian excellence comes into the equation – was a well-managed society capable of being mobilized into mass corporate endeavour. And this seems to have been what Egyptian society was.

For the most part, ancient Egyptian society was a peasant agrarian culture, with houses made of mud and the population shackled to the fields, but out of this peasant society rose a strong middle class and an overall hierarchy vested with divine status. When cities began to appear, they were not cities in a true sense but palace complexes, temples and monuments dedicated to these divinities and locked into this form of monumental expression for some 3,000 years. It is this huge expanse of time that explains the magnificence of the pyramids, for no other culture has ever been locked in a single cultural expression for so long.

The interior of the Great Pyramid is as enigmatic as its structure. You enter it via a tunnel which leads to a single underground chamber. At one point you can leave this main tunnel and enter a second. This soon forks off to two chambers nearer the centre of the pyramid construction, known as the Queen's and King's Chambers. From each of these chambers a northern and southern shaft rises and travels to the exterior of the pyramid.

The Great Pyramid was first breached by Al Mamun, a young caliph of Baghdad, in AD 800. He had heard the stories of the pyramid, and how great knowledge and wealth were sealed inside. Ancient Egyptian society was regulated by a single impulse – their belief in the afterlife. Upon death, Pharaohs entered the afterlife, and in order to maintain their wealth and power, expressions of these were buried with them, as was found in the tomb of Tutankhamun. The pyramid itself was seen as nothing more than a burial site for the Pharaoh. But Al Mamun was to be disappointed, for when he entered the King's Chamber all that he found was an empty and lidless sarcophagus, or stone coffin. If the Great Pyramid was simply Khufu's tomb, then it never carried out its purpose.

Much of the modern mythology of the Great Pyramid began with the conclusions of Englishman John Taylor, son of the editor of the *Observer* newspaper, in the 1860s. Analysing the dimensions of the pyramid, he surmised that the builders knew the Earth was a sphere and, by observing the movements of heavenly bodies, had worked out its circumference. This led to the later, and startling, claims that the Great Pyramid was a record of the universe and a history of man, as well as being invested with many technological abilities. For instance, also in the nineteenth century, French physicist Jean Baptiste Biot argued that the pyramid was a huge form of sundial, and British astronomer Richard Proctor pointed out that one of the tunnels was precisely aligned to the Pole Star.

During the twentieth century, ideas concerning the pyramid became more fantastic. American psychic Edgar Cayce and philosopher Manly P. Hall associated the pyramid with Atlantis. Soon, because of the pyramid's magnificence, it was said to have been built by Atlanteans who survived the destruction of this mythical land, the pyramid being a monument to their culture and technology, including their power of prophecy, with the shape and hieroglyphics recording the future history of the world up to the Second Coming in 1998.

Even stranger was Czech radio engineer Karl Drbal, who in 1959 claimed that razor blades placed under a pyramid structure would resharpen due to some mystical or cosmic power. Such an idea has associated the pyramids with Earth energies, or alternatively New Age spiritual forces that can heal a person if they sit inside such a structure.

Recently, however, authors Graham Hancock and Robert Bauval have come up with a much more intriguing theory (see Bibliography). Using computer simulations of the positions of the stars in 2500 BC, they calculated that one of the southern shafts would have pointed to the star Sirius and the other to the lowest star in the three-star belt of Orion. Bauval later noted that the three pyramids at Giza were a perfect match for the belt of Orion, with the third and smallest pyramid out of line with the others in the same way as the third star in Orion's belt. However, going back to computer simulations, they attempted to explain why the pyramids at Giza were offset with the actual belt. They then discovered that the pyramids were an exact match with the belt of Orion as it would have been in 10,500 BC. Many researchers see this as proof of the antiquity of the pyramids and that they *were* built by the Atlanteans. Hancock and Bauval themselves have been inspired by such ideas to propose technical and mystical attributes far in excess of the facts, reaching back over 12,500 years. However, what do these apparent facts really tell us?

The positioning of the southern shafts to Sirius and the belt of Orion in 2500 BC tells us that the official dating of the pyramids is correct, and that they were not built in 10,500 BC but in 2500 BC. However, the offsetting of the belt of Orion tells us that the site the pyramids were eventually built upon was first laid out in 10,500 BC.

Because of the retreat of the glaciers at the end of the last ice age, Egypt became temperate much earlier than more northern lands, and therefore the agricultural revolution also came earlier. Hence, it is valid to say that the earlier ancient Egyptians turned to the sky as early as 10,500 BC and began to build monuments reflecting this new knowledge in a similar way to the ancient Britons when they began to build Stonehenge in 3500 BC. This possibility allows for an unbroken cultural expression in Egypt over 10,000 years, beginning with Stonehenge-like structures which, like Stonehenge itself, were added to and readapted over millennia. Such an idea addresses the alignment with the belt of Orion in 10,500 BC, and the Egyptians eventually achieving definite astronomical alignment in the final expression of the site 8,000 years later with the Great Pyramid.

This idea requires no mystical nonsense associated with Atlantis, and no remarkable mathematical abilities. It requires nothing more than unbroken cultural achievement of great length, thus suggesting that the Great Pyramid was simply the final readaptation of a building form that had been ongoing for millennia. Indeed, the pyramid itself can be seen as symbolic of the stone age cave decorated with images, or hieroglyphics, and the construction of the tunnels and chambers suggests a final expression of a form of labyrinth. We do not see these previous constructions because the pyramids were built on top of them. In looking to the possible mythology behind the pyramids, as identified in part by Graham Hancock, we can see evidence of this sociological progression.

The association with Orion and Sirius is telling, for Sirius is thought to be the celestial home of the goddess Isis, and the belt of Orion is the celestial home of the god Osiris. Egyptian mythology tells us that Osiris was the first king of Egypt and became the god of agriculture, teaching humanity the secrets of farming and civilization. He married his sister, Isis, and his rule was threatened by the forces of chaos, represented by his brother, Seth. Osiris was eventually drowned in the Nile. This deed was done by Seth, who took on the form of a crocodile or hippopotamus (in a variation, Seth turns into a bull and tramples Osiris to death).

Isis went in search of her dead husband and used magical powers to revive him long enough for her to be impregnated by his sperm. Discovering this, Seth found the now divine Osiris and ripped him to pieces, his remains being buried in sites all around Egypt.

The now pregnant Isis fled from Seth and hid in the Nile marshlands. Here she bore a divine son, Horus. By this time Seth was king of Egypt, and when

Horus grew up, Seth challenged him. Horus eventually won and was crowned king, while Seth was sent to the sky to become the god of storms. From that time on, Osiris would be reborn every year with the growing of the crops.

In this myth, we can see how agriculture, the fertility goddess Isis and her divine son, Horus, destroyed the old hunter-gatherer deities along with the 'animal' god, Seth. Their eventual representations in the sky go on to associate fertility with the stars, and in the seasonal return of Osiris we see elements of the death/rebirth ritual. In other words, we see a different cultural expression which is nevertheless identical in form to the already suggested shamanic ritual and religion (see page 58). As with Stonehenge, we can see the social, religious and seasonal knowledge aspects coming together in the construction of the pyramids, which became grand cultural expressions of the society that built them. But with the Egyptians, the sheer length of this cultural expression led them to attempt a symbolic marriage of the worlds of the physical and the spiritual by placing the belt of Orion upon the land itself. Indeed, it has been suggested that the entire pyramid-building enterprise of ancient Egypt was an attempt to place the stars upon the land, for to walk in ancient Egypt was to walk upon the land and within the stars. And the same idea can be applied to the other puzzling construction at Giza, the Sphinx.

Egyptologists are adamant that the Sphinx was constructed at the same time as the Great Pyramid, but evidence suggests not, for this great monument with the body of a lion and face of a man has fissures running down it that can only be explained by the erosion of running water such as rainfall – and Egypt has not experienced significant rainfall for over 7,000 years.

Using the ideas above, we can see the Sphinx as a much older adaptation of Egyptian cultural building, first constructed at a time when Egypt was lush with greenery and used to torrential rains. But what was the Sphinx symbolic of? The most unusual feature of it is the human head, for this is much too small in comparison to its huge lion body. However, as researchers have pointed out, perhaps when it was first built its head was that of a lion. Then, as the cultural expression changes from animal spirits to the later man-gods of ancient Egypt, the face was restructured to express the face of a man. It is here that we find the continuing evolution of society and, by implication, its religions.

We have seen how Egypt was an expression of a prolonged period of agricultural society. Unlike Mesopotamia, or later Greece, this society never developed into the great city-state. Arguably this is because of its static nature, locked as it was into the central death and rebirth of Osiris, bringing the seasons each year in a never-ending cycle.

In other regions this was not the case. In Mesopotamia society advanced, investing absolute divinity in a definite god-king. And in the god-king, the human ego can be seen to have become a distinct divine force that rose above the nature fertility religions. In such a new religious form, the feminine aspect of divinity was suppressed in favour of superhuman males such as Zeus or Hercules. This led to shorter periods of divine cultural expression and faster, more intense periods of cultural expression through building. It is here that sacred geometry, first expressed in structures such as Stonehenge and the pyramids, really became a cultural force.

Sacred Geometry and Culture

■ Much of this section has been about sacred geometry, but I have not yet explained exactly what sacred geometry is. The word geometry means 'measuring the Earth', and this is a suitable starting point for understanding. In the ancient eastern practice of geomancy, known as *feng shui*, the design, placing and construction of all buildings had to comply with both the lie and 'feel' of the land. The Earth was filled with contradictory forces that had to be held in balance and harmony to guarantee the correct function of the building. This required the use of natural design methods that could better be understood today as ecological. In this way, man's technological achievements existed in harmony with nature.

In the western architectural tradition, this was taken a stage further. For instance, to the builders of Stonehenge and the pyramids, everything that their society could do in the physical world had a prime cause in the supernatural. Today we know that the sun rises in the morning because of the rotation of our planet, but in ancient times the sun rose because a god directed it to rise. This supernatural direction existed throughout life.

In order to achieve success in both the physical and supernatural worlds, every physical event became a form of ritual. In this way, the gods placed a magical intervention upon the action, and success was a result of this rather than of the endeavour of the 'physical' person.

As rationalism began to replace superstition and supernatural beliefs, this idea was formalized into a logical philosophy. This can be seen in the ideas of Plato, who believed that everything had a 'form' in a timeless universe. For instance, a chair can exist as a physical thing, but to Plato before you could build a chair, the 'form' of the chair had to exist in some ethereal plane. Hence, when the chair was invented, it was not a design of man but an intuition of the 'form' of the chair in this ethereal other-world.

To Plato, everything that existed, and everything that could ever exist, already existed in this ethereal 'form'. This idea was a direct progression from the power and absoluteness of the supernatural over the physical world, and in such a world it was natural that these ideas formulated into societal ceremony. But in order to enforce the power of the supernatural, as well as the ceremony itself, images of the supernatural were required.

In deep prehistory, such images were based upon natural formations such as the prehistoric cave, which eventually came alive with art. However, as technology advanced, people began to build their own representations. It is here that sacred geometry comes alive as mankind's attempt to make their buildings harmonize with the world in which they physically lived, while at the same time expressing the 'truths' of the supernatural world that intervened within it.

In this way, sacred geometry replaced shamanic ritual by representing in physical form that which used to be hallucinated by the shaman. Such reverence was placed upon the buildings that were constructed that they not only became the cultural centres of society, but in a way became the culture itself. It is here that we can understand the fanatical endeavour that went into their construction, for without their cultural centre the people could exist only in the physical world; without a temple they were denied access to the supernatural, because they did not have a 'doorway' to allow entry.

With such an impulse to motivate them, it was inevitable that construction would turn into a form of science at an early stage of human civilization, providing, first, constructions such as Stonehenge, and then, as this science developed, monumental temples such as the pyramids. But what is the main difference between these two constructions?

In the pyramid, design had become more symmetrical, and in this its degree of perfection had increased. This was an important point to early civilizations. Their gods were perfect, so it was natural that their representations would have to move in the direction of perfection. Plato gives us a hint as to what was considered a greater perfection. If geometry reflected the harmony of the Earth, and sacred geometry added supernatural harmony to the equation, then 'forms' must exist in the ethereal world to reflect this harmony. To Plato, the 'forms' that best reflected harmony were geometrical, such as the cube, tetrahedron and so on. This was because their sides were in exact proportion to each other, thus reflecting absolute harmony. It is therefore no coincidence that the pyramid gained its shape, for the pyramid is, of course, a tetrahedron.

We can see here that sacred geometry is not so much an exact way of doing things, but rather an impulse to invest design with supernatural qualities. However, it is important to realize that, to the ancients, by constructing a building with supernatural form, they were not creating supernatural form itself. We say that God made man in his own image. As our knowledge advances and we leave superstition behind, we can see that this should really be reversed, and in actual fact man made God in his own image. While this may also be true of the ancients, they did not believe this to be the case. Hence, the cultural image portrayed in design was not the supernatural itself, but a symbolic representation of the supernatural; symbolism was therefore of primary importance to the ancients. It is here that we can see the most important function of ritual, existing from early shamanic ritual, through sacred geometry, to the modern day.

Today we live in a material world where supernatural forces are scoffed at. Society itself has been degraded, and we live the life of individuals. Yet is this really the case? Society is expressed through its culture. Individualism reduces culture, for in revelling in individualism we see history as the history of ourselves, rather than the history of society. However, we still bow to cultural influences, even if those influences are no longer deeply historical.

The modern world is exemplified by the United States of America. Here, individual enterprise and self-expression are the primary influences. However, it is interesting to note that when an individual reaches absolute fame, people in their thousands express their individuality by emulating them. Most starkly, this is done through fashion, where thousands wear the style of clothing preferred by their 'hero'.

Such cultural expression has an important outlet in the United States. The country is interesting in that it has a distinct culture factory. Everyone knows this factory, and everyone has been affected by its expressions. It is called Hollywood, and throughout most of the twentieth century it has poured out symbolic cultural expressions in the form of movies – expressions that have defined the way we view the world. Hollywood is very different to the prehistoric cave in which ritual and cultural expression began, but this difference is only technological. In an anthropological sense, the purpose of Hollywood is exactly the same as the purpose of our prehistoric cave. We may have advanced technologically, but in regard to cultural motivation, we have not advanced one iota.

Hollywood and similar centres of culture churn out role models. We call such role models stereotypes. These representations of cultural form are said to define what we are, but in reality they do nothing of the sort. A stereotype does not tell us what we are, but what we should aspire to be.

This is a subtle, but vitally important difference. To the ancients, supernatural forms also represented what we should aspire to be. Because the gods intervened in the physical world, their actions were important to us, but those actions were perfect, because they themselves were perfect. So why should they bother helping us mere mortals? Because we deserved their help – and we deserved their help because we aspired to be as one with them. In this aspiration, society became imbued with an urge towards perfection.

By looking at the world of the ancients in terms of modern life, we can see that the supernatural was not so much an existent supernatural power as a sociological force, which is just as much in evidence today as it was in the past. This force affects us through subtle psychology.

One of the best examples of this continuing sociological force can be seen in the changing stereotypical image of the perfection of womanhood. Her first definite appearance came with the advent of agriculture. Cultivation became as one with fertility, and in a supernatural sense this gave rise to the Goddess, first expressed as the Earth Mother, or Mother Earth.

We have seen how the prehistoric cave was most likely thought of as a womb, through which rebirth occurred. This was important, because the Earth allowed a supernatural rebirth each year with the seeding of the ground, through which new life sprang up in the fields. This idea of supernatural rebirth found expression in a new cultural goddess, Isis, for Isis mothered Horus through supernatural intervention.

As man's religions took on a more human form, so the Earth Mother took the form of the beautiful and fertile Gaia, and later the many-breasted Demeter. But as societal interaction moved towards a family-based rather than tribal system, the female stereotype took on a more appealing, sexually oriented form. Here we can see the perfection of womanhood manifesting in goddesses such as Aphrodite.

With the advent of Christianity, the sexual side was suppressed, but the importance of supernatural fertility was maintained in the Virgin Mary, who, like Isis, birthed a god through supernatural means in Christ. The stereotype led to the nun, through which the perfection of womanhood expressed itself in chastity and obedience to a male God.

The next full expression of the perfection of womanhood came in a world where the supernatural was in decline, but the importance of chastity and obedience was maintained. She appeared as the stereotypical housewife in early television commercials, becoming ecstatic when a new washing powder came along to make her life of obedience that much easier. However, feminism was rising as a cultural force, and Aphrodite was again in the ascendant with the Hollywood female predator epitomized by such as Marilyn Monroe, the new stereotype of the sex goddess.

As for today, she can still be seen. She has begun to take on the form of geometrical perfection, and can be seen on many a catwalk. For she is the supermodel, still exerting her sociological and psychological power of conformity on many a young girl who aspires to be as perfect as she is by starving herself through anorexia nervosa.

The cultural requirement of the stereotype changes to express the cultural 'needs' of society, but its role as a means towards perfection has remained the same throughout history and stretches way back into prehistory. We may have denied the supernatural, but we cannot deny the urges that led to it in the first place. The continuing use of supernatural forces can be seen to echo societal change as society progressed from a basic agrarian system to the city-state which was, above all else, an expression of man's growing power to rule and subjugate the people.

One of the earliest known divine representations of a city-state culture was the Babylonian Tower of Babel. A high, narrow structure known as a ziggurat, the tower was built in seven distinct stages, representing the seven heavens of Babylonian cosmology. By this time, the definite man-god had come into being, and it was *his* power that had to take absolute form. Hence, unlike the ancient Egyptians who represented the celestial gods on the ground in the pyramids of Giza, man's new confidence required a high, towering structure aimed directly at allowing the man-god to ascend up to the celestial gods.

The difference was subtle but all-consuming. Gods still existed in the supernatural, but their powers were directly enhanced by a ruler, who himself became divine. In political terms, it led to absolute power over life and death – a privilege previously allowed only to the supernatural – and the total regulation of society and, by implication, culture – the place where true psychological power was held.

The natural progression of this man-god urge eventually led to western society embracing monotheism. The central aim of all culture is to regulate an ordered society through morality and psychological pressures. Hence, as more and more man-gods appeared to maintain power, it was inevitable that this would lead to so many contradictory gods that society would echo such supernatural chaos through anarchy in the physical world. But in monotheism, the man-god was banished in favour of the image of a man who *was* God.

First expressed by the Hebrews, the one God became a truly potent force. As the Hebrews moved from being nomads to the city-state, the principles of sacred geometry expressed themselves first in the mobile cultural centre known as the Ark of the Covenant, and later in the symbol of early monotheism as a cultural force which was the magnificence of King Solomon's Temple. Later still, as Christianity became a progression of the monotheistic tendency, the gap between physical man and supernatural man-god was bridged in the divinity of

Christ and his representation in the cross. The eventual development was the perfection of sacred geometry in the nave-and-transept design of the Christian church in the shape of the cross, or a man, his arms outstretched. The man, the doorway, and the God had become one in perfect harmony, and represented the harmony of the universe, the supernatural and the physical world of man.

Freemasons

■ How did the shaman fit into this increasingly technological cultural expression of the divine? We have seen how the Druids demonstrate the societal progression of shaman-like individuals. As tribes amalgamated to forge the early kingdoms, the shaman seemed to specialize, thus forming the foundations of the professional middle class. It would be convenient at this point to follow this societal evolution and see how the most surprising professions can be traced back to the shaman.

A more refined Druid-like order arose in ancient Egypt. The most obvious is the Egyptian priesthood, who continued to perform ritual in their temples. Indeed, we can imagine an Osiris-based death/rebirth ritual actually going on inside the Great Pyramid of Giza. But sacred geometry offers evidence that the builders of such temples were also mystically inclined.

To this day there exists a mystical-based middle-class organization known as Freemasonry. Shrouded in secrecy, it has attracted a great deal of suspicion in modern times, being seen as a form of old-school-tie network to foster professional and entrepreneurial benefits for its members. It would be surprising if some members didn't use it in this way, but the stated function of Freemasonry is to foster spiritual development and fraternal charity.

Members are often known as Masons, and are given one of three grades, known as degrees. These are Entered Apprentice, Fellow Craft and Master Mason. They meet in Lodges or Temples. The inside of the Lodge is a four-sided rectangular shape decorated with Masonic symbols and with a black and white chequered floor, representing the dark and light sides of human nature. Rituals are carried out in the Lodge using symbols such as the compass and plumb-line, and participants wear white leather aprons that can be traced back to the garb worn by ancient stonemasons.

There are strict rules of secrecy in Freemasonry, and identification is carried out with the use of secret signs. During the Middle Ages membership had to involve a strong Christian belief, but by 1723 this was changed. Members have to believe in a God, but the choice of religion is left open. Due to this, Masons have a symbolic supreme being known as the Great Architect of the Universe.

The mystical aspect of Freemasonry, as well as its great antiquity, is evidenced in its most powerful symbolic representation – the Great Pyramid of Giza. However, the image is flat-topped, as if incomplete, and represents the incomplete nature of mankind. Above the pyramid is a single eye which bears a great resemblance to the symbolic eye of Horus, son of Isis and Osiris. This is seen as the All-Seeing Eye of the Great Architect, and reflects divine perfection above mankind.

The general view of Freemasonry is that it was first formed in the Middle Ages, during the building of the great medieval cathedrals. Stonemasons were few in number and wanted to guard their practices, and thus formed themselves into craft guilds, which eventually formed into Freemasonry proper. Due to the practices of sacred geometry, mysticism was obviously involved in such constructions, and as middle-class skills increased, Freemasonry opened its doors to these new trades.

By the eighteenth century a Lodge could be found in most towns in Britain, usually in a back room of a public house. In 1717, four London Lodges merged into the Grand Lodge of England, causing the creation of the Masonic Grand Master. With the move away from strictly Christian membership, the Vatican condemned Freemasonry in 1738, and today a Freemason can be excommunicated from the Catholic Church.

With the colonization of America, it was inevitable that Freemasonry would travel to that country. George Washington became a Freemason in 1752, and eight signatories of the American Declaration of Independence were Masons. Masonic influence in the early American establishment was so complete that the pyramid and All-Seeing Eye appear on the dollar bill.

While Freemasonry is *thought* to have begun in the Middle Ages, we can, however, suggest an earlier Masonic tradition shrouded in secrecy and mysticism. This is hinted at by the fact that the three 'degrees' are said not to be the only grades of membership. Indeed, there are supposedly 33 degrees in all, rising in secrecy and deep mysticism. Further, the fact that little monumental building went on from the end of the classical world until the Middle Ages suggests that history would not have been bothered with the existence of ancient mystical orders during this period.

Bearing in mind the obvious implications of sacred geometry used in the medieval cathedrals, we can again hint at an unbroken mystical line to the sacred geometers of earlier times. Indeed, many consider the building of King Solomon's Temple to be the starting point of actual Freemasonry, and a story surrounding its building is fundamental to Masonic ritual.

The Bible tells us that the architect and builder of the temple was a man called Hiram. We find out nothing else about him from the Bible, but in Masonic ritual he becomes Hiram Abiff, and he is murdered by three of his workmen when he refuses to reveal the secret Word of God hidden in the temple structure. This story speaks of a guarded and secret form of sacred geometry, and the essence of the central ritual of Freemasonry involves the death of the Mason and his rebirth into the spiritual ways of Freemasonry.

This ritualized death confirms Freemasonry as linked to the sacred geometry of the ancients, and the distinct death/rebirth ritual finds its roots in shamanic ritual in the prehistoric cave. The architect and builder of today may have lost his sacredness, but there is little doubt that he can trace his profession back to the shaman. Perhaps if they realized this generally, building practices might return to a more sacred form, being more at one with man's psychology and the natural lie of the land.

Another modern profession that can be traced back to the shaman is the politician. He was previously known as a prophet. Typical was Moses, whose greatest achievement was the moulding of a nomadic, tribal people into a distinct political nation. The wisdom that allowed him to do this can be seen to have come from an hallucinatory experience where he talked with God, during which his old way of life 'died' and he was 'reborn' as a wise, old man. This Hebrew prophetic tradition was finally formulated into the ultimate expression of death/rebirth in the crucifixion and resurrection of Christ.

Prophets also existed in ancient Greece. The most famous of these was the Oracle of Apollo at Delphi, on the southern slopes of Mount Parnassus. This was, in fact, an order of prophets housed in a circular construction of stone columns supporting a number of stone slabs. Within this circle was an inner circle. The similarities of this construction to Stonehenge are obvious.

The chief priestess of the Oracle, known as the Pythia, would be asked questions by the rulers. To answer, she would sit in the centre of the circle, with sulphuric fumes rising from the volcanic chasm upon which the construction was built. Here she would go into a shamanic-type trance and be possessed by Apollo, who would answer the question. Often the answer was so garbled that priests would debate her words and come to a final meaning.

Such prophetic practices were thought to be a means of foretelling the future, but is this really the case? We must remember that to the people of the classical world every event was supernatural as well as physical. To this extent, free will was not seen to exist, so contemplating the future was not regarded as a human practice, but a preserve of the gods. Hence, human beings did not appear to reason a particular outcome of a human event. But what was really happening with the garbled words of the Pythia and the eventual meaning provided by the priests?

Employing the Pythia as a mouthpiece for the gods, the priests used supernatural authority to analyse an outcome themselves. In this way, they did not foretell the future as such, but rationalized the possible outcome of a political decision. In other words, the Oracle at Delphi was the first known expression of a political 'think tank', with the priests as political advisors.

The advancement of this process can be seen in British political history. As the Dark Ages came to an end and a distinct political tradition began based on kingdoms ruled by hereditary lineage, it was soon realized that many kings did not have the political abilities to rule. To answer this problem, a council of advisors came into being, known as the Witan – the word actually means 'to know'. The Witan itself was made up of the 'elders' of the still-existent tribal regions, who were not political chiefs, but revered 'wise men'. Their obvious descent from the Druids, and thus the shaman, goes without saying.

As British political life advanced, the Witan took on a distinct advisory role, and after several centuries it formulated into a 'parliament', which selected as its spokesman a Prime Minister. With the continuing decline of monarchical powers in favour of democracy, the Parliament eventually assumed the political sovereignty of the monarch, and in doing so became the cultural centre of society, thus confirming that not only can politicians be traced back to the shaman, but their role as centre and arbiter of society remains the same.

■ We have advanced a great deal from those dark, primeval days when a controlled schizophrenic carried out ritual in a damp cave through the hallucination of animal spirits. But in one sense we have hardly advanced at all: rather, we can see that the supernatural entities he manifested were an expression of the paranormal. That paranormal force can now be seen as an extension of psychological forces involved with cultural expression, and from prehistory to the modern day, this psychological definition of the paranormal has continued to define what we are, and what we continually aspire to be. Above all else, the control that culture imposes upon us tells us that our individuality is an illusion, for through mechanisms that we class as paranormal, we become fundamentally communal beings.

· THE CABAL ·

Early Magicians

■ The rational world is a direct descendant of the 'madness' of shamanic practices. The priest, the doctor, the scientist, the architect, the psychologist, the artist and the politician can all find their genesis in the shaman. And like the shaman, they assist communal life and define what cultural expression becomes.

The form our cultural expression takes changes constantly, but without the culture to define who we are, we are nothing. We may have free will *within* the cultural expression, but cultural change is achieved through communal transition. It can be sparked by an individual act, but if this act is not transposed into communal symbolic influences such as the stereotype, communal change does not occur.

We can see here how culture becomes a form of omnipotent god-force which impinges upon the individual through a form of psychological possession. For instance, social forces seem to compel the individual to live according to a norm, or to aspire to ape a stereotype. It may be subtle, but this is nevertheless a form of 'possession' by outside forces.

This social mechanism may well hint at paranormality, but it can work against acceptance of paranormal forces if the prevailing culture decrees that such forces do not exist. This has proved a damaging cultural force for many individuals throughout history who have retained the original idiosyncrasies of the shaman. History has branded such people as magicians, wizards, alchemists, mediums, healers and occultists.

Typical was Apollonius of Tyana, now part of Turkey. Regarded as a philosopher and miracle worker, most of what we know of him has been handed down through legend. Born around AD 40, he entered Rome during the reign of the emperor Nerva. Taken in by the academics of the day, his reputation became so powerful that some considered him a god. This was, of course, too much for the emperor, who considered himself a god. Apollonius was arrested and put on trial, his hair being cut off to decrease his magical powers. The trial did not last long, however, for Apollonius disappeared during it and was never seen again.

Several extraordinary feats of magic were attributed to Apollonius. At one stage, Antioch was apparently infested by scorpions. Apollonius was called for. He found a bronze statue of a scorpion and, carrying out a magical ritual, he buried it somewhere in the city. Shortly after this, the scorpions disappeared.

Ephesus also had reason to thank Apollonius. At one time there was a great plague in the area. When Apollonius arrived, he knew exactly what to do. To the people of the time, illness was as much a part of the supernatural as anything else. In a great magical ceremony, Apollonius called upon the spirits who brought the plague to show themselves. This they did, and he directed the population to stone them, thus removing the plague.

In Apollonius of Tyana we can see a survival of the tribal shaman, using ritual to assist society. But what strange powers did he use to carry out his magic? The most obvious answer is that these events never took place. They are simply the result of legend and gullibility. This could well be the case, but the methodology I will follow here is to continue as if they did happen. This is not due to gullibility on my part, but is rather an attempt to show how such feats could appear to have been carried out through magical, shamanic rites.

Consider the scorpions at Antioch. Like most creatures, scorpions are seasonal in habit. In particular, they feed off the juices of arachnids and insects. Often nature provides an imbalance in such insects, and the balance of nature is such that when this happens a predator seems to breed at a similar rate. This usually leads to a short period of infestation. Hence, we must consider the possibility that Apollonius realized this and performed his ritual at the time that the infestation was in decline. In other words, he used 'magic' to bring about an event he knew was about to happen.

Alternatively, we can look at the possibility of there being no infestation. Rather, a few individuals had simply been stung by scorpions in quick succession. Consider a quiet street in any town today. One night a house is burgled. News spreads like wildfire. Everyone begins checking their houses more carefully at night, and stories circulate of others in the street who knew someone elsewhere who was burgled, and in no time at all one burglary transforms into the idea of a crimewave. This natural social predilection towards exaggeration would have been far greater in more superstitious times, so in the Apollonius ritual we can see an easing of fear rather than infestation. In easing the fear, by implication, the infestation wanes.

What about the plague in Ephesus? First of all, not all 'plagues' in ancient times *were* plagues. Due to lack of medical knowledge, any infectious illness was classed as a form of plague, and due to lack of preventive measures, death could often ensue from the mildest infection. This inability to fight infectious illness led to extreme melancholia in the sufferers. In today's world we know that this can add a psychosomatic element to the illness, with the sufferer losing the ability to fight against it.

Along comes Apollonius and, being a clever chap, he decides to raise the spirits of the people in a literal sense. Carrying out a form of hallucinated ritual as described on page 49, he raises the 'spirits' who, to the people, caused the plague. In a symbolic way, he gets them to fight back by stoning them. The people thereby gain the confidence to fight the illness themselves, and the 'plague' is soon over.

I do not know whether or not these explanations of the events at Antioch and Ephesus are correct. I do not even know if the events took place. But such explanations can be seen to be valid, and in offering them we can see that no magic was involved, other than the subtle use of existing social and cultural forces brought together into a form of communal psychology. These rituals worked because the culture of the people told them that such magical rites could work.

As tribal society gave way to the classical world of ancient Egypt, Greece and Rome, magic became so refined that ritual was not always needed. Cultural forces manifested into all-pervasive superstition to such an extent that a single word could induce a magical event. Known as 'word magic', the most famous example appeared on a Sumerian tablet: *Abrada Ke Dabra* means 'perish like the word', and it became infamous as a word that can harm the hearer. By Roman times it had metamorphosed into 'abracadabra', and to this day the word is known; although today, like magic, it is ridiculed.

This shows that it wasn't the word that was important, but the cultural interpretation of the word, which itself suggests that the power of such words lay in the emotion they could induce in the individual. In this sense, word magic survives to this day with words such as Auschwitz. The word may no longer induce hallucinations or curses, but it is easy to imagine it doing so in a more superstitious people who knew of the absolute evil associated with it.

The ancient Egyptians perfected word magic to the point that an incantation upon an object could transfer the power on to it. These became 'power symbols', the magical amulet being a popular one; stage magic today celebrates this power in the magic wand. Such symbols defined the magician as the investor of supernatural power he was thought to be. This subtle use of symbol and garb to define position in culture is still used today, with jewellery to define wealth – and few of us have not heard of 'power dressing'.

Word magic and power symbols continue to tug at our communal emotions, particularly in religion. The dog collar, the cross and the mitre can all find their power in such ancient concepts. Prayers and the chanting of words known as mantras in eastern religions are used today to cleanse the mind and allow peace to settle within. This is magic: yet the magic is not supernatural, but the subtle use of communal emotion brought out by cultural interpretation.

As the classical world gave way to the Dark Ages, definite knowledge of magicians and magic waned, but the fact of its continued existence is celebrated through the mythologies of sorcerers such as Merlin. However, by the fifteenth century magicians began to make an appearance in the official record once more.

Abramelin the Jew was one such magician. Believed to have been born in Würzburg, Germany, in 1362, he lived much of his life there before dying at the grand old age of 98. Abramelin claimed to see 'angels', who instructed him in harnessing the supernatural. Among his feats he was said to be able to manifest devils, tame demons, produce spirit soldiers, control the weather, turn men into animals, demolish buildings, raise the dead and have visions of the future.

Such powers appear ludicrous to the rational mind – but consider the time he was said to raise 2,000 spirit cavalrymen to assist Frederick, Elector of Saxony, in battle. Such 'spirit' soldiers are not uncommon. In 1914, the British Expeditionary Force was said to be aided by such soldiers, known as the Angels of Mons. Dozens of anecdotal tales exist of these ghostly knights in armour coming to the aid of the soldiers as they attempted to hold out against the German onslaught.

What caused such hallucinations? Many researchers, including myself, put the episode down to a story by Arthur Machen called 'The Bowmen', which appeared in a popular newspaper at the time to boost morale. In the story, medieval archers come to the aid of British soldiers and victory is achieved. We can envisage the story carrying out its function to the point that the fear of the British forces turned the story into a communal hallucination, and we can see a similar social interaction taking place from Abramelin's suggestion that the 'spirit' cavalrymen would be seen. Such a vision would, of course, improve morale to the point that the soldiers' fighting efficiency would increase.

At one time in his life, Abramelin decided to tour the world in search of tales of magic and instruction as to how to perfect his talents. He is said to have travelled through most of Arabia and much of central Europe. The knowledge he gained he wrote down in *The Book of Sacred Magic*, published in 1458. However, from this book we can see that Abramelin was significantly more than a simple magician.

He recounts the time he met a young woman in Linz who rubbed a potion into his hands and feet in order to make him fly. Falling asleep, he did have the sensation of flying, but the experience left him with a feeling of depression. To test her abilities, he asked her to rub the potion on herself, travel 200 miles (320 km) to visit a friend of his, and bring back news. The woman did so and fell asleep for a number of hours. Upon awaking she confirmed that she had travelled to the friend and gave him news. Abramelin checked this out and it was shown to be a lie.

He goes on to dismiss the case as a simple dream. Today we have a better explanation. Whatever the potion was, it seems to have been some form of psychedelic hallucinogen such as LSD: Abramelin and the woman had simply been on a drug-induced 'trip'. However, of most importance was the fact that Abramelin had studied the case logically.

We can see here an early case of psychical research, with talents being put to the test. In this, we have an extension of the magician from superstitious hysteric to more of a scholar, complete with an urge to understand the powers involved rationally. Such an approach was continued by such notable scholars as Cornelius Agrippa and Dr John Dee, who devised a distinct occult philosophy which grew alongside the slowly evolving sciences. However, as the Christian church began to split during the Reformation, theological heels dug in and magic was seen as a power to suppress. From this point on, magicians were not tolerated and were regarded as charlatans – a fact that is demonstrated in the mythology that grew up around the character known as Faust.

From Faust to Home

■ In dealing with Faust, it is difficult to separate fact from fiction. A magician of extraordinary abilities, there is little doubt that he existed. For instance, it is known that in 1509 a Johannes Faust received a degree in theology from Heidelberg University. Later references show him to be a widely travelled man, indulging in prophecies by communicating with the dead.

Immortalized in the writings of Johnann Spies, Christopher Marlowe, Goethe and, as late as 1947, Thomas Mann, Faust emerges as a brilliant man with a thirst for spiritual knowledge. On the other hand, Martin Luther and others dismissed him as a 'common charlatan.' Indeed, a Georg Faust who lived at the time became known as the 'demigod of Heidelberg'.

This is the essence of Faust. To his contemporaries, he became known as a hard-drinking lout and confidence trickster – there are even references to his being a sodomite. Faust could have been a great intellectual, but instead he committed himself to gaining knowledge through a pact with the devil. In other words, at a time when Christianity was becoming increasingly entrenched, he refused to toe the academic line and had to be put down, for any knowledge gained outside Christian authority *had* to be demonic.

Here we have the explanation of both his vilification by his contemporaries and his hallowed position in a continued literary tradition. Faust was a man with a thirst to know, but also a refusal to accept the established wisdom. In this sense, Faust is alive today. He exists in me and in nearly every writer on the paranormal; he exists in every medium, healer and psychic superstar, for as one we say that the present established wisdom is incomplete. Our pact with the 'devil' may be symbolic, but in searching for knowledge outside the accepted world view, we step into the world of the unknown. And what people don't know, they fear, as they once feared the devil.

The answer to such people is to ridicule them; to build up a mythology of charlatans, fools and conmen – for established wisdom has never been able to discredit the existence of the paranormal. It is true that some supposed psychic superstars may be conmen, and occasionally they are caught, but the general existence of the paranormal has remained intact throughout history, and is just as strong today. It is this niggling existence that fascinates the literary man and turns the Fausts of history into legend.

Faust is said to have been born in 1491, the son of German peasants living near Weimar. Moving to Wittenberg, he was brought up by a rich uncle. As he showed signs of high intelligence, the church seemed to be the right place for him, but the young Faust turned instead to studying magic. However, he eventually gained a degree in theology as well as a medical degree. It was even thought that he would go on to be a famous doctor.

Evidence suggests that in 1507 he gained a teaching post at a boys' school near Frankfurt, but had to flee amid allegations of seducing pupils. Little else is known of him, but he is thought to have died around 1540. Upon his death, his corpse turned face down, hinting that his destination was hell. Five times it was turned on its back, but each time it flipped over again.

As with Abramelin the Jew, there are a number of stories concerning Faust's magical abilities. Visiting a moneylender, he saws off a leg and gives it to him as security for a loan. Later, the moneylender throws the leg into a river in disgust. Faust then appears again and demands his leg back. Unable to comply, the moneylender ends up paying Faust extra money in compensation.

On another occasion, Faust stops a wagon loaded with hay and asks the wagoner how much he can have for a few pence. The wagoner jokes that he can eat as much as he likes – after all, men don't eat hay. When Faust has eaten half the load, the wagoner pays him a gold piece to leave the rest alone. He accepts and goes away, leaving the wagoner baffled when he sees his load intact once more.

We may again be tempted to dismiss such tales as the invention of a superstitious population at a time when scientific understanding was almost non-existent, but similar fantastic tales continue to be told concerning people of high paranormal ability. In the late nineteenth century, many such stories were circulated regarding the physical mediums involved with spiritualism. Undoubtedly some were fraudulent, but let us consider the most famous of them – Daniel Dunglas Home – and compare such tales with those of Faust.

Throughout the 1850s, 60s and 70s, Home fascinated audiences throughout the United States and Europe with the most amazing paranormal feats. He performed in well-lit rooms and wore tight-fitting clothes so that no 'gadgets' could be involved, and he intrigued royalty, aristocrats, intellectuals and scientists alike.

His most famous performance took place in December 1868 in front of Lord Adare and notable scientist Lord Lindsay. In the top-floor flat of Ashley House in London, 80 feet (25 m) above ground, he levitated out of a window, floated through the air, and came back into another room through a window.

Elizabeth Barrett Browning was a particular admirer of Home. At one seance, Home produced flowers out of thin air and laid them on a table. A spirit hand appeared and floated the flowers to a position above her head. Once, in Massachusetts, he agreed to hold a seance for a delegation from Harvard. Suddenly the table they were using reared up like a horse on two legs. Several of those present sat on the table to try to force it down again, but failed. In Florence, a countess was playing a grand piano at one of Home's performances. Suddenly, piano and countess floated to the ceiling, the countess continuing to play.

In March 1871 Home agreed to be tested by the scientist Sir William Crookes. In front of the scientist, Home stirred a number of hot coals in a grate with his bare hand. He picked up a piece and held it while he blew it until it was white hot. In another experiment, Crookes placed an accordion in a large copper cage and asked Home to play it without touching it. The accordion rose from the base of the cage and played.

Many of these 'performances' far exceeded the talents of Faust, and while most rational people today will dismiss them totally, we simply have to accept that Home had paranormal powers. But of what order were those powers?

There are hints within the literature. First of all, he refused to perform in front of large audiences. Hostesses could sometimes fly into a rage regarding his refusal, but always they relented and cleared out much of the audience, with Home rarely performing to more than half a dozen people. So why did his audience have to be so small?

A further hint is offered by the occasional detractor, such as the poet Robert Browning. Browning loathed Home, particularly because of his wife's affection for him. So, too, did Charles Dickens. But neither of these detractors denied that phenomena happened: Dickens's annoyance concerned his failure to explain them, and Browning simply failed to accept the evidence of his eyes. If phenomena didn't happen, surely such observers would have said they didn't happen? But no – they saw them happen; they simply tried to deny them.

The obvious answer to Home's powers is that he used psychokinesis – an ability to affect matter through the power of the mind. Alternatively, many researchers, such as Brian Inglis, suggest that Home had relearned the ancient powers of the shaman. But as we have seen, the shaman, while having some form of extra-sensory ability, simply induced mass hallucinations.

In recent years a new phenomenon has hit the entertainment world – stage hypnosis. Audiences delight in watching hypnotized stooges making fools of themselves. The most famous of these hypnotists is Paul McKenna, although his work goes much deeper than simple stage hypnotism, for he uses hypnosis as a therapeutic tool too.

As McKenna has his own series on British television, the stooges are often interviewed after the show. They speak of times when they were given one type of food and instructed to 'taste' a different food. Under such hypnosis, they speak of a clash within the mind, knowing that what they are tasting is wrong, but unable to deny it. A similar problem occurs with what they are hypnotized to see. They readily experience hallucinations, but at some logical level they know it isn't real; yet they are compelled to believe, and so they do. The problem is only resolved when the trance is broken, and they can speak logically about the actual reality. But what would happen if a really gifted hypnotist induced a trance without their knowing, and also broke the trance at the end of the performance without their knowledge? It is logical to assume that a true believer in the power of the hypnotist to hold paranormal abilities would remain intact. A detractor, on the other hand, would suspect something untoward, but be unable to put their finger on exactly what it was.

These abilities can provide a logical explanation of the powers invested in magicians and mediums such as Home and Faust. With Home, audiences had to be small so that he could produce the hypnotic state in them and control them. In such a state they would believe anything, for they actually saw what he suggested to them, and any detractor such as Robert Browning would be left unable to intuit what was going on.

So can we come to the conclusion that Home and, if correct, Faust were nothing more than conmen using hypnosis to dupe a stooge? This is an attractive deduction to make, but is not necessarily the case, for even as late as the turn of the nineteenth century, the ability of hypnosis to produce hallucinations was not understood. Hypnosis was used at the time of Home, but only as a tool to get into the deep inner mind. As far as hallucinations were concerned, the phenomenon had not been associated with them. Hence, we can envisage Home understanding that he had a magnificent talent, but there was nothing in academic literature to suggest that the talent was psychological. Indeed, it is even acceptable to suggest that Home, thinking the power was supernatural, believed the hallucinations he induced himself.

There are two important points to be understood here. First of all, the hint is given that supernatural talents are only supernatural until such time that logical theory shows them to be psychological. It is that devil again, making us fear that which we do not yet understand. And second, when such misunderstood abilities are shown to produce events, we either believe completely or we deny their existence, putting such talents down to fraudsters, conmen and liars. And as history moved out of the superstitious Middle Ages and Reformation, such motives continued to be placed on shamanic survivors such as the enigmatic count known as Saint Germain.

Saint Germain

■ Occasionally, the paranormal produces a person of such enigmatic idiosyncrasies that, having failed to explain him, most researchers end up ignoring him. To accept such a person as genuine is to invite ridicule, yet to attempt to explain him requires such a massive leap of faith that the task becomes intolerable. One such person was the eighteenth-century Count Saint Germain.

As with Abramelin and Faust, it is impossible here to differentiate between fact and legend. Even though Saint Germain lived during the Enlightenment, when reason had taken over the intellect and the historical record is complete, he remains a total enigma. The most obvious course here is to cede to the general view of him as a charlatan, fool and swindler, yet annoying commentaries exist such as that of Prince Charles of Hesse-Cassel, who considered him 'perhaps one of the greatest sages who ever lived'.

Saint Germain is said to have been born around 1710. One story says he was born in San Germano to a tax collector. Alternatively, he was the third son of Prince Ferenc Rakoczy II of Hungary, the son of a Portuguese Jew, or the bastard child of a Bohemian nobleman who dabbled in Rosicrucianism. The first known record of him is in 1740 in Vienna. The French Marshal de Belle Isle had been campaigning in Germany and had been taken ill. The nature of the illness was unknown, but suddenly he was miraculously cured by the curious Saint Germain, who had begun to move in fashionable Viennese circles.

In a society that dressed colourfully, Saint Germain stood out by always wearing black. Such drabness was countered by a huge diamond ring on every finger, and the story arose that he carried loose diamonds in his pockets which he used as money. He was never seen eating in public. He claimed he did not eat, for he had discovered the fabled elixir of life which, among other things, would keep him at the age of 30 for eternity. As well as being a healer, he claimed he could speak over a dozen languages, was a collector of fine art, played violin and harpsichord, painted and was an accomplished alchemist. And, if the stories are to be believed, he went on to be a gifted spy, statesman and soldier.

Upon recovery, the Marshal showed gratitude to Saint Germain by taking him to Paris, where he paid for an apartment and equipped him with a laboratory in which to continue his alchemical experiments. The legend began to take on extreme form when he attended a function given by the Countess von Georgy. Saint Germain told the ageing lady that he remembered her when she was a young girl. The countess said this was impossible, so he began talking of some of his experiences from the past, including being alive at the time of Christ. The countess called him 'a devil', whereupon he was reduced to a trembling hysteric and ran out in terror.

Soon Saint Germain was moving in royal circles, befriending Louis XV and his mistress, Madame de Pompadour. Within a year he moved to London, where for two years he was thought to be a spy. He was arrested in 1743, but somehow escaped to France, where he began to put out feelers hinting that he could ease diplomatic relations between France and England. Louis was convinced that Saint Germain was going to betray him, so Saint Germain fled back to England, and eventually Holland.

In Holland he set up another laboratory and eventually moved to Belgium, supposedly after defrauding a nobleman of 100,000 gilders. Setting up yet another laboratory in Belgium, he had to flee again, finally turning up at the court of the Russian queen, Catherine the Great, in 1768. Now known as General Welldone, he became a diplomat and soldier, but in 1770 he decided to move once more.

In 1774 he turned up in Nuremberg, setting up a laboratory once more and claiming to be a Freemason of a high mystical degree. By 1779, still in Germany, he appeared as an old man, and is thought to have died on 27 February 1784. His last patron, Prince Charles of Hesse-Cassel, burnt all of Saint Germain's papers after his death for fear of their being misinterpreted. That is provided, of course, that Saint Germain had died.

Such confusion arises because after his supposed death he turned up at the court of Louis XVI, offering prophecies of the French Revolution, and in 1822 he made a last appearance, advising that he was going off to the Himalayas for a life of peace and meditation. However, this didn't stop him turning up in America in 1930, where spiritualist Guy Ballard formed the 'I Am Religious Activity' based upon his appearance, and in 1972 he was said to have turned up again in Paris, in the character of supposed alchemist Richard Chanfray.

Of course, these 'afterlife' appearances pale into insignificance when compared to the legends of his existence prior to the eighteenth century. Saint Germain's claim to have been around at the time of Christ is just one of many that have impinged upon his legendary existence, for to believers he is part of a distinct occult tradition that sees him as a great, immortal adept, a member of the Great White Brotherhood who protect the wisdom of the ages.

Saint Germain is said to have first walked on Earth 50,000 years ago, where he was the High Priest of a cosmic race that lived in a paradise which is now the Sahara Desert. Eventually these peoples succumbed to the pleasures of the senses, becoming trapped in physical existence and beginning the present evolutionary state of the human race. Saint Germain left them to their fate, but vowed to return again and again to keep them on the true path of knowledge.

His next appearance was in 1050 BC, where he was the prophet Samuel, who anointed Saul. He returned again as Joseph, husband of Mary, mother of Jesus, and in the third century AD he became St Alban, the first British Christian martyr. However, Christianity wasn't the only movement that survived only with his help. After Plato, he became Proclus, head of Plato's academy in Athens. Next, he was Merlin, overseeing the transitional phase of the Dark Ages. The thirteenth century saw him appear as Roger Bacon, one of the principal players in the move towards rationalism. Later, he discovered America as Christopher Columbus, and helped science along once more as Francis Bacon in the seventeenth century.

With such a legend behind him it is easy to see why most rational researchers ignore Saint Germain, but this is an error. We cannot understand the paranormal unless we are prepared to consider every facet of it, and such an approach must include Count Saint Germain. So what was he: charlatan or immortal sage?

The central problem with Saint Germain is that we see him in terms of the Enlightenment, during which he lived. The Enlightenment was the time of the great transition from religion and monarchy to reason and political power invested in the people. It was the time when the supernatural was banished intellectually, but underneath this established view it was also the time of a growing intellectual interest in a reasoned occult. Soon the world was to hear of occultists Francis Barrett and Eliphas Levi, who would go on to write major occult texts, causing the formation of a myriad of occult organizations. Although the rational world tries to ignore this tradition, it has continued to this day, and we must see Saint Germain in terms of such occultism.

If we do so, Saint Germain need no longer be seen as an Enlightenment contemporary, but as a survival of the idiosyncrasies of classical shamanism. Saint Germain could well have been a complete charlatan – I don't know – but we can also see him as invested with the madness associated with the shaman, yet living in a world where it was thought correct to understand. It is in this light that I will offer Saint Germain the benefit of the doubt, and see if the paranormality of the man can be understood in rational terms.

If the legends are correct, Saint Germain claimed to have been on Earth many times and thought himself to be immortal. However, we have already seen how past life regression can cause people to believe they have lived before (see pages 38–39). Of course, such regression is a recent phenomenon, an idiosyncrasy of an understanding of hypnosis – but consider the possibility of a man having the ability to attain a shaman-like trance state manifesting past lives at a time when such trances were not understood. For such a man, the idea that he had lived before and was, indeed, immortal, would not only be attractive, but logical.

We can immediately see the possibility that Saint Germain wasn't a charlatan, but genuinely believed he *had* been on Earth many times. His belief may well have been based upon inner fantasies, but just as many people today believe they have lived before, we can attach the same explanation to Saint Germain.

What would such a belief do to the psychological state of such a man? Living at the time of the Enlightenment, he would have a need to understand himself, and this would involve a thirst for knowledge in the form of reading and experiment. But what form of experimentation would he be most likely to indulge in? His mania for creating laboratories offers the key, for many secret laboratories existed at the time. They were involved in discovering the fabled philosopher's stone, which in turn led to the formula of the elixir of life, through which immortality was achieved. This was the search of the alchemist, and as Saint Germain most probably thought himself immortal, he would inevitably turn in this direction.

Alchemy

■ We are all aware of the image of the medieval wizard: pointed hat atop his head, long robes encompassing his body and a huge, bushy beard hiding his face but allowing manic eyes to stare. Sometimes he has a wand, but often he is in a closed, secret, darkened room surrounded by thick and dusty books. In the middle of the room is a table, and on this table is a host of glass receptacles with bubbling concoctions within. By the side is a bellows to blow a fire to an inferno, and above it further concoctions will boil.

This image is not, in fact, that of the wizard, but of the alchemist. The forerunner of modern chemistry – most of the chemist's equipment was devised by these seekers after knowledge – the alchemist was involved in the search for the philosopher's stone, a substance that could transmute base metals such as lead into gold. Should the alchemist succeed in his quest, then he was also said to be close to the formula of the elixir of life, which, if imbibed, could banish illness and lead to immortality.

Alchemy is known as one of the Hermetic philosophies, in that it is believed to have been devised by the god-like magician Hermes Trismegistos. It is unlikely that such a character actually lived, for he is regarded as representing the ancient esoteric teaching traditions of both ancient Egypt and Greece. In Hermes Trismegistos we therefore have a form of genesis of occult knowledge.

Principal to this knowledge was the idea that the world was created by a divine force which placed order upon the initial chaotic mass of the universe. This state was called *prima materia*, or 'first matter'. Everything within the universe was made up of this matter, and the idea grew that the properties of this first state could be produced again by a process of dissolving and combining elements and transmuting them into something more desirable. As gold was the most perfect of all known elements, this became the ultimate goal of the alchemist. In changing a less desirable substance into gold, perfection was achieved, and the alchemist moved closer to the perfection of God.

The ancient Egyptians became master goldsmiths, the worker in gold holding a similar mystical position to the builder. Hence, we can see an impulse similar to sacred geometry behind the idea of gold being symbolic of divine perfection. This is why gold was so often used by the Egyptians in funerals.

In the seventh century AD Egypt was invaded by the Arabs. They called the country Khem, and they were amazed by the Egyptian gold working, which they called *al-kimiya*, or 'the art of the land of Khem'. The word 'alchemy' is said to have come from here. Such gold working fitted ideally into the Arabian mystical and academic structure, for they had already begun to experiment to try to find the root of physical existence, the practice being well established by the fourth century AD.

The main intellectual stimulus behind Arabian attempts to find the 'first matter' – which to all intents and purposes we can take to be the philosopher's stone – was based on the ideas of the Greek philosopher Aristotle. He believed that the material world was made from 'prime matter'. This was not a physical property as we understand today, but an esoteric substance. Physical 'forms' could, however, be impressed upon it, and it was these physical 'forms' that led to the physical world. Such 'forms' were created from four 'qualities', which Aristotle took to be wetness, dryness, heat and cold. These qualities gained physicality with water, air, fire and earth. These becoming fundamental elements, all physical matter was composed of various amounts of them.

For hundreds of years the Arabs broke down physical elements in their laboratories in order to find the Aristotelian 'prime matter'. Unlike today, however, where scientific knowledge tends to be open, the alchemist guarded his knowledge jealously. He devised codes and secret symbolism to disguise his notes, and it is from this practice that alchemy descended to become one of the occult sciences. The word 'gibberish' comes from the practice, named after the alchemist Jabir ibn Hayyan.

With the end of the Muslim occupation of Spain in the twelfth century, Arabian alchemical knowledge was passed on to Europe, where it was taken on board by the existing occult fraternity. Many European intellectuals joined the search, including Albrecht, Roger Bacon and Paracelsus, the man who is accepted as the father of modern chemistry.

Paracelsus superseded Aristotle's four elements with three ideal substances from which physical matter was made. These were mercury, sulphur and salt. While there were chemical precedents for these elements being fundamental to the physical world, the main impulse in their choice was mystical, for mercury was seen as analogous to the 'spirit', sulphur to the 'soul' and salt to the 'body'. In this way, the physical world echoed the Trinity of Christ, who was also seen as spirit (Holy Father), soul (Holy Ghost) and body (the Son in human form).

This suggests that alchemy was as much a mystical search as a physical one. Indeed, alchemical literature is full of instances of personal revelation based on visions and dreams. Such an idea falls into the pattern developing in this book: that occult knowledge is based upon the requirement to walk within the spiritual and physical worlds at the same time.

Psychoanalyst Carl Jung spent many decades studying alchemy, and came to the conclusion that it was aimed not at the transmutation of base metals into gold, but at the transformation of the soul. Placing an essentially psychological process on the practice, alchemy becomes a spiritual process aimed at transmuting normal consciousness into a higher state. The process of destroying one element in order to discover a more perfect one such as gold is analogous to the death/rebirth ritual.

Jung's analysis is instructive, in that we can see alchemy as a progression of shamanic-type ritual in order to achieve a higher trance state. The association with the physical world is seen here as purely symbolic, for if gold was achieved in the physical world, then a higher, mental state was achieved in the mind.

With this knowledge, we can return to Count Saint Germain and, rather than seeing him as a charlatan, we can envisage a process whereby, through his obsession with laboratories, he was attempting to purify his mind in order to bring out shamanic qualities. In so doing, his trances involved in the alchemical search produced in his mind 'spirits' of past individuals involved with furthering human knowledge. In this sense, the spirits by which he seemed to be 'possessed' were analogous to the shamanic animal spirits, the only difference being one of cultural interpretation. And in finding these spirits in his head, he considered himself immortal.

Channelling

■ Carl Jung removed alchemy from the physical world and put it into the psychological. In doing so, he allowed a new interpretation of the philosopher's stone and the elixir of life, for in a real sense the philosopher's stone is now no longer a physical property of a physical world, but an understanding of ritual in order to cleanse the mind so as to purify it. Once purified, the mind reaches a higher state where the individual walks as one with the gods. He thus enters an immortal world, and it is this realm of insight that can be seen as the elixir of life.

Alchemy therefore becomes a different cultural method of achieving the age-old shamanic state. In this sense, the alchemical quest has remained alive throughout history and finds its latest expression in the phenomenon known as 'channelling'. A development of the mediumistic talent of contacting the dead, channelling moves beyond this spiritualist ideal and involves the 'possession', through trance states, of higher entities similar to those involved with Saint Germain.

One of the earliest occultists with a definite recorded channelling ability was Violet Mary Firth, who is best known by her magical name, Dion Fortune. Born in Llandudno, Wales, in 1890, she was brought up by a Christian Scientist mother, and by the age of four she claimed to have begun having visions. As with our earlier cases of reincarnation (see Minds Possessed), the visions led to feelings of possession, and the first of these was a remembrance of being a temple priestess on Atlantis. Fortune understood that this entity was not physical, but a being who inhabited a form of 'inner plane' within the mind, similar to a superconscious.

When she was 20 years old, Fortune's psychic abilities became more pronounced when she worked at a school. Supervising her was a bad-tempered woman who had studied eastern occultism. According to Fortune, the clash of wills between the two led to a form of psychic warfare, where the woman attempted to lower Fortune's self-esteem by attacking her inner mind.

Turning to psychoanalysis, Fortune realized that her abilities which had manifested held important lessons for psychology, and she was to spend a lifetime trying to understand her 'gift'. However, prior to World War I she had a dream in which she understood that the inner plane was populated with immortal 'masters' who directed human affairs. During the dream she met two of them in the form of Jesus and, now elevated to an immortal, Saint Germain. Fortune became a pupil of Jesus, and he gave her information on her past lives, where, throughout history, she had worked within the occult.

Fortune went on to found the Fraternity of the Inner Light, an organization dedicated to understanding the esoteric nature of Christianity. By this time she was steeped in occult ritual and began to perfect her magical abilities. In 1923 she went on a pilgrimage to Glastonbury, and it was here that she contacted three more 'masters', including the Greek philosopher Socrates. These masters went on to help her perfect her magical abilities, which reached their ritual apotheosis during World War II, when she organized a mass magical ceremony aimed at awakening King Arthur to come to the aid of Britain. Fortune died in 1946, but for years after her death many mediums claimed to have contacted her. Perhaps, like Saint Germain, she too had become immortal.

Dion Fortune was not classed as a channeller *per se*, for the term had not come into use at that time. Jane Roberts, however, was. Born in 1929 in New York State, she married a painter, Robert Butts, and began a not-too-successful literary career writing poetry and short stories. However, one evening in September 1963 her writing was curtailed when she went into a form of trance state and her mind was suddenly flooded with ideas. She was unaware of where they came from, but they seemed to take her over and compel her to write them down. Wanting to know more about the source of these ideas, Roberts and her husband began experimenting with the Ouija board.

Communications soon began to flow from the board, first of all from her deceased grandfather and then a deceased English teacher called Frank Withers. By December 1963 Withers had advised her that he preferred to be known as 'Seth', saying that he was a 'personality essence'.

Communications with Seth continued for a while using the Ouija board, but after a time Roberts realized that she could go into a natural trance state and Seth would possess her directly. During such trances she would speak in a man's voice, and occasionally Seth would manifest close to her in hallucinated form.

Over the following years until her death in 1984, Seth dictated several books to Roberts, and small groups would meet in her house to watch as Seth possessed her, passing on his messages. Indeed, at one stage a group of entities would possess her, including the American philosopher and psychologist William James. As with Dion Fortune, following Jane Roberts's death several other channellers claimed to receive communications from Seth. But what was the purpose of Seth's communications?

Seth claimed to be a personality with a message. A non-physical being, he had, however, lived many lives on Earth in order to learn about human beings. He was now using Roberts to advise humanity of the absolute scope of their consciousness; including their ability to construct reality through thoughts, actions and beliefs. In particular, human beings were reincarnated many times – Seth himself had once lived on Atlantis, this being just one of many lives – and it was the purpose of the soul to perfect psychic focus. In this way people could come to know God, who lived a multi-dimensional existence and was much more than any system ever devised to understand him.

Christ, Seth advised, was actually three individuals. The third person of Christ would not appear until the Second Coming. When he did arrive, he would be a great psychic and would renew Christianity, which would be in great decline before his appearance.

What are we to make of Seth's message? First of all, if we take away his references to Atlantis and Christ, we are left with the idea that reality is a construct created by human consciousness. This is simply a restatement of occult and mystical philosophy throughout the ages and offers nothing new. The sharp reader will already see how this book is developing into a logical restatement of the idea, with culture taking the place of reality *per se*, constantly remoulded by our thoughts, actions and beliefs. Seth thus becomes a simple reflection of occult knowledge, clinging, as many occultists do, to one of the earliest, and most persistent future, mythologies in Atlantis and the Second Coming.

This allows us to intuit the true reality of Seth. Rather than some great non-physical being from the supernatural, we can see him as a split-off element of Jane Roberts's own mind. Roberts aspired to be a great writer, and when her abilities failed to realize her dream, her frustrations led to a mind fragmentation similar to multiple personality, manifesting a 'personality' with a message based on an already existing cultural expression of the occult. However, while we can put Seth down to a delusion, we have in him a vital cultural force that has had a far greater effect on humanity than any other, for his manifestation can be allied directly to similar manifestations throughout history.

The story is a typical one. An individual grows up either in obscurity or aware that the life he is leading is inadequate. The reason for such inadequacy is that the individual realizes something is wrong with the world, and this realization causes frustrations which eventually lead to a spiritual experience. During the experience, a God-force communicates and goes on to dictate a new way of living and a new understanding of reality. The individual is then driven to communicate the message and convert others.

We are talking of the genesis and progression of religion. Applied to the Judaeo-Christian tradition, the story is almost exact in Abraham, Moses, Jesus, St Paul and St Augustine of Hippo, the main players within it. In less hallowed traditions, the process can be applied to Armageddon gurus such as David Koresh and even Shoko Asahara of the Japanese Aum Shinrikyo cult. In each case, the insight brought out by the spiritual experience is based on cultural expression. In 99.9 per cent of cases, the experiencer is classed as mad, schizophrenic or simply a charlatan, but when we have an instance that strikes a note in a particular culture, a great religion such as Christianity is born. And the world is fundamentally changed by a paranormal experience.

The process is steeped in death/rebirth, in that the spiritual experience leads to the death of the old way and instigation of the new, and in being new, it is more perfect, and is thus alchemical in process. However, this alchemy is both psychological and sociological, in that an individual spiritual experience goes on to change not just the experiencer, but an entire society. Can such a process be explained by our present understanding of culture as a simple, chaotic grouping of ideals?

Returning to Carl Jung, he thought that the ultimate expression of the higher alchemical state involved a transformation of consciousness into absolute love, personified by the image of the hermaphrodite, which is a blending of the male and female opposites. The mythology of alchemy actually claims that the successful alchemist is transformed physically into an asexual being, being neither male nor female. Eastern philosophy is steeped in the idea of male and female opposites, highlighted in the concept of two opposing but complementary natural forces in yin and yang. Yin is thought of as the female principle, and yang the male: the perfect balance of the two leads to prolonged life, which again hints at alchemical immortality.

We can, of course, dismiss such ideas as mere mystical claptrap, but the idea of a kind of 'superforce' within the universe has remained constant throughout history – and the world's most famous alchemist was well aware of its possible existence.

Sir Isaac Newton is known today for his monumental work on calculus, optics and, most importantly, universal gravitation; the reality of his life is that these were physical breakthroughs based on his understanding of Hermetic philosophy. One of the greatest disgraces of modern science is the way in which it has chosen to ignore the bulk of his work, for Newton spent much of his life in secret laboratories breaking down chemicals in search of the 'prime matter' and wrote over a million words of alchemical text. He is considered the first great scientist, but one should read over and over again the telling words of the British economist John Maynard Keynes (quoted by John Barrow in *The World Within the World* [see Bibliography], who said of him:

> Newton was not the first of the age of reason. He was the last of the magicians, the last of the Babylonians and the Sumerians, the last great mind which looked out on the visible and intellectual world with the same eyes as those who began to build our intellectual inheritance rather less than 10,000 years ago.

Keynes was wrong. As this book will show, he was not the last great mind to contemplate such esoteric concepts. The problem is that, as with Newton, science has simply ignored those minds. So what was the basis of Newton's real philosophy?

Fundamental to it was the belief in an original wisdom concerning the order of the universe, given by God to the ancients. Reason caused this knowledge to be first ignored, and then lost, but Newton was convinced that this original wisdom could still be found in mythology.

This led him to Hermetic philosophy. He devoured alchemical texts in search of this wisdom, becoming convinced that alchemical transmutation would lead to 'prime matter', within which the truth of the universe would be unfolded.

He soon realized that the Cartesian view of the universe, in which reason had separated body from mind, was wrong. Such an idea denied the existence of 'spirit' in the universe. To Newton, 'spirit' *was* the universe. Nature was not a machine, and the universe could not be explained by its physical existence alone but was a living thing – an actual, existent being. However, Newton was not prepared to accept simple beliefs. He also wanted evidence.

He never found his absolute evidence. His search offered physical side-effects such as gravity, but he remained true to his search throughout his life. Had science remained true to him, the principles of Hermetic philosophy may well have been proved, for the simple fact is that most of its basic principles have been vindicated by science itself.

Alchemy was wrong in the assumption that reality was made up of four, or later three, fundamental elements. The atomic periodic table eventually identified 92 such elements of which the universe was made, thus validating the basic idea. These elements, or atoms, are themselves made up from smaller particles that exist in an electromagnetic field. This field is ethereal and formless in an exact physical sense, validating the alchemical ideal of a formless 'prime matter'.

Hermetic philosophy argued that 'prime matter' was first sculpted out of chaos by a universal force. Science tells us of the 'big bang' which produced matter in a chaotic state. Universal forces such as gravity worked on this matter to form the universe as we know it. Hermetic philosophy argued that this 'prime matter', while not 'physical', could have physical form impressed upon it. We now know that the physical reality of the universe, including ourselves, is made up of stable electromagnetic patterns; thus physical form is impressed upon a 'prime matter'. And of course, principal to alchemy is the idea of the transmutation of one element into another. We now know that an atom is made up of a nucleus orbited by electrons. The nucleus is itself made up of neutrons and protons, and the number of such particles within the nucleus defines what element the atom becomes. Such atoms can be 'split', and in so doing, the element is 'transmuted' into something else.

At the fringes of today's science are other concepts, such as the search for an understanding of how particles can affect each other simultaneously without physical contact, and scientists are having to come to terms with a possible role for consciousness within the universal construct. We will return to such concepts later. For the moment, we can say that if either of these concepts is ever proved, then Newton's 'spirit' within the universe will also be proved. A superforce will be seen to exist, and its properties will be nothing less than a form of superconscious.

Healing

■ Science is slowly, and begrudgingly, beginning to prove the ideals of Hermetic philosophy. A superconscious that marries the physical to the spiritual may not be far from our understanding; if ever proved, it will show how the properties of the universe reflect the idiosyncrasies of the individual. Such a concept was immortalized by the mythological instigator of Hermetic philosophy, Hermes Trismegistos, in the saying 'As above, so below'. Perhaps Newton was also right concerning the original wisdom within mythology.

This universal superconscious can be allied to shamanic trance states, for if consciousness *does* permeate both the universe and the individual, then it would be valid to say that we connect with the universal superconscious through a descent into our own minds. However, I have shown how such trance states can cause 'possessions' from outside the personal mind in the form of cultural expression. Does this suggest that such possessions could be both personal and also tinged with an element of the 'universal' forces hinted at? If so, such a God-force could be exactly that – God. His actual expression may be cultural in nature, but an overall God above culture and existent in the universe could be valid.

There is, of course, a further phenomenon involved with shamanic principles that has not yet been discussed. This is known as spiritual or faith healing. The phenomenon is said to be rampant among religious prophets and mystics, and shamanic survivors such as Count Saint Germain were said to practise it. Could such healing give us further indications of the existence of a superconscious?

Spiritual and faith healing are thought by many to be separate disciplines. The latter is the preserve of God, whereas the former is thought to involve charlatans, or to be the province of more demonic forces. Many Biblical prophets were healers and healing was central to the ministry of Jesus. As the Christian church developed, the idea grew that illness was caused by the devil. Hence, as with sin, it would yield to the power of prayer. As the Church grew, many saints were canonized due to their power to heal. Upon death, the saint's bones or other body parts were often preserved as relics, and to this day cases continue to arise of believers being healed by contact with such relics.

During the Enlightenment, belief in faith healing waned, but with the growth of the Christian Scientists and Pentecostalists in the nineteenth century, faith healing was popularly revived. Today, charismatic movements hold mass healing sessions, the Toronto Blessing being an example. However, the distinction between spiritual and faith healing seems to be more of a cultural idiosyncrasy than a valid reality.

A spiritual healer does not have to believe in God. Rather, most accept that they act as a form of conduit for a universal healing energy. The most usual form of healing is the laying on of hands, where the healer places a hand on the patient or holds it close to their body. Patients report feeling heat, tingling or other similar sensations emanating from the hand. Such healing can alleviate pain and cause a reduction, or sometimes complete cure, of most illnesses, from back complaints to cancer.

In Britain, many healers join organizations that are themselves allied to the Confederation of Healing Organizations. Through such organizations a large number of medical authorities now hold lists of registered healers, with doctors beginning to take healing seriously as a complementary element of orthodox medicine. Most would argue that healing doesn't really work, in that any benefit is psychosomatic, but, they are beginning to say, belief in healing can go a long way towards increasing a patient's well-being, which can only be good for them in the long run.

Healing is mainly holistic, in that the healer treats the whole body, and several factors have shown themselves to be important in its success. First of all, the patient is assisted if they believe the treatment will work. Relaxation has also been shown to be vital. A third factor involves the relationship between healer and patient. Compassion must be present in the healer, or success is significantly reduced. And finally, bolstering the healer's energies with beliefs in some form of higher power seems to increase benefit. In this way, many healers claim to be guided by spirits in their work. However, in the final analysis most healers accept that it is the attitude of the patient that is of greatest importance. If they believe that a higher healing force exists, they can heal themselves.

One of the most famous healers was the American Edgar Cayce, although he claimed not to heal, but to diagnose and offer a course of treatment that could lead to a cure. Born in 1877 in Hopkinsville, Kentucky, he never studied medicine, but began work as a salesman. However, a persistent laryngitis caused him to stop working. Soon after, he was hypnotized, and the hypnotist asked him to describe the cause of his problem and a probable treatment. Cayce astonished himself when he did just that. He went on to perfect the ability in himself.

Becoming known as the Sleeping Prophet, he began trance diagnosis in 1901. Using diagnosis at a distance, he required only a name and address to offer a reading, and he went on to provide some 30,000 during his life. For cures, he advised a whole host of treatments including massage, relaxation, tonics and diet. In 1928 he set up the Association for Research and Enlightenment in Virginia. In August 1944 he collapsed from exhaustion and died in January 1945.

With Cayce, we can see a form of remote viewing similar to ESPionage (see page 25) at work, suggesting a kind of superconscious behind the practice. However, Cayce's philosophy behind his work is interesting. He saw the body as an interconnected network of organs and tissue similar to a 'system'. If one element was not working correctly, it would affect the rest. Behind this holistic system was his belief that every cell had consciousness, allowing them to communicate with each other within the body and with Cayce during his readings, telling him what was wrong.

As for the cause of most illness, Cayce was a believer in reincarnation and illness was usually caused by deeds or emotions during past lives. Cayce himself had had many past lives, including one as a celestial being which first came to Earth prior to Adam and Eve, and he also claimed to have lived, later, on Atlantis.

In Cayce's trance states and past lives we can identify the idiosyncrasies of shamanism. Indeed, as a youth he claimed to see many non-physical beings, many of them becoming his friends. The contemporary, and much more orthodox, healer Matthew Manning shared many of these idiosyncrasies.

Manning was born in 1955, and from an early age he had remembrances of objects moving about around him. In 1967 these phenomena exploded around him into a protracted and virulent poltergeist outbreak that went on intermittently for several years. During this time he also had an out-of-body-experience, communicated with and saw dead occupants of his house, and was possessed by dead personalities who brought out in him automatic writing and painting, where his hand was compelled to perform for them.

Manning came to the attention of the media, and when he discovered that he could psychically bend spoons, he was dubbed Britain's answer to Uri Geller. Achieving a high media profile, he performed on television throughout the world, but by 1976 he realized he was becoming nothing but a freak show. He disappeared from media view and went off to India in search of enlightenment. In the foothills of the Himalayas he underwent a mystical experience where he felt he had become part of the mountains. Sensing a form of universal presence, he felt at one with a sympathetic and connected world, and realized intuitively that his future was to channel his chaotic powers into a force for good through healing.

Over the following few years Manning trained himself in healing practices, perfecting these through the laying on of hands. Since then, from his home at Bury St Edmunds, he has held healing sessions and travelled to various healing workshops, passing on his techniques.

To Manning, his healing abilities constitute a passing on of universal love. His sessions last for 15–20 minutes, during which he passes his hands over the patient's body. During the session he experiences sensations of heat emanating from his hands, and symbolic pictures of the medical problem formulate in his mind. In tests, it has been found that often his brain wave patterns synthesize with those of the patient. As to the absolute secret of his ability, Manning claims that he gives patients permission to heal themselves – something that orthodox medicine disallows, by adopting a negative attitude that reinforces the patient's illness.

In Matthew Manning we can again ally healing to other shamanic abilities. Uncontrolled, his power was destructive, in that it led to poltergeist activity and possession, but in learning to control the ability he focused it, using it for good – provided, that is, that such abilities actually exist, and are not mere delusions which produce nothing but psychosomatic responses from the patients.

To find out whether such abilities actually are real, the researcher Dr Bernard Grad decided to test healer Oscar Estebany under laboratory conditions at McGill University in Montreal. He was so impressed by the results that he repeated the experiment a second time, again achieving positive results. For the test, Dr Grad made a small wound under anaesthetic on a number of mice. Estebany was not allowed access to some of the mice, but was allowed to practise healing on others. In both tests, the 'healed' mice recovered from the wound significantly faster than the others.

Such tests seem to validate healing, but also tell us quite clearly that the process cannot be psychological in nature, in that psychosomatic factors cannot be involved. Rather, some form of 'invasion' by a channelled force seems to be taking place. As to the nature of this ability, an experiment performed in 1971 can be instructive – an experiment, incidentally, that had nothing to do with healing.

It has often been thought that when several women live together, they tend to synchronize their menstrual cycles. Researcher Martha McClintock of the University of Chicago decided to test whether the belief had any basis in fact. Finding a 'control' subject who menstruated on an exact 28-day cycle, McClintock collected sweat from her armpit. Three times a week she would dilute a drop of sweat in alcohol and place it on the upper lip of a number of subjects. As a control, she applied the same technique to a second group of women but using pure alcohol, with no sweat. After four months of treatment, the second group was in total disarray, but 80 per cent of the group treated with the 'control's' sweat menstruated on exactly the same day.

The most likely explanation of this 'invasion' was hormonal, in that the sweat caused the synchronization of the hormones of others. Menstruation is, of course, regulated by hormone levels but, interestingly, so are many other body functions involved in our ability to fight disease and illness. Endorphins, for instance, are vital for fighting pain, while adrenalin is often used to fortify the body in order to fight infection.

Hormones are produced by a number of glands within the body which, together, are known as the endocrine system. These are the pituitary, thyroid, parathyroid and adrenal glands, the testes in males, the ovaries in females, and parts of the pancreas. These are the least understood parts of the body, and their actions are known to include psychological factors. For instance, a state of mind can affect the menstrual cycle, or a pornographic picture can produce a male erection without physical stimulant.

The hormones produced by the endocrine system are thought of as chemical messengers which co-ordinate vital body function. However, there is one such chemical messenger that defies explanation. Thought to be associated with scent, this is the pheromone, and it defies explanation because it can leave the body and become airborne, passing on a chemical message that can affect hormones in another life form.

How this happens is unknown, but the fact that it does is well established within science. For instance, when a dog goes wild due to a bitch being on heat, it is reacting to pheromonal actions. Colonies of ants leave pheromonal trails to allow others to follow, and the queen bee produces pheromones within the hive to prevent the development of further queens.

It is debatable whether or not humans actually give off pheromones, but if we decide we do, then it is attractive to see the laying on of hands during healing as a process of pheromonal 'invasion', passing on healing through hormonal interaction. However, to many eastern healers, it is not hormonal action that causes cure, but energy levels within the esoteric concept of chakras.

Chakra is the Sanskrit word for 'wheel'. Thought to be invisible energy centres within the body, they pass through the body a universal life force that is said to produce physical, mental and emotional health in the person. The chakras are analogous to spoked wheels that whirl at various speeds as they process the life force. Within this very ancient and esoteric concept, if the energies are blocked, the outcome is illness.

There are said to be hundreds of chakras within the body, but only seven major ones, most of which are along the spinal column. The root chakra lies at the base of the spine and is said to be responsible for self-preservation. Next we have the sacral chakra near the genitals, responsible for reproduction and sexuality. The solar plexus chakra lies above the navel and is associated with emotion. The heart chakra is in the centre of the chest and influences our immunity to disease. The throat chakra is identified with creativity and self-expression. Next we have the brow chakra, sometimes called the mystical third eye, which is responsible for intuition, intelligence and our psychic abilities. Finally, the crown chakra exists just above the head and governs our conscious evolution.

As with most ancient and esoteric concepts, the chakras are scoffed at by science, but their close proximity to the main endocrine glands suggests that the ancients could have had knowledge of hormonal interaction, identifying the concept as a universal life force – which, in a sense, it is. However, we can look deeper into the human body than hormonal action, and in doing so we can identify a further concept that could well offer valid evidence of a true form of universal life force. To approach such a concept, we need to move away from healing *per se* and enter the world of alternative medicine.

According to a 1995 report by Mintel, sales of alternative medicines such as herbal and homoeopathic remedies have risen by a quarter since 1992, amounting to sales worth just over £62 million in Britain alone. In 1986 the British Medical Association had discounted alternative medicines as a passing fashion, but a 1994 report indicated a change of mind, with some three-quarters of British family doctors prepared to refer patients to alternative practitioners if necessary.

However, identifying the archetypal user of alternative medicines as female, middle-aged and middle class, medical authorities tend to identify users as the 'worried well'. In surveys, four out of five users claim to receive benefits, but in the main these are thought to be psychological, with the patient finding comfort in a medical approach that treats the whole person, including state of mind and well-being, rather than seeing them merely as an organic repository for chemical cures. However, even the Royal College of Physicians has noted that trials of homoeopathic remedies for hayfever can show benefits.

The argument that homoeopathic remedies simply make use of the 'placebo effect', in that the benefit is purely psychological, has taken a battering from several sources. For instance, placing a few drops of a homoeopathic solution in a dairy herd's water each day has cut down the prevalence of mastitis in some herds by over 70 per cent. In such areas, a placebo effect cannot be behind the success.

Herbal remedies seem to gain more acceptance among doctors than homoeopathic. This is due to the fact that many herbal remedies are present in conventional drugs. The main fear with alternative herbal remedies concerns the lack of skill and competence of many practitioners, for the simple fact is that such herbal remedies can be as potent as conventional chemical drugs. The lack of safety precautions in their availability and use has led to thousands of cases of worrying side-effects.

However, homoeopathic treatments are harder to understand. Indeed, logically, they should be of no use at all. Homoeopathy comes from the Greek word, '*homoios*', meaning like, and '*pathos*', meaning disease. Developed by the nineteenth-century German physician Samuel Hahnemann, the concept is based around two central ideas. First, he decided that an ailment could best be cured by treatment with the same substance that would produce the disease in healthy people, and second, that such substances would best work in minute proportions. The homoeopathic practitioner goes to the natural world in order to find the required substances for the patient to take.

When Hahnemann decided that minute proportions would work best, his words were really an understatement, and it is here that homoeopathy seems to become a nonsense. The substances are diluted in water to a hundredth of their capacity, and then diluted by a hundredth once more, then again and again to as many as a thousand dilutions. This process makes the factor of its dilution an absolute nonsense in terms of ordinary mathematics. In fact, it makes the consistency of the medicine sub-molecular.

Few explanations have been offered as to how such minute quantities of the substance can possibly assist the body to fight illness. In the 1980s, the French scientist Jacques Benveniste suggested that water could act as a form of magnetic medium, retaining a 'memory' of the substance, and it was this memory that provided the effect. Benveniste was derided by the scientific community, but he may not have been far wrong.

The problem with medicine is that we see it in terms of chemical interaction upon a biological organism, the chemicals allowing the cells and organisms within the body to provide cure. With homoeopathy, we perhaps need to go beneath the idea of the body as a biological organism, for underneath this structure of reality we can be seen in terms of an electromagnetic field. This is the 'prime matter' that even science accepts lies below physical form. At this level we are not a biological organism, but a field of electromagnetic 'information', and due to the dilutions involved in homoeopathy, the substances become so slight that they, too, can be seen to exist in terms of this electromagnetic field.

Could it be that homoeopathy works at this level? Could it be that it does not provide a biological cure but works at an 'information' level, interacting with the 'information' in our electromagnetic field? In other words, if we think of our fundamental sub-atomic structure as analogous to the software of a computer, homoeopathy inputs a new program, working on illness at this more subtle level.

Before discounting such an idea, we must realize that we already know of illnesses and cures involved within the electromagnetic field. The sub-atomic structure of the field constitutes radiations. We know that large doses of radiation can cause cancer, and equally that radiations involved in radiotherapy can assist in curing it. Laser surgery is a further electromagnetic bombardment of the body. And as for the electromagnetic field's ability to hold information, this is proved every time you turn on a radio or television.

This electromagnetic field is, of course, interactive with reality outside our bodily structure. According to particle physics, the whole universe exists in a foam-like, interactive field of sub-atomic particles. At present we understand the passing of information within the field only in terms of radio waves, but the known ability of particles to react spontaneously at a distance suggests that an as yet unknown form of information 'transmission' must also exist. So could it be that, in healing, the healer passes on a new program through this suggested mechanism? Perhaps the patient is revitalized by a healthy program of the healer's healthy body, and, as suggested for homoeopathy, this works upon curing the patient.

Of course, this is all highly speculative at our present level of understanding of the universe, but it offers indications of the actual existence of a universal life force. Except, of course, due to its permeating the entire universe and not just life, it is a far more fundamental concept – perhaps even a God. But even if we look upon it in less esoteric ways, it would still constitute an existent form of superconscious.

◼ In this section we have looked at some of the most ridiculed individuals in history. Seeing them as shamanic survivals of tribal culture, however, we can regard them as following a distinct anthropological and sociological pattern. They display powers that have until now been classed as supernatural, but we have analysed them in more rational terms, showing how hints exist in science regarding their real abilities.

I chose to call this section The Cabal, and for a very good reason. The word 'cabal' means 'secret' or 'intrigue', and we can see how the characters herein have been treated with suspicions worthy of the word. But are they really the cabalists of this section? Sir Isaac Newton would have been honoured to have been associated with them. He would not have accepted characters such as Saint Germain at face value, but he would have had the guts to look at his claims rationally – for he, too, believed in the reality of alchemical principles and Hermetic philosophy, but an intransigent scientific establishment forced his real views into secrecy.

Today that enforcement is far greater, even though science itself is providing hints of the true reality of such powers. Perhaps the real cabalists are the sceptics who deride such powers, maintaining their own secrecy and intrigue in an increasingly defunct material view of the universe.

However, the word 'cabal' comes from the 'cabbala', which was the essence of Jewish mysticism. It was a way of seeing God which was distinctly different to the orthodox Judaic view of Him. Within the cabbala, God had many faces. The true God was above these faces, and we can see that the many expressions of God within the cabbala are really expressions of the many different cultural interpretations of his existence.

The cabbala went on to form a large part of western occultism, and in this sense we can see the occult search for knowledge as being a search above culture, and an understanding of the universe above the egoism and hopes of mankind. Our present cultural interpretation of the universe is similarly based on our egoism and our hopes, and in this sense it is essentially wrong. However, such a statement needs to be analysed further.

Newton was an Hermetic philosopher. In searching out the holistic and spiritual side of the universe, he identified many concepts that could, indeed, be seen in a material sense. Principal among these was gravity. We must see science in a similar way. Like Newton, it, too, provides many factual ideas of how the material universe works, but unlike Newton, scientists cannot look above these mechanisms. In their distinct specialized fields, their discovered mechanisms *do* reflect a true universe, but scientists fail to look at the universe outside their specializations. They fail to see the higher living connectedness of the holistic universe above their cultural myopia, and until they are prepared to do so, the absolute reality of the universe will not be known.

This book indicates that that true reality is a universe held together by a form of superconsciousness. Such a concept permeates the entire universe and all that exists within it. In this sense, we have seen how such superconsciousness moulds men together into societies by the formulation of culture. Until the advent of reason and science, such a superconscious was viewed, culturally, as the supernatural, and nowhere does culture express this supernatural concept more than in the superstitions that culture has consistently provided. Can these, too, cede to logical understanding?

· SUPERSTITION ·

Superstition and Culture

■ A warning for all actors. I am about to use the most magical word in the history of theatre. I must use it; some readers may not know what it means, so I have to be precise, to explain. It is the title of the – you know – the Scottish play. Close your eyes if you must. It's coming now *Macbeth*.

No play excites such emotion as this one. To an actor, even to utter its name can bring bad luck – hence, it is known only as 'the Scottish play'. Many believe that it is the inclusion of witches that give it its sinister air, and the superstitions concerning it were said to begin on its first opening night.

The actor who was to play Lady Macbeth was taken mysteriously ill, and it is said that Shakespeare himself had to stand in for the role. The play was originally commissioned by James I: he attended the opening night and hated it. It was never performed, never even uttered, again for 50 years, and from that day to this disaster has struck at dozens of performances.

Two episodes of this mythology will suffice to describe the awe the play inspires. In 1849, it is said, *Macbeth* was being performed at the Astor Place Opera House. For some unknown reason a riot broke out and 31 people were killed. Playing Macbeth at the Old Vic in London in 1937, Laurence Olivier lost his voice. It was a prelude to disaster: the theatre boss died on the opening night, and shortly afterwards the director was killed in a car crash.

How do we account for such anecdotes? How do we account for the irrational fear such tales induce? Is there a real force at work, wreaking havoc, chaos, death and destruction in its wake, or are we back to that glorious thing called culture once more?

The obvious answer is the latter. Throughout history, cultures have directed how we behave individually. While we have free will within culture, it

117

nevertheless defines how our behaviour is understood, and what that behaviour will be. In this respect, culture is a higher collective entity in its own right. Yet such an awesome, omnipotent concept as this can be seen as a 'force' in the way it compels us. In a real sense, we can see it as a psychical mechanism that possesses and consumes – and it is through this mechanism that superstition works. As to how all-pervasive such superstitions can be, let me take you from conception to death in a Britain of not so very long ago. By doing this, we can see that when the supernatural is within society, it *is* culture.

Life begins at conception, but for the first nine months of that life, the beautiful child that will eventually be born takes on an almost vampiric form, sucking the life from, and even the iron from the blood of the mother. Today, medicines and exercises allow most pregnant women to live an increasingly comfortable life, but in times past the main emphasis seemed to be on making the woman as uncomfortable as possible and turning her into a nervous wreck.

The land was full of demons, devils and witches, and they desired nothing more than a child soon to be born. Constantly using their supernatural powers, they forced the pregnant woman into almost ceremonial seclusion, surrounded with charms to keep these powers at bay.

Should she be allowed out, every step had to be taken carefully, for if she stepped on a grave, the child would die. Even opening her eyes could be catastrophic, for she might see a demon. She could not hide the fact if she did, for when born the baby would have a birthmark in the shape of the demon the mother had seen. And, influenced by a demon, the child could well be a demon itself. Most fearful of all was if the woman met a hare. Then the child would surely be born with a hare lip, for the hare would not have been a hare but a witch's familiar, and a hare lip was, of course, the sign of the devil.

The naming of the future child was equally steeped in superstition. A name was more than a name – it was the essence of what the individual would become. Eventually brought into the church through baptism, the name and the individual would be protected by God from sinister forces, but until baptism the name was protected by the family, never uttered lest a witch discover it and use it to charm the baby. For this reason, false names were used before baptism, and it is here that we find the beginnings of what became known as nicknames.

Naming a baby after a loved or respected individual was thought to invest the child with the idiosyncrasies of that person. For this reason, many future parents would open the Bible at random and name the child after the first Biblical person they saw of the right sex. However, if the baby was named after a brother or sister who had died, the dead child was thought to return to claim the newborn.

A newborn child had to be protected particularly from fairies, who scoured the land in search of babies to kidnap and take to fairyland. The way a baby was handled and dressed was also of prime importance. Most women gave birth downstairs, for a baby's first journey had always to be upwards. In this way, it was guaranteed that upon death its first journey would also be upwards, to heaven. Take the baby downwards for its first journey, and it was condemned to eventual hell.

Purity was also considered an important matter. For this reason, it was thought sensible always to have a virgin present at a birth, for if a virgin is the first to hold a newborn, the baby would be protected from evil and was guaranteed a virtuous and honourable life.

One powerful superstition survives to this day in the idea that you must cross a baby's palm with silver. Placing a silver coin in a baby's hand was considered a form of divination. Placed in the right hand, future character could be ascertained. If the child held it tightly, he (or she) would be careful with money. If he held it loosely, he would be a generous soul. But if he dropped it, he would be for ever a spendthrift.

Following baptism, the next most important event for the individual was marriage. The wedding ceremony was steeped in magical symbolism, for the success of the ceremony was passed on to the marriage itself. Most Christian ceremonies involved an absolute ban on weddings, for no other ceremony could be carried out during Easter, Advent and so on. Cultural word magic is still remembered in phrases such as 'Marry in Lent, you'll live to repent.'

May was an unlucky time to get married. This cultural ban goes back to the days of the Roman empire, when during May offerings were made to the dead. As for the picking of the actual day, Thursday was thought to be unlucky, with most marriages taking place on a Monday or Tuesday.

The most remembered wedding superstition is still popular today, where many brides wear something old, something new, something borrowed and something blue. Most of the bride's attire had to be new to signify a new life. Something old, however, symbolized the continuance of age-old traditions; something borrowed, particularly from a lucky person, transferred the luck to the bride; and blue was a particularly lucky colour, and caused a double dose of luck. The wedding dress itself could be of any light colour except green. This was associated with fairies, and the wearer would soon be swapping the dress for funeral black.

The last item the bride donned had always to be the veil. This was a magical garment and was never worn before or after the wedding. Should the bride do so and see herself in a mirror, it was a guarantee of an unhappy marriage. Today it is also considered unlucky for the groom to see the bridal gown before the marriage, or to see the bride on the morning of the wedding. Just to show that we can still create superstitions, the reader may like to know that this is a recent addition to wedding mythology. In times past, the bride and groom usually walked to the church together.

Their journey to the church was a precarious affair, offering many advantages for good or bad luck. Setting out from the house, the bride had to place her right foot first. It was considered extremely lucky if the sun shone on her, and encountering a black cat or a chimney sweep added to the luck. The modern idea of being kissed by the chimney sweep is also new, however, no doubt a product of the modern promiscuous society, for no man but the groom could kiss a bride. Should she encounter a pig or a funeral, on the other hand, she might as well turn around and head for home, for the marriage was doomed.

The most magical element of the ceremony was the wedding ring. This was nothing less than a magical symbol, and its handling was almost sacred. If dropped by the bride or groom, the clumsy one would be the first to die. If dropped by anyone else – beware, best man – the marriage was doomed to failure. If dropped and it rested on a gravestone, the clumsy one had literally caused the eventual death of one, or both, of the pair. Even after the wedding, losing or damaging the ring foretold the end of the marriage through death or infidelity.

Following the wedding ceremony, the wedding cake was eaten. The mixture had to be as rich and fruity as possible, for its richness decided the fertility of the bride. The first slice had to be cut by the bride, with the groom holding his hand above hers. If this magical ceremony did not take place the marriage would be childless. All guests had to eat a piece of the cake or they would bring ill luck on the marriage. However, young girls at the wedding often kept a piece and slept that night with it under their pillow. In this way, the girl dreamed of her own future husband.

Following the wedding day, the couple settled down to a hopefully happy marriage with many children. Throughout this life, charms and spells continued to keep them free from supernatural harm, but eventually, as the candle of life began to flicker, it was the destiny of every human that lived to end up in that vast and ominous supernatural land known as death.

Of course, the body did not go anywhere but into the ground. The soul was a different matter. This was a supernatural entity in its own right, and had to be treated with care. Indeed, the soul became of primary importance even before death.

For instance, it was often thought that very serious illness was caused by the soul beginning to dislocate itself from the physical body. This left the loved ones in a bit of a dilemma: they obviously loved the ill person, but when they thought it clear that death was imminent, it was bad to impede the soul's journey in any way. The outcome of this idea was that the ill person was often helped on their way by strangulation or smothering. In a more modern and secular world we still debate a variation on this practice, deciding whether a person has a right to a dignified death. Today we call it euthanasia.

As death came, it was important to allow immediate escape for the soul. Hence, it was thought prudent to loosen any garments the person was wearing and make sure that all locks in the house were open. After all, if access to heaven was impeded in any way, the family could find themselves haunted by a disgruntled spirit.

Of equal importance during this period was the need to safeguard the departing soul from demons intent on transporting it to hell. For this, the usual practice was to put a heap of salt on the dead person's breast. A further need was born from the idea that sometimes the soul did not fully depart until burial. For this reason, the corpse was never left alone. Day and night, family members would sit with it, guarding it from demons. At the dead of night this could often be a frightening experience, so the practice of holding a party – known as a wake – by the corpse was born.

A certain amount of self-defence was required during this period, too. The soul could find its final journey a lonely one, and the longing to be with its loved ones again could cause it to act selfishly. As the most supernaturally vulnerable part of a living person was their reflection, it was thought expedient to cover up all mirrors until after burial.

While it was generally accepted that it was the soul that went to heaven, certain rituals often accompanied the body up to its burial. The best known is the practice of shutting the eyes of those who die with their eyes open. The reason for this is that you must not look upon the eyes of a dead person, lest they see you and decide to take you with them.

Possessions often accompanied the body to the grave. Some peoples believed the corpse eventually *did* make it to the afterlife, where it lived in a similar way to how it had lived on Earth. Hence, symbols of wealth were important, so its position in society could immediately be known. Some societies even placed a hammer or other tool in the coffin so that the corpse could bang on the gates of heaven if it experienced any difficulty getting in.

Mourners were also very aware of the need to assist the corpse come Judgement Day. Burial shrouds were always loose, so that the corpse would have little difficulty in raising itself. One additional requirement for some societies was to place a mirror in the coffin of a pretty girl who had died. This allowed her to tidy her hair on Judgement Day so that she wouldn't look a mess.

The means by which the corpse was taken to the funeral was vitally important. It had always to be carried out of the house feet first and through the front of the house. As in many religions, it is thought wrong to offer a bare head to God, and to leave by the back of the house was an indication that the person was heading for hell. If the front door was too narrow, the corpse passed through a front window. If these were also too narrow, it was not uncommon for a hole to be knocked out in the front wall to allow access.

A corpse had always to be carried to a grave, a practice sometimes insisted upon today where it is the usual practice to use a trolley. The grave itself had to be dug facing east–west, and the corpse was laid with its feet to the east. This was because Judgement Day was thought to come from the east and it was therefore wise to allow the corpse to rise up facing the dawn at the time of resurrection.

■ Over the last few pages we have taken a look at just some of the superstitions surrounding the main rites of passage of the individual in Britain. Most of these were being honoured well into the twentieth century, and some remain important today, even though we will offer more secular reasons for their practice. Indeed, some societies are so steeped in superstitious culture that paranormal phenomena can still be found to exist.

Spiritism

■ The cultures of Brazil and the Philippines are heavily steeped in superstitions. This is due to the overall influence of a relatively modern religion called Spiritism, which originates from *The Spirits' Book* and *The Mediums' Book*, written by nineteenth-century Frenchman Allan Kardec.

Kardec was the pseudonym of teacher Hippolyte Rivail. As spiritualism swept through Paris in the 1850s he became extremely sceptical of the practice, but was shocked when he experienced spiritualist and poltergeist phenomena for himself. Of particular interest to him was the medium Mademoiselle Japhet, who was often possessed by spirits and manifested the phenomenon of automatic writing.

Kardec decided to see if he could become an automatic writer himself, and after much practice discovered that he was a natural. The experience changed his life, and although he never intended to start a new religion, his automatic writings did just that, beginning when the Brazilian statesman Adolfo Bezerra de Meneses introduced Spiritism to Brazil.

In order to understand the phenomena he witnessed, Kardec devised a whole spiritual philosophy, which was well established by his death in 1869. According to Kardec, a person is composed of three elements: a body, a soul and what he called the perispirit – an element that held the body and soul together in life. At death the body corrupts, but the perispirit takes the soul to an afterlife, full of spirits.

Once in this spirit world, the soul reviews how successful it had been in life. This process is vital, for it is the function of the soul to seek a higher existence. Should this higher existence still evade it, it is allowed to return to a newborn body to continue its process of achieving the higher existence.

We can see in the above that Spiritism is essentially identical to spiritualism in regard to the existence of a spirit world, but has the belief in reincarnation attached to it. Indeed, in this respect, Spiritism became a breeding ground for mediums who went on to achieve trance states in order to communicate with the spirits. However, belief in such spirits attached itself to existing Brazilian and Filipino tribal religions, giving birth to the idea that many of these spirits could be malevolent.

Kardec made it easy for tribal beliefs to attach themselves to Spiritism. He pointed out that sometimes the dead attempted to hold on to the material world. When this happened, the perispirit held the soul in a form of limbo, and the deceased person could create spiritual havoc for the living in the form of poltergeist phenomena, a subject we will look at later on (see pages 149–153).

Alternatively, some souls take a definite decision not to seek a higher existence. These become immensely troubled, and when reborn into another body their negative attitude causes possession by 'evil spirits' from past lives, and psychiatric problems such as schizophrenia.

In a way, this was an ingenious addition to Spiritism by Kardec, for within the concept he marries the spiritual with the psychological, allowing psychiatric treatment in terms of a supernatural culture. This has two important side-effects. First of all, it takes away any taboo of psychiatric illness being the fault of the person – a position that is held by many in western cultures. And second, it elevates the treatment of the mentally ill to important status. Consequently, Brazil has many excellent, well-staffed Kardecist psychiatric hospitals which are the envy of the world.

A further fundamental element of Spiritist philosophy concerns wealth. The requirement of the soul is to achieve higher spiritual existence. As such, wealth accumulation, which is the requirement of a higher material existence, is shunned. Clearly, many Brazilians and Filipinos attempt wealth creation. Spiritism is not the main religious movement in either country – both are predominently Catholic – but in Spiritist communities, wealth is said to reduce spiritual existence and powers.

Few religious movements become as humble as Spiritism, for wealth destroys their ability to reach higher existence. In such a culture we have mediums such as Chico Xavier, who, through automatic writing, has written over 100 books, yet lives in poverty. And even in a country with no welfare state, the Kardecist psychiatric hospitals accept all comers, regardless of their ability to pay.

However, there is one further element of Spiritism that constitutes the most ridiculed area of the paranormal, and that is the phenomenon of psychic surgery. The problem with psychic surgery is that it is so plainly ridiculous and fraudulent that it is hard to take it seriously. Usually performed by uneducated peasants with no knowledge of anatomy at all, the patient is laid on a table in a room full of germs. The surgeon, who is often 'taken over' by a spirit for the operation, then plunges either his hands or an unclean knife or scissors into the body, takes out an offending organ in a spurt of blood, and magically covers up the wound. The operation takes place without anaesthetic, yet the patient feels no pain, and afterwards simply stands up and walks out without as much as a scar on the body.

Typical of such psychic surgeons was José Arigo, who was imprisoned for eight months for practising medicine illegally in 1964. Born in 1921, Arigo claimed his talent began in 1956. He was with family and friends comforting a woman dying from cancer of the uterus. Arigo did not remember what happened – he claimed he went into a trance – but suddenly he rushed from the room and came back in with a kitchen knife. He plunged the knife into the woman's vagina, twisted it and extracted a tumour the size of a grapefruit.

This was the beginning of his life as a psychic surgeon, which was interrupted by his prison sentence, and then his death in a car crash in 1971. Having no medical knowledge whatsoever, and using nothing but a rusty knife, he carried out thousands of operations, possessed, he believed, by the spirit of a German doctor called Dr Adolph Fritz. His only form of cleanliness was his habit of wiping the knife on his shirt before and after surgery.

During the 1960s, psychical researcher Andrija Puharich became interested in psychic surgery and investigated Arigo. Indeed, Arigo actually performed a small operation on Puharich himself. He removed a benign tumour from his arm in seconds with his knife, totally without pain.

Teacher and journalist Guy Lyon Playfair also became interested in Spiritism while living in Brazil. Indeed, classing Brazil as the 'most psychically oriented country on Earth', his research led him to become one of the most distinguished psychical researchers of the late twentieth century.

Suffering from a long-term stomach complaint, Playfair was operated on by a psychic surgeon called Edivaldo. Unbuttoning his shirt, he lay down. Edivaldo ran his hands over his stomach and then pressed. Playfair felt a plop and a wet feeling on his skin, followed by a tickling sensation actually inside his stomach. He felt no pain, and moments later he was told he could go.

Playfair was incapacitated by a stiffness for some time, and had a second operation later on. The complaint didn't go away, but it was eased considerably. Deciding to research Edivaldo further, he spent a year attending his 'surgeries'. During one session, Edivaldo grabbed Playfair's hand and actually thrust it into a patient's open stomach.

What are we to make of such stories? Are we to class Puharich and Playfair as just as 'mad' as the psychic surgeons they investigated? Austrian researcher Gert Chesi spent time in the Philippines in the early 1980s investigating psychic surgeons. Attending many 'bloody operations', as they are known, he even photographed surgeons in action, and the experience left him totally bemused.

Most bemusing of all was the variety of objects taken from the bodies of patients. For as well as bloody organs, it was not uncommon for surgeons to extract such things as leaves, nails, worms, string and coins. Other researchers have noted that extracted organs have come not from the patient, but from animals such as pigs. Some patients have been later X-rayed, and the organ that was supposedly extracted was still there.

This evidence is damning. The only viable explanation is to class psychic surgery as fraudulent, achieved by nothing more than sleight of hand. Indeed, magician and sceptical researcher James Randi has reproduced all such phenomena in this way. I will therefore make a definite statement and condemn psychic surgery as absolute fakery, but in doing so, I will also make it clear that this fakery is totally beside the point.

What must be understood with psychic surgery is, first, that Chesi noted that most psychic surgeons did not accept payment, so fakery for financial gain is nearly always out of the question. And second, Playfair testified that the operations he underwent did lead to a lessening of his complaint.

At this point we must look to two areas already covered by this book. These are spiritual healing (see pages 108–112) and the role of culture in defining superstitions. Yes, the 'drama' of the operation is clearly faked, but the question that has to be asked is this: in a superstitious society where spirits are real and can possess the person, could the fakery convince the patient, through superstition, that the operation would lead to a cure?

I would therefore suggest that faked psychic surgery is a clever form of spiritual healing. The various artefacts that are removed from the body can be seen as symbolic of the ailment. For instance, Chesi witnessed one operation where a psychic surgeon removed three American quarters and a number of staples from a patient's stomach. The patient had complained of a horrible metallic taste in her mouth.

Playfair did not have an absolute cure, but then again, Playfair is a westerner, and not totally consumed by the superstitious culture of Spiritism. If he had been, he could well have been fully healed for, as Allan Kardec understood very well, the spiritual world and the psychological idiosyncrasies of the person can be seen as one and the same. And as with the psychiatric hospitals in Brazil, fully trained psychiatrists continue to use 'spiritual' realities to con the patient into a cure.

Voodoo

■ While Spiritism is known mainly for its more benevolent attributes, the same cannot be said for a similar contemporary religion, practised mainly in Haiti. This is, of course, voodoo.

A more exact name for voodoo would be 'vodoun', which derives from '*vodu*' which, in the Fon language spoken in parts of Nigeria, means 'spirit' or 'deity'. Although centred in Haiti, some 50 million people practise Voodoo worldwide. A syncretic religion, it is based on African tribal rites synthesized with Catholicism. Indeed, most of their spirits are analogous to both tribal African deities and Catholic saints.

The main tenet of voodoo is that reality is a façade, behind which spiritual forces work. At the head of these forces is a supreme being called Gran Met. However, he is too remote to be worshipped personally. Hence, worshippers have a whole host of lesser gods called 'loas', many of which are ancestral.

The oldest of the loas is Damballah, or Great Serpent. Based on an old African deity, he created the world and the universe. The essence of voodoo concerns a form of pact with the loas and worshippers, whereby worshippers seek to please the gods in order to receive favours.

The most famous of the loas is Baron Samedi. He oversees death and graveyards and represents the sinister side of Voodoo. Symbolized as wearing top hat and dark tailcoat, he is associated with the coffin. However, his fame overshadows the majority of voodoo practices, which are essentially benevolent.

Voodoo ritual takes place in isolated outside locations at night, close to a small building, or temple, known as a 'hounfour'. Containing an altar and a small room for deep meditation, sacred relics are kept here. Rituals involve drumming, chanting and dancing, leading to ecstatic trance. During trance, the lucky ones who have achieved the state will be possessed by a loa. This will involve a change of personality, speaking in strange tongues, and eventual unconsciousness. Voodoo rituals are initiated to bring good fortune, ward off evil, appease a troubled spirit of the dead, consecrate a new priest, or effect a spiritual healing.

A voodoo priest is called a 'houngan'; a priestess, a 'mambo'. They are, in effect, classic shamans, instigating ceremony through hysterical mechanisms. To achieve this, the houngan has two magical tools. First is a large ritual rattle containing sacred stones and snake vertebrae. He shakes this to call the spirits to come down. He also has a ritual sword, decorated with sacred symbols. He slashes at the air with this, symbolically cutting away the material world, leaving the spiritual world to be accessed.

While most people see voodoo in sinister terms – the religion of zombies and curses involving wax images – throughout most of its history it was the saviour of the people. It comprised part of the old Hispaniola, when the Christopher Columbus discovered the area that became Haiti in 1492. European growers saw its potential for sugar cane production. As colonization had involved the total genocide of the indigenous Indians, it was decided to repopulate the land with West African slaves.

These slaves arrived with nothing but their African religion, and in order to maintain it they included Catholic elements to hide the essentially tribal nature of their ritual. In this sense, the voodoo which eventually evolved was secret, and very much a part of the occult, but this secrecy was required in order to allow the slaves' cultural expression to remain intact.

In the eighteenth century, the area was handed over to the French and Haiti came into being. By the time of the French Revolution colonial power was in tatters, and the half-million black slaves revolted against the 40,000 French. Voodoo priest-warriors, such as the legendary Boukman, now came into being, leading to total anarchy.

By the mid-nineteenth century Haiti had become independent, but the anarchy continued. The principal reason for this is that various voodoo sects had grown into powerful political forces, and none wanted to give up their new power. However, in 1957 voodoo evolved into a single, cultural force under Dr François Duvalier, better known as Papa Doc. A total dictator, voodoo worked alongside his secret police, the infamous Tonton Macoutes, to turn Haiti into the most superstitious country on Earth. A religion that at one time had been its people's saviour had become their gaoler.

Is there a reality to the stories of zombies and curses that seem to infest voodoo? Haiti is now free of the excesses of Papa Doc and the son, Baby Doc, who succeeded him. Similarly, the main controls that voodoo had on the people are lessening. However, superstition is a hard force to keep at bay and certain voodoo sects, such as the Bizango and Cochon Gris, work their sinister ways to this day. Headed by dark priests known as 'bokors', stories exist of human sacrifice, calling up the dead to harm others through curses, and turning people into zombies. Indeed, throughout the history of voodoo stories have continued to be told of people identifying dead relatives working, as if automatons, in the fields.

Culturally, zombies are a dark manifestation of the death/rebirth ideal. As with most other religions, worshippers have a soul, known as the 'ti bon ange'. Upon death, the soul hovers above the body for seven days until separated from it through ritual. It then goes to live in the afterlife, known as the 'dark waters', for a year and a day. The family then raises the soul, which is now spirit, to live in the trees and rocks until it is reborn in another body. After 16 such incarnations, the spirit goes off to live as part of a great cosmic energy for ever.

The first seven days after death, when the soul hovers over the body, are important. It is at this time that the bokor can capture the soul and turn it into a zombie. Such a process involves placing it back in the body and resurrecting the corpse. Hence, to prevent this, families often decapitate the body before burial. Rather than mere superstition, however, it seems there is an actual reality to the zombie – but not, I might add, involving the supernatural.

Africans were first transported to Haiti in order to work the fields as slaves. As slavery was abolished, it seems that the bokor decided to use voodoo cultural expression to continue the slave tradition with zombies. Following an idea first put forward by anthropologist Zora Hurston in the 1930s and perfected by Harvard anthropologist Dr E. Wade Davis in 1980, it is believed that the bokor administers a poison to suitable candidates which causes a form of suspended animation.

Made up from various poisonous plants, the bouga toad and puffer fish, the poison apes death. A couple of days after burial, the bokor opens up the grave and administers an antidote known as the zombie cucumber. This revives the zombie, but the initial poison was so strong that brain damage is done. In this way, the zombie is physically healthy, but mentally nothing more than an automaton. Such a person makes an excellent, cheap field worker, and the bokor goes on to sell him to a landowner.

In the above, we can see how cunning and enterprise can attach to cultural superstition, creating a belief in a definite supernatural existence. And if

The Brown Lady of Raynham Hall (photographed 1936). Some researchers think ghosts are a physical energy that can be captured on film. *Fortean Picture Library*

TOP Cave painting discovered at Lascaux, France, depicting a shaman with a bison speared through the stomach. Some researchers believe these ancient paintings are simply art for art's sake, but was there a deeper ritual motive involved? *The Ancient Art and Architecture Collection*

BOTTOM The 'ghost dance' of the Sioux. Did this really lead to mass hallucinations of dead ancestors? *Mary Evans Picture Library*

OPPOSITE Rolling Thunder, American Indian medicine man, 1984. The shaman, or medicine man, has long been regarded as a bridge between the physical world and the supernatural. *Dr Elmar R Gruber/Fortean Picture Library*

ABOVE Stonehenge. The most enigmatic monument in England. *The Ancient Art and Architecture Collection*

OPPOSITE TOP Maze north of Visby on the island of Gotland, Sweden. What strange phenomenon drove early societies throughout the world to recreate this labyrinth image? *Lars Thomas/Fortean Picture Library*

OPPOSITE BOTTOM Greek vase from the fourth century BC depicting Theseus warding off the Minotaur in the labyrinth at Knossos, Crete. What cultural force is being re-enacted here? *The Ancient Art and Architecture Collection*

RIGHT Paul Devereux, leading researcher in Earth mysteries. *Paul Devereux*

BELOW Pyramids at Giza, Egypt. Latest theories suggest that, seen from above, their formation represents the belt of stars in the constellation of Orion. *The Ancient Art and Architecture Collection*

OPPOSITE Did the medium Daniel Dunglas Home really levitate, or is there a simple explanation for his paranormal talent? *Fortean Picture Library*

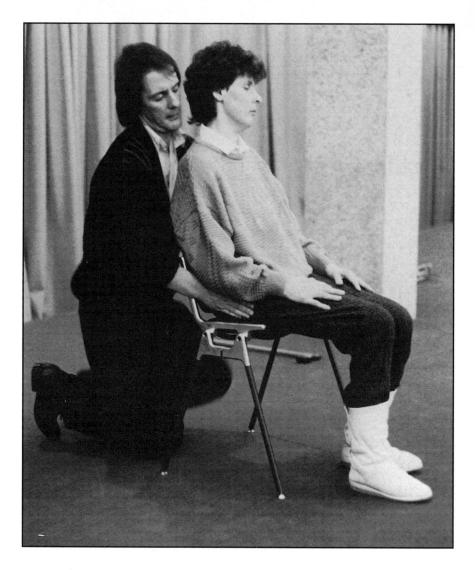

ABOVE The greatest contemporary healer, Matthew Manning (British), at a demonstration in Baden-Baden, Germany. Are we now in a position to understand his uncanny powers? *Fortean Picture Library*

OPPOSITE TOP Artist's depiction of Cagliostro's interview with Count de Saint-Germain at Holstein 1785, from Louis Figuier's *Mystères de la Science*. The Count was ignored by most serious researchers when he claimed to be immortal. Was he really as enigmatic as people believed? *Mary Evans Picture Library*

OPPOSITE BOTTOM Sixteenth-century engraving of medieval alchemist at work. Did alchemists really transmute lead into gold or was this symbolic of the transformation of the soul? *The Ancient Art and Architecture Collection*

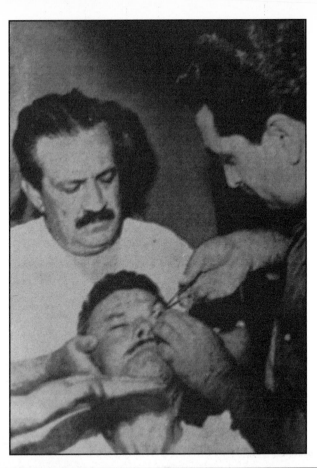

May Frances Turner   June Bailey

A. J. Linzmayer

T. Coleman Cooper   J. G. Pratt

Mr. Pratt (assistant) was photographed while experimenting.

Extra-Sensory Perception

J. B. RHINE, Ph.D.
Associate Professor of Psychology
Duke University

With a Foreword by
Professor WILLIAM McDOUGALL, F.R.S., D.Sc., M.B.

And an Introduction by
WALTER FRANKLIN PRINCE, Ph.D.
Research Officer, B.S.P.R.

MARCH, 1934

BOSTON SOCIETY FOR PSYCHIC RESEARCH
719 Boylston Street, Boston, Mass.

Printed in U. S. A.

ABOVE Tomb of Allan Kardec, founding father of Spiritism, at the Père Lachaise cemetery in Paris, France. *Mary Evans Picture Library*

OPPOSITE TOP Psychic surgeon Jose Arigo performing an eye operation. Arigo was put to trial in 1964 for carrying out operations with a rusty knife. *Mary Evans Picture Library*

OPPOSITE BOTTOM Title-page and frontispiece of J.B. Rhine's first published account of ESP, with portraits of the experimenters. *Mary Evans Picture Library*

ABOVE Harry Price, psychic researcher, from his book *Search for the Truth* (1942). Although Price was dismissed as a showman and self-seeking publicist, he was nevertheless a pioneer in the field of psychical research. *Fortean Picture Library*

RIGHT Carl Gustav Jung. Known as a founder of psychoanalysis, was he a survival of the great shamanic tradition? *Fortean Picture Library*

OPPOSITE Engraving of a poltergeist at work, from Figuier's *Mystères de la Science*. Are poltergeists best understood as a supernatural entity or as a psychological anomaly? *Mary Evans Picture Library*

ABOVE Chinese Buddha figurine from the seventeenth century. Did he hold the secret of paranormal power? *The Ancient Art and Architecture Collection*

OPPOSITE TOP The three major arcana from the Italian tarot deck: the stars, the pope and the moon. Known as the 'Devil's picture book', tarot cards are a popular form of divination. *Fortean Picture Library*

OPPOSITE BOTTOM Charles Darwin finally banished God from the scientific world, but can evolution really work without a form of intelligent guiding principle? *The Ancient Art and Architecture Collection*

LE STELLE

IL PAPA

LA LUNA

Rupert Sheldrake. In his theory of 'morphic fields' Sheldrake has come the closest so far to offering a mechanism through which paranormal powers can work. *Fortean Picture Library*

zombies are 'real', then why not the rest of voodoo magic? Indeed, some voodoo 'sorcerers' have reached legendary status. Typical was Marie Laveau, who in the late eighteenth century became known as the Witch Queen of New Orleans.

Voodoo moved to New Orleans with the black slaves taken there by the French, and many black ghettos grew in the city. Laveau was born here and became a powerful mambo, mainly by offering services to the white population. She died around 1875, leaving behind stories of curses and fortune telling. Thought to possess a 'magic' shawl, she also carried out rites with various charms, fetishes and Catholic symbols.

The most famous story surrounding her involves a rich white family whose son was to be put on trial for a crime. The evidence against him was damning, but Laveau placed three peppers in her mouth and prayed. When the day of the trial arrived she placed the peppers under the judge's chair. The man was released scot-free.

The most likely explanation of this anecdote is that the family paid off the judge, Laveau making up the story around the event. However, giving her the benefit of the doubt, it is equally possible that her 'magic' involved charming the judge through a form of hypnosis, the peppers being just part of a process which would have included actually facing the judge in order to hypnotize him.

With such an idea, we can again see how the supernatural gives way to the psychological – and a similar psychological scenario can be offered to account for the many curses associated with voodoo.

A typical case was that of retired US Marine Colonel Robert Heinl. In 1971, he and his wife wrote a book about Papa Doc. Enraged, Papa Doc's widow ritually cursed the book. Shortly after this the manuscript was lost: it turned up in a locked room at the publishers' too late for publication. Soon afterwards, a journalist who was to interview the Heinls for the *Washington Post* newspaper fell ill with appendicitis. About to give a lecture, Heinl injured his leg on the lecture platform and was forced to cancel. Later, he was badly bitten by a dog. Finally, in 1979, the colonel dropped dead while on holiday close to Haiti.

How do we account for so many catastrophes? One important element of a curse is the fact that the cursed person must know, or at least suspect, that a curse has been placed. A second important point is that the cursed person must live within, or be exposed to, a prevalent culture that accepts the reality of curses.

Both Heinl and the publisher were aware of the curse, and in researching the book Heinl had been exposed to voodoo culture. With this information, both psychological and sociological factors can be seen to play a part in how the curse unfolded.

Such factors can work in two ways. On the one hand, by being cursed the person will be on the look-out for indications of the curse working. In this way, a natural progression of unrelated accidents and mistakes can be seen in an incorrectly meaningful and connected way, thus validating the curse. On the other hand, the curse can upset the natural equilibrium of bodily movement. To be exact, in order to counter the effects of a curse, the person can act so differently and warily that the outcome is that they cause their own accidents.

The above can account for every element of the curse bar Heinl's actual death. However, while he may initially have been sceptical of curses, the continuing evidence of the curse can reinforce its validity to the point where scepticism turns towards belief. Such a psychological process leads to a feeling of inevitability, and this feeling can, indeed, lead to death.

The process can be identified even today. Take the case of Andrew Thomas from South Wales, who died at the age of 27 in April 1997. Andrew was unemployed and became so dysfunctional that he did nothing but watch television. He got dressed once a week to take his only outing from the house in order to sign on for welfare payments. On the day of his death, he had watched television all day until about 2 a.m. Later that morning his father found him dead in his bed. The coroner recorded a verdict of 'death by natural causes'. However, as with many such deaths, the pathologist's report gave the cause of death as 'unascertainable'.

Such deaths are unascertainable because the body simply stops working. The process is known as 'vegal inhibition', and is caused by a sense of total hopelessness. Such hopelessness causes the individual to lose the will to live, and the body satisfies this will by simply slowing down, and then ceasing to function. Thomas's hopelessness was caused by his unemployment. It is not difficult to see the same process in action due to the inevitability of a curse.

Hell and the Devil

■ Voodoo holds an important message for us all, and that is that superstitions can be seen to contain a valid reality – but not a reality that can be classed as supernatural. With curses, we can see how they are valid in terms of psychology, and in the zombie we have a perfect example of how human cunning can manipulate superstition to the benefit of the shrewd.

Papa Doc Duvalier tells us something more, for in a real sense he manipulated the superstitious Haitian population to such an extent that its controls became both political and sociological. Using the religious requirements of superstition, he provided mass social control by literally frightening the people into obedience – and a similar process was used by religious leaders in Europe for many hundreds of years.

Europe is essentially Christian. The popular God may well be on the wane today, but throughout recorded history He was the main cohesive force in a religious and social sense. However, as monarchs ruled during this time through 'divine right', God can also be seen to have taken a leading political role, too. The political system defined in his name – the hierarchy of monarch, aristocracy and serf – was fundamentally geared to keeping the monarch powerful, the aristocracy rich, and the peasantry poor and under absolute control.

To achieve this, superstitions were as important as the physical force used against the people, and the most important of these superstitions involved the devil and hell. However, you can read the Bible as much as you like, but you will not find the eventual images of these two concepts within its pages.

The devil has many names: Satan, Lucifer, Old Clootie, Mephistopheles, Old Nick, Beelzebub, even the number 666. His most recent media appearances offer a changing view of him in a less superstitious world. His last sinister ones were in the early 1970s, where he provided safe titillation by possessing Linda Blair in *The Exorcist* or hiding behind the innocence of youth in *The Omen*. By the late 1980s he still retained his trickiness, but our general fear of him had gone with Jack Nicholson's portrayal of him as a sexual trickster in *The Witches of Eastwick*. Yet even these are exaggerations of the Biblical devil.

First appearing as the snakish tempter of Eve, his only other major role was in the tempting of Jesus in the wilderness, where he was essentially undescribed. The popular image of cloven hooves, spiky tail, scaly body, pointy ears and, of course, his trident, didn't even begin to appear until the tenth century, at about the time that medieval social controls became predominant. But if not from the Bible, from where did these images emerge?

Most of these images actually come from Greek mythology. The trident was borrowed from Poseidon, lord of earthquakes and destruction. In this sense, the trident represented the chaos that could result from following his ways. Yet intriguingly Poseidon was also god of the waters that fertilized the soil, and in *this* sense he was a survival from the pre-Christian fertility religions. It is in a further survival of these religions that we find the essential character of the image.

The devil comes from the Greek *diabolos*, meaning 'slanderer'. We can therefore see the devil as someone who speaks against the truth of God – but who, at the time of the formulation of Christian society, would speak against God? History tells us the answer: the fertility religions and pagan ways that had to be suppressed in order to allow Christianity to grow. And in Greek mythology, the pagan fertility religion found expression in the god Pan.

Pan was the guardian of flocks and herds, and his general description apes closely the eventual character invested in the devil. His appearance playing pipes and leading a dance of nymphs (young, beautiful, virgin maidens) would cause 'panic' in those trying to change the old ways. The word 'pan' means 'all', and in this sense he embodied the holistic nature of pagan religions. Indeed, he was the very personification of nature.

With this information, the devil is exposed. He is not some evil fallen angel, but an expression of a way of life that Christianity had to suppress. And hence, anything that disagreed with Christianity became part of his domain, turning people evil only in that they spoke or acted against the Christian authority. And if for a moment you think that we have escaped this politically motivated superstitious concept, let me offer a magic phrase – satanic child abuse. It seems the power exists even today to turn delusional concepts into an apparent, if superstitious, truth.

The devil was overlord of hell. The land of brimstone, fires and rivers of boiling blood, this was the afterlife location of those who ceded to the devil's ways, living out existence in eternal torment. In *The Divine Comedy*, written in the fourteenth century, Dante located it in a cone-shaped hole in the Earth, caused by Satan's impact as he fell from heaven. Dante divides it into nine regions, each more fearful as you descend down into the bowels of the Earth.

To John Milton, who in the seventeenth century wrote *Paradise Lost*, hell is a separate universe surrounded by formless chaos and called Pandemonium. A place of sorrow and darkness, here flames lick and torture rules, while sulphurous odours pervade from a volcano, in which the devils built their palace.

Such images are far removed from the Biblical description. In the Bible, hell is not active punishment in any form, but annihilation. It is simply an absence of God; an afterlife that was, quite simply, nothingness. But to a Christian establishment intent upon obedience from the masses, this just would not do.

Judaic mythology offers a slightly more horrible view of the afterlife for sinners in the concept of Sheol. This is a shadowy world placed underground, inhabited by spirits of the dead who exist listlessly on a diet of dust. But for the really horrible view of an afterlife we have to go to those hardy and imaginative ancient Greeks once more.

The Greeks gave us Hades, god of the underworld, which took his name. This is a shadowy, listless world, a prison for bad Titans such as Sisyphus, Ixion and Tantalus, who are eternally punished. Tantalus attempted to trick the gods into eating the flesh of his son. In Hades, he can see grapes and water, but is condemned to starvation and thirst by never being able quite to grasp them.

Ixion was accused of attempted rape, and in Hades is tied to a burning wheel. As for Sisyphus, he was a trickster who, even in Hades, tried to con his way out. For punishment he must roll a rock up a hill, only to see it roll back down to be rolled up again, *ad infinitum*.

The evolving mythology of Hades introduced whip-wielding, vengeful spirits to punish those who lived bad lives. Plato later added judges to decide who would rise to the beautiful afterlife of the Elysian fields, and who would be condemned to Hades.

The Romans added to the mythology of Hades. Their hell was the domain of Dis, lord of the dead. He inhabited a three-walled citadel full of clanking chains, poisonous fumes and eternal screams of anguish. Virgil went on to add the concept of Purgatory, which Roman Catholicism interpreted as a place where the bad dead lingered until they were pure enough to enter heaven.

Like the devil, hell can be seen here to have little to do with the Bible, but much to do with social controls to frighten the superstitious into obedience. And as with the manipulations of voodoo by Papa Doc Duvalier, it turned what were essentially mythologies into an all-pervading cultural force.

Taboo and Mythology

■ How could an essentially beautiful religion such as Christianity be turned into an almost totalitarian social and political force in this way? Perhaps the answer to this lies in understanding that religion has two components. Initially, a religion is born from insight from a shaman-like individual. In practically every case, the religious creed forthcoming is benevolent and pure. However, it is also naive, in that religions initially look for the good in people and the universe – and this allows a second component into the equation, which can best be understood as the 'power urges' of those who follow, using and manipulating the beauty of the creed into a tool of control.

I cannot think of a single organized religion that was not pure at conception – nor can I think of a single organized religion that was not perverted by the egoistic urges of those who claim to speak in its name. Always, those who wish to seek power will manipulate the superstitious element of religion for their own good at the expense of others. The process through which these mechanisms are allowed to work can be traced back to the earliest known religions of tribal society.

Essential to those early religious were the guardian spirits, expressed in the cave paintings of stone age man. The first guardian spirits were animal in nature, and their purpose was to protect either the individual or the tribe from danger, both physical and supernatural. Venerated as the first gods, they were found in the hallucinations and vision quests of the shaman.

To the Amerindian they were known as totems, and few people will not have seen the image of their representation in the totem pole. However, the guardian spirit was a much wider concept than simply a protector, for in order to protect, the spirit had to be seen as a form of organizer of the individual and society. Hence, in the spirit's possession of the shaman, the shaman learned of certain prohibitions handed down from the spirit to the tribe.

Such prohibitions became known as 'taboos', and one of the earliest was a condemnation of incest. This was essential, for family life – which forms the foundation of society – can exist only where sex with kinfolk is disallowed. The formulation of this taboo can be found in all early religious texts, including the Old Testament, and in demanding restraint from the practice, superstitions were placed in the way of incest literally to scare the people from participation. Even well into the twentieth century such superstition remained, in the view that a child born from an incestuous relationship would be mentally impaired.

The process whereby the shaman decreed taboos continued well into religious formulation. For instance, Moses learned of the Ten Commandments through a similar supernatural means, dictated by God in a Biblical form of automatic writing. Today, this social control is generally invested in the legislative powers of parliaments. In this way, we can see that early religious forms were all to do with societal control through superstition, and in their formulation they were essentially benevolent.

As society progressed to a more agricultural living and, eventually, the city-state, such controls and superstitions became more subtle, with the use of 'mythologies' to show us how we should live. In this way, myths can be seen as the wisdom of culture. Today, that wisdom is again vested in the legislature, but in a time without democracy, where symbolism was all-important, mythologies and their taboos were iron-clad, and were invested with sociological insight. Indeed, Carl Jung realized that myths were not inventions, but symbolic representations of insight born from experience.

Famed twentieth-century American mythologist Joseph Campbell spent a lifetime analysing myths. He noted that in all cultures, mythologies had four main purposes. First, they were involved with the moral ordering of the individual to his culture and environment. Second, they defined the requirement of individual integrity. Third, they bridged human consciousness to the supernatural realm. And fourth, they provided symbolic images of universal consciousness.

In these four points we can see how myths married taboos to an understanding of spiritual existence. However, psychoanalyst Sigmund Freud also noted another important aspect of mythology, in that psychological idiosyncrasies were often portrayed in mythologies.

Typical is the story of Oedipus, son of King Laius of Thebes and his wife, Jocasta. A prophet tells Laius that his son will grow up to murder him and marry his wife. Oedipus is thus cast out, but the prophecy comes true, for Oedipus returns to kill Laius and marry Jocasta. The event leads to the destruction of Thebes. While again demonstrating the sociological taboo against incest, Freud saw the myth in psychological terms and formulated the Oedipus complex, where a child unconsciously desires the parent of the opposite sex and harbours aggressions towards the parent of the same sex.

The Oedipus complex has never been proved to exist, but the idea that myths could be seen as a form of unconscious psyche was championed by Carl Jung, as we shall see in the next section. Consider the myth of Narcissus, the beautiful youth who fell in love with his own reflection. Frustrated that he could not possess himself, he withered away and became a flower. In Narcissus, Freud discovered the ego, and while it may be unproved, the result of egoism, or self-love and importance, has been shown to be a psychologically destructive force of the inner psyche. Such comparisons indicate that mythology, as well as being a social control, is a symbolic, cultural history lesson combined with an understanding of our deep psychological idiosyncrasies. The gods, demons and spirits of the supernatural portrayed in myth are not inventions, but symbolic elements of our individual and cultural inner mind. Indeed, it is often argued that if mythologies were still important, the way in which they bind us psychologically to nature would take away our psychological ability to cause environmental damage.

In seeing myths as echoes of our mind, we must also consider the possibility that they *are* our mind. Campbell helps us along this path with his monumental work *The Hero with a Thousand Faces* (see Bibliography). Looking to all mythologies and all supernatural cultures ever devised, he finds a single, key concept within them all. This is the myth of the 'hero'.

The hero is the centre of all mythology. Throughout the world, he has appeared in almost exact form. He is a single man who realizes errors in his society. Through supernatural means he discovers how society can be improved, and from that point on he dedicates himself to a single journey to transform. His success becomes the success of society, in that social evolution takes place.

The supernatural transformation of the myth is shamanic, and his, and later society's, transformation is death and rebirth. As for the hero, he is Moses, he is Jesus, he is Buddha, he is Muhammad. In a less awesomely supernatural sense, he is every hero from Hercules to Luke Skywalker of *Star Wars*. Indeed, as a friend of film-maker George Lucas, Campbell was advisor for the creation of the deeply mythological *Star Wars* trilogy.

This exact pattern of societal evolution – of *all* societal evolution – is just as prevalent today without supernatural overtones. The hero exists in the likes of Charles Darwin, who, through deep thought, changed society with his theory of evolution, as well as in Lech Walesa, the single individual who transformed Poland and began the destruction of Communism. And in being such an exact mechanism, it echoes other exact idiosyncrasies throughout all cultures, such as the incest taboo.

We are said to be individuals, full of individual ideas and ways of living life, but the exactness of mythologies and the way they formulate society tells us this may not be the case. Rather, mythologies and the superstitions they produce can be seen as overall orchestrators of the societies and cultures they evolve. They are our psyche, but not an individual psyche. Rather, they are communal, and above the thoughts of an individual man. In other words, cultures, and the myths that produce them, are superconscious. And the way they direct us can be classified by only one word. That word is 'paranormal'.

MODERN MYSTICS

Psychical Research

■ The supernatural has existed in all cultures through all time. Today we know it as the paranormal, meaning 'beyond' normal. This definition moves phenomena away from a definite after-life and beliefs in forces from 'other worlds'. Rather, the emphasis is now upon the fringes of psychology and the role of consciousness within the world.

As science cannot attach definite mechanisms to paranormal phenomena, they are classed as occult, but rather than carrying the sinister connotations usually applied to the word, we should remember that occult means, simply, 'hidden'. Seen in this way, the phenomenon associated with electricity was 'occult' until science understood it.

Evidence of such phenomena can be found throughout history, and even from prehistory stories of supernatural powers have come down to us through mythology. What this historical and prehistorical inheritance tells us is that such phenomena were so universally identical that it suggests the existence of a form of superconscious. Defining, through mythology, what culture should be, the paranormal can be seen as a universal mechanism – a form of psychological gravity, to use a simple analogy.

Although mythologist Joseph Campbell was not interested in the paranormal *per se*, he understood the exactness of the mythologies it produced. As he often quoted from the Hindu Vedas: 'Truth is one, the sages speak of it by many names.'

Understanding of this universal paranormality has evaded us for a very good reason. Culture may well be formulated through paranormal experience, but its expression comes in the form of understanding of culture alone, and not the universal mechanisms above it. Hence, a paranormal possession is of a cultural entity such as God, rather than a non-cultural higher force.

Such an idiosyncrasy impedes examination of this more general higher force.

Only mystics, such as the Cabbalists, understood that God had many cultural faces, his higher reality hidden by experience – but they were only occultists, and could be ignored.

As religious cultural expression waned, the world came to be viewed in terms of science and reason. Great minds such as Sir Isaac Newton began to look beyond culture to this higher force, but as cultural expression began to ignore the supernatural as religious hogwash, a true understanding was again impeded by cultural precedent. However, all that was to change in 1848.

In that year, spiritualism was born. In a wave of cultural expression, shamanic abilities manifested themselves in trance states through which mediums were 'possessed' by the spirits of the dead. In seances, a subtle form of tribal cultural hallucination broke out in sitting rooms throughout the western world.

Science's answer to this phenomenon was predictable: spiritualism was one big confidence trick. But while many mediums were blatantly fraudulent, a small band of brave intellectuals began to realize that something strange was, indeed, going on.

By 1870 the London Dialectical Society had decided that there was something worthy of study in spiritualism, and for the first time academics began to take the subject seriously. One such was British physicist Sir William Crookes, who went on to study famed mediums such as Florence Cook and Daniel Dunglas Home. Crookes was to be lambasted by his academic colleagues for his foolishness; however, a group of Fellows of Trinity College, Cambridge, also began to take an interest.

Principal of these was academic Frederic W. H. Myers. Attending a seance held by the medium C. Williams, Myers witnessed a huge, hairy hand materialize near the ceiling. It slowly floated down to the ground, and Myers actually caught it and held it in his hand. This experience convinced him of the reality of spiritualism. His colleague, Henry Sidgwick, was more sceptical, but agreed that the subject was perhaps worthy of study. By 1874 Myers had convinced a group of highly respected, wealthy intellectuals to form a group to study the supernatural phenomena associated with spiritualism. Becoming known as the Sidgwick Group, they included Edmund Gurney, Walter Leaf, Lord Raleigh, Arthur Balfour and Sidgwick's sisters, Eleanor and Evelyn.

In 1876 prominent Irish physicist Sir William F. Barrett also became interested in spiritualist phenomena, but realized that his studies were impeded by a lack of support. Joining forces with leading spiritualist Edmund Dawson Rogers, Barrett called for the creation of a society dedicated to investigating the paranormal. In 1882 he joined forces with a host of mediums and the Sidgwick Group to form the Society for Psychical Research. Based in Kensington,

London, the first president was Henry Sidgwick, and the society exists to this day, dedicated to investigating the paranormal. Early members included Sir William Crookes, Arthur Conan Doyle, physicist Sir Oliver Lodge, psychoanalysts Sigmund Freud and Carl Jung and the soon to be famous researchers, Frank Podmore and Richard Hodgson.

As well as publishing vast surveys of phenomena, such as their 1886 survey *Phantasms of the Living*, the society concentrated on the study of mediums such as Leonore Piper and Eusapia Palladino. However, their occasional lapses into suspected fraud caused the society to abandon their study of mediums in 1895. This led to many spiritualists leaving, the result being that the society moved towards a much more scientific and sceptical approach. In later years this would prove of benefit in exposing the falsified results of leading researcher S. G. Soal, but the poet W. B. Yeats highlighted their scepticism when he said: 'If your psychical researchers had been about when God Almighty was creating the world, He couldn't have finished the job.'

While this general scepticism has pervaded the hierarchy of the society, the statement must be qualified. The general opinion of psychical researchers with an academic background is that proof can only come in terms of scientific procedure. It is here that scepticism rises, and they are absolutely correct. But sadly, as we shall soon see, our scientific culture is perfectly attuned to ignore all but definite observable and experimental evidence. Phenomena have proved too shy to satisfy this definite requirement, so while the procedure is academically right, it condemns paranormal research to the fringe, never grasping the absolute proof that is required.

Saying this, however, at the turn of the twentieth century elements of the society did descend into a most remarkable period of investigations known as the cross-correspondences phenomena. Myers had died in 1901, but before his death he declared his intention to communicate from 'beyond the grave'. By 1905, with Hodgson's death, all the main players in the Sidgwick Group were also deceased. In 1906 the society's research officer, Alice Johnson, noticed a strange phenomenon unfolding. Monitoring the output of a number of automatic writers, including Rudyard Kipling's sister, Mrs Fleming, in India, Dame Edith Lyttelton in Britain and Leonore Piper in the United States, they seemed to be receiving elements of overall messages from the afterlife.

Designating a specific team to analyse their work, including Sir Oliver Lodge, Alice Johnson made sure that none of the mediums knew what the others were producing. Over the following years they came to the definite conclusion that Myers and the other founders *were* communicating. Indeed, Hodgson went on to come back as Piper's 'spirit guide'.

As the cross-correspondences continued, the 'entities' spoke of their diffi-culties in getting the messages through. Gurney: 'You never seem to realize how little we know . . . sometimes I know and can't get it through, but very often I don't know.' Myers: 'The nearest simile I can find to express the difficulties of sending a message – is that I appear to be standing behind a sheet of frosted glass – which blurs sight and deadens sound – dictating feebly to a reluctant and somewhat obtuse secretary.'

Such evidence was, of course, discounted, for the scientific culture could not comprehend the possibility of survival beyond bodily death. However, using the theorizing in this book so far, we can perhaps account for such cross-correspondences: if we see the deceased members of the Sidgwick Group as an overall cultural entity in its own right, we can see the communicating mediums exhibiting a split-off personality of their own mind, tuning in to the cultural expression of the Society for Psychical Research. Put simply, knowing that Myers broadcast his intention to communicate after death, mediums involved with the society manifested phenomena suggestive of that proof. In a more superstitious time, the deceased Sidgwick Group would have been hailed as a 'god', and a new religion would have been created.

However, such a theory requires the existence of a superconscious above culture, but formulating the culture through which it expresses itself, and as the Society for Psychical Research pressed on for such an understanding, similar moves were being made in the United States. Leading the academic assault was Harvard psychologist William James. James had a good pedigree – his father was the philosopher Henry James and one of his brothers was Henry James, the novelist. Principal to James's philosophy was a deep sense of pragmatism (James was one of the founders of this school of philosophy). How-ever, while pragmatism is usually involved with materialist living and a truly scientific methodology, he felt science should expand to the study of all phenomena, whether it can be answerable to the experimental aspect of empiricist science or not.

Taking the lead from London, James and William Barrett formed the American Society for Psychical Research in 1885, with astronomer Simon Newcomb as its first president. In that same year, James began his own inves-tigations of Leonora Piper, becoming convinced of her abilities. For the rest of his life, until his death in 1910, James investigated mediums, satisfied that telepathy existed but never accepting the possibility of life after death. As to the scientific search for proof of what he called instances of 'supernormal knowledge', he laid out the requirement in his famous 'white crow' speech in 1890:

To upset the conclusion that all crows are black, there is no need to seek demonstration that no crows are black; it is sufficient to produce one white crow; a single one is sufficient.

To James, the single 'white crow' was Leonora Piper. If her abilities were real, then such abilities existed and, to him, were proved to exist. However, as in Britain, the general academic mood was to ignore the evidence, and the American Society for Psychical Research settled down to the problem of dedicated research without academic credibility.

In 1887 Richard Hodgson moved to the United States and took over the reins of the society until his death in 1905. Researcher James Hyslop took over from him, with the society moving away from experimental research and appealing more to lay researchers, the investigation of mediums being of primary importance to them. Hyslop's death in 1920 led to a power struggle within the society, and while Hyslop's son, George, took over as president, the 'science' faction won the struggle, with psychologist Gardner Murphy moving the society away from researching mediums and towards a more laboratory-based culture. By 1938, Murphy was carrying out controlled tests to discover statistical evidence of extra-sensory perception, helping to formulate the science of parapsychology.

The term 'parapsychology' had been coined in 1889 by researcher Max Dessoir. It slowly took over from 'psychical research', giving the practice a more credible air and fixing research in scientific terms. In 1927, Scottish psychologist William McDougall convinced the authorities of Duke University in Durham, North Carolina, to form the first parapsychology laboratory. In that same year, two young plant physiologists joined the team. They were Joseph Banks Rhine and his wife, Louisa.

Rhine popularized the terms ESP and PK. The former involved all forms of extra-sensory information input such as telepathy, clairvoyance and precognition, and the latter stood for psychokinesis, or the ability of the mind to affect the physical world, more commonly known as 'mind over matter'. Convinced that most people could exhibit signs of both ESP and PK, he devised statistical tests in order to provide evidence of such abilities.

Rhine's eventual results were positive, but the degree of statistical proof was so slight that it could be easily ignored by academe. This, combined with insinuations of fraud – insinuations that are unproven to this day – condemned parapsychology to failure. When Rhine retired in 1965, Duke University formally cut connections with the work, but an unofficial laboratory carried on his work off-campus, at what became known as the Institute for Parapsychology.

Taking a lead from Rhine, in 1948 Gardner Murphy opened a 'medical section' of the American Society for Psychical Research. Formulating the term 'psi' to denote evidence of paranormal activity, he integrated research with psychiatry and depth psychology. This led to an understanding of how to enhance paranormal abilities through meditation and trance states. The term 'altered state of consciousness', or ASC, came into being. It was soon discovered that the dream state could be considered an ASC, so could paranormal abilities manifest during dreams?

Researchers Montague Ullman, Stanley Krippner and Charles Honorton took up the challenge by forming a dream laboratory at Maimonides Hospital in New York in 1962. Devising experiments in which subjects attempted to 'transmit' information and images to the mind of a sleeping person, significant results were again achieved, but were essentially ignored. In an attempt to devise more sophisticated tests, Honorton significantly advanced parapsychology by devising the 'ganzfeld' technique, where information was 'transmitted' to a receiver who was lying relaxed with 'white noise' playing through earphones and half ping-pong balls over their eyes. This cut the receiver off from the outside world, allowing them to concentrate upon their inner mind, thus inducing a form of ASC. Significant results were again achieved, and were replicated in Cambridge, England, by researcher Carl Sargent. However, such successes were shadowed by some spectacular failures to provide evidence by other researchers.

Why was this? One answer – and an answer clung to by the more sceptical researchers – was that Honorton and Sargent had cheated. However, a more intriguing answer came from the research of parapsychologist Gertrude Schmeidler in New York. She noted that success was more likely to be achieved if everyone involved in the test believed that ESP actually occurred. Devising the term 'sheep' for believers, and 'goat' for sceptics, her ideas formulated into what has become known as the 'experimenter effect'.

This is the most important finding that has ever come out of the scientific approach to the paranormal, for the effect tells us that phenomena are more likely to occur within a 'culture' that expect them to occur. Such information ties in with many of the views expressed in this book, in that phenomena and culture are interlinked. We have seen this effect particularly with superstition, where a belief that a curse could work is the main element of the curse's success. However, it also condemns the paranormal to the fringe of understanding, for it allows a sceptic to pollute an experiment to the point that the experiment will fail – and if sceptics never see the paranormal in action, it can never be validated to a degree acceptable to academe.

Research into the possibilities of PK have been equally impressive and equally ignored. Rhine used to test for PK by getting subjects to try to influence the fall of dice by mind power. By the 1960s the technicality of the approach had been advanced by physicist Helmut Schmidt, who devised the 'random event generator'. Based upon the unpredictability of radioactive decay, the idea was to affect the randomness by mind power. Again, slight but consistent statistical evidence was accumulated, but ignored. The leading figure in the search for proof of PK today is rocket-propulsion engineer Robert Jahn. Working from a basement laboratory at Princeton University, he has devised dozens of tests for PK and consistently provided the same statistical proof as Schmidt. When he published his research in 1986, the Princeton authorities rewarded him through demotion and tried to cover up their embarrassment.

Apart from the obvious implications of the experimenter effect, this short history of the scientific approach to the paranormal offers a telling story. Modern scientific culture is hostile to the idea of the existence of the paranormal. Evidence has been consistently offered, but science's answer is to become totally unscientific and deny its existence. One way out of this problem is to devise acceptable theory through which the evidence can be validated, but this will not come from the scientific approach, and it is unlikely that academe would accept any such theory in the first place.

The result of this scientific dogma is that scientific research of the paranormal is starved of both resources and cash. Up to 1983, only three universities in the UK allowed parapsychology as a credible area of postgraduate study. The situation is only marginally better today. However, in that year parapsychology did receive a symbolic boost when the writer Arthur Koestler bequeathed an estimated £700,000 for the creation of the first British chair of parapsychology. This was set up at Edinburgh, and in 1985 researcher Robert Morris became the first Koestler Professor of Parapsychology.

Apart from this, inroads into the paranormal are sparse. The Institut Metaphysique International was set up in 1914 in Paris, followed by the Institut für Parapsychologie in Berlin in 1928. In the late 1940s, the very first chair of Parapsychology was established at Utrecht University in the Netherlands, but the only truly breathtaking research going on in the later part of the twentieth century was that of physicists Russell Targ and Harold Puthof at the Stanford Research Institute in California. They devised the term 'remote viewing' (see page 25), but their research was made possible only because the American intelligence community thought there might be value in the paranormal in terms of national security.

This bleak picture leads many researchers such as myself to the conclusion that while scientific research into the paranormal has provided valid evidence and insight, it is essentially a lame duck. Far more valid is research in the field, and one of the most famous researchers in this area of study was the maverick, Harry Price.

Harry Price

■ Harry Price – a short, stocky, balding man – was born in London in 1881, the son of a grocer. A natural showman, up to the age of 40 he had a variety of jobs including commercial travelling and journalism. In addition, he studied engineering, chemistry and photography. In 1908 he married a girl he had known since childhood, and they remained happily married throughout their life.

In addition to these more normal pursuits, Price had been fascinated by stage magic since he was eight years old. As a youth he sought out conjurors, quack doctors, hypnotists and fortune tellers, learning their trade and becoming something of an expert magician himself. This experience left him well equipped to identify fraud in his later days of psychical research – a career that was also helped by a small private income received by his wife.

Through most of his life, Price suffered from heart trouble. It was this that kept him out of World War I, and was eventually to lead to his death from a massive heart attack in 1948. Treated with suspicion by the more scientifically minded researchers, he was, however, the first to introduce scientific monitoring at the site of hauntings, and the Harry Price Library is regarded as one of the best collections of literature and evidence upon the paranormal in the world.

In the mid-1920s Price opened his National Laboratory for Psychical Research in a blaze of publicity. Unfortunately, his showmanship could often get the better of him, such as the time that he and the famous philosopher Dr Joad conducted a magical ritual on top of Brocken in the Harz mountains of Germany in full evening dress. The ritual, which Price had come across during his researches, was supposed to turn a billy goat into a handsome young man. Predictably, the goat remained a goat.

Such antics led to his dismissal as a self-seeking publicist who would attempt any fraud to get himself into the papers. However, while much of the criticism was deserved in terms of his publicity stunts, if not fraud, a great deal of it can today be seen as based mainly upon academic snobbery.

Price's most famous research concerned Borley Rectory, a house dubbed the 'most haunted house' in Britain. (I hope the reader will forgive me for not going over this case again. It is the most written-about case in the history of psychical research, and I have dealt with it myself in my previous book, *The Paranormal: A Guide to the Unexplained* [see Bibliography].) This one aside, Price investigated many of the most fascinating cases of paranormality from the early and mid-twentieth century, and a history of paranormal research could not be seen as complete without identifying them. Indeed, they offer strong indications as to where paranormal theory lies.

The young Harry Price had his first encounter with the paranormal when he was 15 years old. In an old manor house occupied by a vicar and his wife in a village near Shrewsbury, strange things had begun to happen. Locked stable doors would be found opened in the mornings, pans of milk would be overturned and logs disturbed. In case an intruder was doing the damage, servants were posted to guard the manor all night, but no one was seen.

Eventually the phenomena moved into the house, and knockings and shriekings were heard, forcing the family to vacate the property. However, young Price convinced the caretaker to let him and a friend spend the night there. Setting themselves up in a downstairs room, Price rigged up rudimentary photographic equipment in the hall. At about 11.30 p.m. his companion thought he heard a noise upstairs. A couple of minutes later there was a loud thud. Half an hour later the noise was heard again, and it felt as if something was coming downstairs. The young men were too frightened to look, and nothing further happened until about 1 a.m., when they heard definite footsteps coming down the hall. Price pressed a button to take a photograph. There was a flash and a huge explosive sound, but by the time they rushed into the hall, there was nothing there.

This experience convinced Price that his future lay in psychical research. During his career he studied many gifted psychics, including a young nurse called Stella Cranshawe. Price met Stella on a train in 1923. Charming and good-looking, Stella had nothing to read on the train and asked Price if she could take a look at the magazine he was reading. The magazine concerned psychical phenomena, and in the conversation that ensued Stella said she was objective about such things, but had to admit that occasionally she would be sitting in a quiet room when a breeze would get up and small objects would take to the air about her.

Although Stella had no interest in mediumship, Price asked her if she would take part in a series of seances to see if she really was psychic in any way. Over the following five years Price conducted many seances with Stella Cranshawe, who produced numerous physical phenomena. These began from the first seance, when a table rose into the air, rappings and flashes filled the room, and the temperature dropped considerably. At a further seance, a table hit Price on the chin and then demolished itself, ending up as so many pieces of wood.

Stella married in 1928 and refused to help Price any longer, but by this time he had already carried out further research on an amazing psychic called Eleonora Zugun.

In February 1925 Eleonora, a Rumanian peasant girl then 13 years old, went to visit her grandmother, who was known locally as a witch. On the way, she found some money and bought sweets. Upon arrival, she told her grandmother about the money, and in order to frighten her not to spend money she had found, the grandmother told her it was devil's money and she might be possessed by the devil for spending it.

The next day, stones rained down on the house, smashing windows, and small objects began to levitate around Eleonora. The grandmother quickly packed her off home, but the phenomena continued, with a jug of water levitating in front of her. Some time later, when a visitor called at the house, a dish flew through the air and hit him, gashing his head.

Eleonora was sent to a nearby monastery, and from there, when the monks could not exorcize her, to a lunatic asylum. However, due to the intervention of a local researcher, she was sent back to the monastery, where a 'spirit' began to possess her. Objects would again levitate about her, and the spirit often slapped her, leaving ugly weals on her skin.

A countess with an interest in psychical research heard of Eleonora and took her back to her home in Vienna. Here, the phenomena continued, with Eleonora beginning to experience the phenomenon of automatic writing, and at one point the spirit spoke through her with a 'breathy and toneless voice'.

In April 1926 Price went to Vienna to visit Eleonora. He was so impressed by the phenomena manifested that he took her back to London for tests. The spirit became increasingly antagonistic towards Eleonora, throwing her out of bed, pulling her hair, stealing her favourite possessions and biting her viciously, teeth marks appearing on her body. Finally, in 1927, the phenomena decreased and the spirit seemed to go away.

Most researchers, including Price, are satisfied that the bodily manifestations that appeared on Eleonora Zugun were a form of unconscious self-punishment caused through hysterical mechanisms similar to those of stigmata, where the wounds of Christ's crucifixion can manifest upon the body due to religious ecstasy.

It is easy to arrive at this theory when we realize that, being from Rumania, Eleonora came from an extremely superstitious culture which gave rise to the vampire mythology. With her grandmother telling the young, pubescent girl that she would be 'possessed', the possession could naturally follow. Indeed, she called it her *dracu*, meaning devil. As for the eventual moulding into an actual 'spirit', this occurred in a monastery where, in attempting to help her, the monks would reinforce the mythology.

However, none of Price's research subjects were as fascinating as the brothers Willi and Rudi Schneider. Born at the turn of the twentieth century in the Austrian town of Braunau, their father was a typesetter. They had four brothers, and their mother, Elise, had a fascination with spiritualism. The family experimented with the Ouija board in the company of a few friends, without success – until, that is, one day when Willi was 14, when he asked if he could have a go. Almost immediately the name 'Olga' was spelt out, and Willi had found a 'spirit guide' through which a whole plethora of physical manifestations would occur.

These soon began in the Schneider kitchen, where water in a bowl began slopping about. Two spirit hands manifested, holding the bowl, and soon the whole house filled with the sounds of clapping. A seance was organized, and during it a tablecloth rose into the air above the sitters. At a later gathering, Olga manifested herself and danced in front of the sitters, Willi being seen to go into a deep trance as she danced.

This all occurred in 1919, and by the end of that year famed researcher Baron von Schrenck-Notzing had practically adopted Willi and taken him to live with him in Munich. The baron went on to observe 124 seances conducted by Willi, who manifested rappings, winds, ethereal black shapes, spirit heads and hands, and successfully levitated a number of heavy objects.

In May 1922, Harry Price went to Munich to visit Willi Schneider, accompanied by researcher Dr Eric Dingwall. Checking the seance room for trap doors and false walls, they also covered Willi in luminous pins so that any movement could be easily observed in the dim light. Going into a trance, Willi produced his usual array of phenomena, convincing Price that he was a natural medium. However, when Price took him to London to continue his investigations, Willi's powers deserted him, and never reappeared. However, Price was not too bothered, for by this time Willi's younger brother, Rudi, was becoming quite a psychic himself.

Rudi's abilities began to appear when he was 11 years old. One night, 'Olga' advised that she wanted him to attend the seance. His parents didn't want this, but shortly after her request Rudi walked into the room in a deep trance state. By December 1925 Rudi was beginning to outdo Willi. At one seance, a tall 'phantom' appeared some 30 times, and he often produced 'spirit hands' and levitated objects.

As with Willi, Schrenck-Notzing took him to Munich to hold seances. However, Rudi was a reluctant medium. All he wanted was to become a car mechanic and marry his girlfriend, Mitzi. When the baron died in 1929, this was exactly what he intended to do, but Price quickly appeared on the scene, offering to be Rudi's mentor.

Begrudgingly, Rudi accompanied Price to London. Organizing six seances, Price offered a reward of £1,000 to any stage magician who could satisfactorily replicate the levitations and manifestations produced. For the seances, Rudi was stripped, searched and dressed in a black leotard. Luminous pins were again used, and even his mouth was inspected for gadgets. However, upon his return home, it was clear that his reluctant efforts were affecting his health.

As with Willi, Rudi's abilities were on the decline. Price convinced him to return to London once more in 1932, when his materializations were poor. Also, a photograph taken during one seance suggested that Rudi was in fact cheating. All these problems led to an argument between Price and the Schneiders. If Rudi was a cheat, he was a very good one; but in the opinion of most researchers who investigated him, he was not – a conclusion that Price eventually came to himself. As for Rudi, his abilities finally disappeared, he became a mechanic and married his Mitzi.

How do we account for the phenomena associated with Stella Cranshawe, Eleonora Zugun and Willi and Rudi Schneider? Did 'spirits' and their appendages really appear? Did objects really float into the air? The obvious explanation is to say that, like Home, they were natural hypnotists, the whole thing being mere hallucination. With the spirit manifestations, I think this is the most valid explanation, but the levitations offer a substantial problem, for there is documented evidence of real effects involved after the event. With Eleonora Zugun, we must remember the smashed table and the injury caused to a visitor by a flying dish. Such incidents allow only two viable explanations: first, we can elect for safety and decide that the people involved were lying; or second, we can admit that real physical effects actually occurred.

A possible explanation of such physical effects is just feasible within the fringes of modern science. Fundamental to our understanding of quantum mechanics is the probabilistic nature of sub-atomic matter. This ethereal world is shrouded in uncertainty, in that science accepts its exact state can never be known. Due to this, quantum theory states that until the observation of a definite existence, a particle could exist in any possible state. In other words, in a fundamental physical reality, all possible realities are equally probable.

Within this fundamental reality, 'events' occur, caused by the interaction of particles with other particles. Let us imagine that these particles are like snooker balls. When we play snooker we hit one ball with another, and the direction of the second ball is determined by the direction and point of impact of the first. In the quantum world, the impact of one particle with another is very different. Here, the second particle can shoot off in any direction, and bears no resemblance to the direction of the first. The mathematics of the event has led physicists to speculate upon the existence of alternative universes, with every outcome of every interaction creating a universe anew.

However, when such an event is monitored, only one outcome is observed. Somewhere, between the probability of the event and its observation, a definite reality has been produced from probability – but what strange, God-like force has created this definite reality?

The most widely held view among scientists is that the definite reality has been produced by the act of observation. Something involved in the observation produces the reality within which we live. As to the nature of this 'something', the most likely answer is consciousness. The definite reality of the world, it appears, is dependent upon observation by a consciousness with an intelligence capable of grasping awareness of the world – and in grasping that awareness, this intelligent consciousness 'creates' the world.

Such a view gives the mind a definite role in creating and ordering reality. The mind and the physical world about us are linked. And within this idea, a glimpse of understanding is achievable.

The Poltergeist

■ Quantum theory offers a tantalizing role for the mind within the physical world. It suggests that the mind is, in a way, the creator of the world. And if it is the creator – or, at the very least, a player in that act of creation – then it is not out of the question to suggest that the mind can also affect the physical world. With such an idea, a glimpse of understanding can be attached to psychokinetic effects involved in the mediumship of Stella Cranshawe, Eleonora Zugun and Willi and Rudi Schneider.

However, while such a theory can account for the effects, it does not account for why the effects occur in the first place. Some understanding of this can be gained if we now extend our investigation into the world of that most baffling phenomenon, the poltergeist.

Harry Price investigated a classic poltergeist case towards the end of the 1920s. Number 8 Eland Rd, Battersea, in London, was occupied by an 86-year-old invalid called Henry Robinson, his son, Frederick, three daughters, and a

14-year-old grandson, Peter. Phenomena began to manifest towards the end of November 1927, when lumps of coal and coins rained down on the conservatory roof. The police were called and a lump of coal bounced off the policeman's helmet. The family's cleaner ran terrified from the wash-house when she found it full of smoke.

As the phenomena progressed, ornaments smashed themselves against the walls and heavy furniture overturned itself. By January 1928 the poltergeist was so destructive that it smashed the entire conservatory. When Price first visited the house, a gas-lighter flew past his head, and when it all became too much for Frederick, a number of chairs 'marched' along the hall behind him as he was taken to hospital following a mental breakdown. Soon afterwards, Henry and one of the daughters also fell ill.

A medium was called in to try to identify any 'spirits' that could be behind the poltergeist infestation, but while the 'feeling' in the house unnerved the medium, the 'spirits' remained unknown. Finally, when Frederick returned from hospital, he moved the entire family out, and the phenomena ceased to bother them.

How do we account for such a case? One logical assumption is to agree with researcher Frank Podmore, who was convinced that the phenomena were caused by mischievous children playing tricks on the family. While this explanation can definitely be applied to some mild cases, it fails to explain long-term infestations, of which there are many among the superstitious population of Brazil.

Guy Playfair investigated a typical case near São Paulo in 1973. The house in question was occupied by a divorced Portuguese woman with an adult son and daughter. The troubles began for the family when the son got married and moved his young wife into the house.

By the time Playfair arrived on the scene, the poltergeist had been present for some six years, and the family had moved house three times to try to escape it, without success. As well as the usual loud rappings, the poltergeist particularly liked setting fire to or soaking bedclothes.

Playfair sat up inside the house on his first night, and just as he was dozing off a series of loud raps sounded, shaking the house. His attempts to recreate these echoing bangs the following day proved ineffective, suggesting that no human agency was involved. On the second night, a stool bounced down the stairs and a drawer full of clothes hurled itself out of a window. Later, a wardrobe full of clothes caught fire.

Eventually, a team of mediums visited the house and tried to exorcize the poltergeist by contacting their spirit guides. The poltergeist calmed itself for a couple of weeks, but then the phenomena began again. In desperation, the family called in a shaman-type individual from one of Brazil's African-influenced cults. He suspected black magic, where spirits had been directed towards the house for malevolent purposes. He carried out a number of rituals and the phenomena ceased, never to return.

The idea that the poltergeist is an actual 'spirit' is well entrenched in paranormal literature. Eleonora Zugun is regarded as being a victim of one such spirit, and the body manifestations and possessions that overcame her are often features in poltergeist cases.

How does the spirit come to haunt people? According to Guy Playfair, a poltergeist usually centres around a 'focus' individual, who is invariably female and at the age of puberty. These girls are full of sexual energies, and if no outlet is found, spirit entities can be attracted to these chaotic energies, thus causing the outbreak.

Alternatively, researchers such as psychoanalyst Nandor Fodor believed that poltergeists are caused by the chaotic energies produced by personality fragments, similar to those expressed in multiple personality. This idea is attractive, in that it can account for the 'possession' in psychological terms, with the role of consciousness upon the physical world producing the phenomena.

Andrew Green, who has spent a lifetime investigating ghosts (see pages 17–18), also sees the poltergeist as quite different to the 'spirit' hypothesis. While the 'focus' can often be identified as a young, pubescent girl, this is not always the case. Like other researchers, he accepts the existence of a 'focus' individual, but he sees the outbreak as a chaotic form of psychokinesis produced by an individual undergoing some form of mental trauma. In this scenario, the reason a young girl is often involved is due simply to the chaotic nature of her pubescent or adolescent mind.

This suggests that the same 'force' was at work with Willi and Rudi Schneider. They both manifested their psychic abilities at puberty, and lost them when they approached adulthood. Their abilities became focused into definite mediumistic talents. Had this not occurred, the chances are that their abilities would have been unfocused, thus causing a chaotic poltergeist infestation.

Such an idea suggests that in the poltergeist 'focus' we have a form of trainee medium – but perhaps 'medium' is the wrong word. If we return to the shaman, I noted that a tribe would identify a future shaman while still young (see page 59). Thus identified, the shaman would be guided to control and use his abilities throughout his life. In this way, a chaotic force would be enhanced and turned into a controlled force for the good of the community. Such a process can be identified in healer Matthew Manning (see pages 110–11).

In his adolescent years, Manning became the focus for a virulent and prolonged poltergeist outbreak. Beginning when his father found a silver tankard inexplicably in the middle of the dining room, the poltergeist often sent knives and forks flying through the air and developed a habit of turning lights on and off. Occasionally it would scribble messages, such as 'Matthew beware', on the wall. One night it even threw him out of bed.

That Manning was responsible for the outbreak, there can be little doubt, for the poltergeist followed him to boarding school, where objects often flew about, and at one time the beds in his dormitory piled themselves up. As his abilities developed and he became a psychic superstar, he found he could bend metal psychokinetically. In Barcelona, he blacked out a seven-storey store when he went for a book signing, and on Japanese television one night, hundreds of people reported ornaments and ashtrays smashing and lamps and bottles exploding in their homes during the broadcast.

As in classic poltergeist infestations, Manning often found himself being 'possessed'. He developed a talent for automatic writing and drawing. He wrote in Russian and Arabic as well as English, and was possessed by post-war minister Stafford Cripps and philosopher Bertrand Russell. That these were some form of cryptomnesic possession is beyond doubt, in that the works he produced by Russell were signed incorrectly as 'Bertram Russell'. With his automatic art, he seemed to be possessed by the likes of Dürer and Picasso, signing the works in their names.

Signs of haunting phenomena also manifested – phenomena that so often, but incorrectly, suggest that 'spirits' are really involved. Manning held conversations with previous occupants of the house, Robert and Henrietta Webbe, from the seventeenth century. At one point, Robert Webbe convinced Manning that they really were hauntings, possessing him through automatic writing and occasionally manifesting in hallucinatory form. Only when Manning dropped out of the psychic circus developing around him did he focus his abilities himself, spending several years training to direct his energies towards healing.

In Matthew Manning, we can see how the poltergeist is an expression of the full myriad of psychic phenomena, including possession, hallucination and psychokinesis, involving information input and manipulation of a form of superconscious. We can also see how these three central elements of the paranormal manifest from the same source, and how they can be allied to the healing powers Manning eventually produced. But most importantly, we can see how their manifestations are not supernatural, but the expression of a possible future shaman-like individual, produced by essentially psychological abilities. However, this is not the complete picture.

Although it cannot always be identified, most poltergeist outbreaks are preceded by an identifiable mental trauma such as a death, family upheaval like a divorce, or – most difficult to identify – some form of child abuse. An additional ingredient of a psychological nature can thereby be identified as the actual prompter for the outbreak. It is therefore arguable that, if the mental trauma had not occurred, neither would the outbreak. And if the outbreak is an indication of a future shaman-like individual (if properly focused, that is), then we can identify mental trauma as vital to shamanic abilities.

Alongside this information, we must introduce a factor identified within the scientific search for 'psi' abilities. For instance, it has been noted that, if they are believers, most people can produce statistical evidence of ESP if they 'practise' the ability enough. Combining these two factors, we can see that shamanic abilities are not a 'gift', in that the person is not somehow special, but rather that they can be seen as a consequence of life experience that anyone can fall into. In other words, we all have the ability to become shamanic.

A further factor must also be identified. In my earlier analysis of the shaman (see pages 57–60), I noted that he was the instigator of a cultural expression of the paranormal through hallucinatory ritual within the tribe. Through his trance state, the shaman brought out the hysterical element of the tribe's mind to produce, with the tribe, an hallucinatory but communal reality. In this way we can see that, while the shaman was the main psychic, he actually brought out the psychic abilities of the entire tribe to produce a communal whole, by expressing a cultural form of the 'supernatural'. Although it is of an involuntary nature, we can see exactly the same process at work in a poltergeist infestation.

While we can identify the 'focus' in such outbreaks, the simple fact is that this person must have an audience that 'shares' the experience. In this sense, the outbreak is also communal – the product not just of the focus, but of the group involved. Put simply, we can see that those around the 'focus' slowly descend into a superstitious sub-culture in its own right, and an involuntary shamanic hallucinatory ritual begins. The focus, it seems, is merely the 'catalyst'.

In the poltergeist we can identify the survival, into modern times, of that original 'supernatural' expression of culture. And the shaman can be seen as a definite psychological factor of society that is with us as much today as it has always been.

Carl Jung

■ We have seen that there have been two central elements at work concerning understanding of the paranormal. These are research in the laboratory and research in the field. Laboratory testing has shown a minor statistical bias for the existence of ESP and PK, but has failed to validate its absolute existence. On the other hand, field research has shown some incredible phenomena at work, but has received academic derision, for without laboratory standards being imposed, the phenomena can easily be ignored.

Most researchers continue to work in one of these two fields, under the mistaken assumption that the constant accumulation of evidence will lead to eventual acceptance of paranormal phenomena. This assumption is mistaken because they fail to understand scientific discipline and methodology. Scientists realized many decades ago that data is of no use whatsoever unless an overall theory exists within which to order the data accumulated, and while psychical researchers may well have offered 'belief systems' within which to rationalize certain areas of the paranormal, few have attempted to provide general theories of the paranormal into which to fit the data.

I do not class myself as either a laboratory or field researcher. Nor do I class myself as a believer in the paranormal or a sceptic. I go for the third option: I look for patterns within the data available in order to provide general theory. If the theory stands up to criticism, it validates the data. If not, the theory is either incomplete or the paranormal is bunkum.

A small handful of researchers have attempted general theory. British writer Colin Wilson is the most obvious example; biologist Lyall Watson another; and, as we shall see later (see page 208), biologist Rupert Sheldrake has also deserved his place on this list. But without doubt the most remarkable of the theorists was Swiss psychoanalyst, Carl Gustav Jung.

Jung was born on 26 July 1875 in Kesswil, Switzerland, the son of a pastor. Caught between the world of the intellect and that of the spiritual, his life was one long search for truth, based as much upon self-analysis as upon empirical study. Classed by some as one of the greatest geniuses of all time – Sir Laurens van der Post described him as 'a universal personality, one of the greatest since the Renaissance' – he was dismissed by others as a manipulative and egotistical misogynist and racist.

This last point is unfair, but his thirst for sex led him to many affairs, and it is fair to say that he treated his wife deplorably. Indeed, endowed with a charismatic personality, he was also vain, infantile, obsessive, a control freak and borderline psychotic, considering himself to be a great prophet. These considerable faults aside, Jung's understanding of the human mind was both phenomenal and revolutionary, offering psychological theory that removed the mind from Freud's dark instincts. As psychologist Henri Ellenberger speculated, if Freud was a sorcerer who reduced man to devilish instincts, Jung was a wizard who could sway the moon.

Jung's early life was full of instances of phenomena that bridged the worlds of the psychological and supernatural. From the age of three he began to have dreams which can only be classed as mystical, complete with what he later identified as pagan symbolism. In addition, he understood that there was a second person living inside his mind, who seemed to be a wise old man. Jung called him Philemon, and as he grew, this second personality began to take him over.

On a psychological level, we can identify a form of multiple personality manifesting in Jung's mind. Alternatively, the voice-like nature of this secondary personality, allied to almost hallucinatory dream images, suggests a rising schizophrenia. Even the cause of this mental trauma can be identified in the fact that his mother suffered a mental breakdown when he was very young, and his continuing relationship with her was based upon the two very different 'personalities' she went on to express herself.

Jung was also surrounded by the supernatural. His grandfather and a cousin both professed to be psychic. In 1900 he began studying his cousin, who had manifested her abilities at puberty, achieving a trance state and speaking in 'strange voices'. When this phenomenon began, the dining-room table suddenly split in half with a loud bang. When a second bang issued from a sideboard, a knife inside it was found to be shattered.

Jung's cousin can be identified as having shamanic abilities, but intriguingly, so can he. While we can place a psychological explanation upon his possessions and hallucinations, we can also see these as shamanic – and whichever explanation you choose, that choice is based upon culture, not reality. The same psychological idiosyncrasies can be seen in two ways: had his family been totally involved in the spiritualist movement, 'Philemon' could well have been his 'spirit guide'; had he belonged to a more tribal culture, his phenomena would have been seen as the first indication of future shamanic abilities, and he would have been trained as such.

This is where most people misinterpret Jung. He is seen as an intellectual who descended into mystical claptrap. Far better, I suggest, to see Jung as a reluctant and unguided shaman, who over a lifetime came to terms with himself in an intellectual way. When we see him in this shamanic form, his social idio-syncrasies fall in line with the 'madness' of the shamanic mentality, and his entire intellectual output fits into an exact and logical pattern.

Jung's lifelong interest in occult phenomena began in 1898, and he soon real-ized that in understanding these, he would understand himself. Intellectually, his interests led him to studies of the mind. Beginning his medical training in 1895 in Basel, Switzerland, in 1900 he moved to the Burgholzki psychiatric clinic in Zurich, where he studied under Swiss psychiatrist Eugen Bleuler.

Bleuler was interested in delusional ideas that rise in the mind, and Jung also threw himself into such studies, for obvious personal reasons. Experimenting in word association, he felt the practice could identify groupings of delusional ideas in the unconscious mind of the sufferer. These ideas rose involuntarily to take over the mind, and thus cause the delusions in the sufferer. Bleuler had Jung's ideas on the subject very much in mind when he termed such delusional illnesses as schizophrenia.

Jung would eventually go on to found Analytical Psychology, a process devised to 'detect the intruders of the mind'. He discovered two states of mind – introversion and extraversion – that had to be in harmony and balance in the mentally healthy individual. Such mind states he saw as idiosyncrasies of personality. Hence, poor mental health becomes a process of the disunity of personality. Where such disunity occurs, it becomes the aim of therapy to convince the patient to experiment with his own nature, for a healthy individual must always engage himself in an understanding of meaning in his life. As for the direction in which this meaning lies, Jung came to understand the importance of dream analysis, for in dreams, unconscious meaning could be identified.

In these early psychological theories we can identify the fact that, rather than basing them simply on an analysis of his patients, Jung had analysed himself. Disunity of personality, dream symbolism and a quest for meaning were all idio-syncrasies of his own mind, and his early studies had been vital for a growing understanding of schizophrenia.

In 1903 Jung married wealthy heiress Emma Rauschenbach, thus guaran-teeing financial stability for Jung to continue his research. On a visit to Vienna in 1907, he met the great Sigmund Freud, and for five years Freud was to embrace him as a disciple. However, in 1910 Jung left the Burgholzki to con-centrate on private practice and his increasingly non-establishment spiritual ideas. For instance, in May of that year he submitted a paper, 'The Psycho-logical Foundations of Belief in Spirits', to the Society for Psychical Research. In it, he argued that there were three main sources for belief in spirits:

apparitions (or hallucinations), mental disease and dream images. In every case, the 'spirit' was created psychologically following the death, manifested by the emotions of the bereaved.

The great split between Jung and Freud has entered the annals of psychoanalysis, and Jung's increasingly spiritual digressions were a primary cause. Jung narrated one almighty argument between the two when, enraged, he felt a heat build up inside him, followed by a loud explosion centred on a nearby bookcase. Arguing that this was proof of phenomena, Freud replied: 'Bosh.' Jung then indicated that the explosion would happen again, and another explosion occurred.

Their split was, of course, due to much more than this. Freud, who portrayed himself as Jung's long-suffering father-figure, thought that early sexual trauma could account for most mental disorder. To Jung, Freud was so entrenched in this notion that he classed it as an article of faith that couldn't be argued with. Jung, on the other hand, thought this sexual trauma to be simply one minor cause of mental illness. To Jung, such trauma found its routes in an historical context, and manifested due to a lack of meaning and misunderstanding of the patient's place in a purposeful universe. Such a view fell perfectly in line with his shamanic leanings, allying psychological idiosyncrasies with the spiritual aspects of religion. And his split with Freud was soon to manifest into a whole new level of spiritual and psychological understanding.

Following the split, Jung descended into a six-year-long mental illness. Some classified it as borderline schizophrenia, but, in line with Jung the shaman, he saw it as a 'creative illness'. The term he used to describe it psychologically is in common use today: mid-life crisis.

Jung began communicating with the 'spirits' within his mind. He classed them as the voices of the unanswered, unresolved and unredeemed. His dreams turned into full-blown visions, where the voices took him on symbolic shamanic quests. He learned and practised how to descend into his inner mind – a process he called active imagination – where hallucinatory images appeared, full of pagan and religious symbolism. In a strict psychological sense, he *had* become a borderline schizophrenic, but in a wider spiritual sense, he was perfecting his abilities as a shaman, inducing trance states through which possessions and hallucinations could be called up at will. The two explanations – the psychological or the spiritual – were equally correct, depending upon the cultural leanings of the assessor.

Jung's illness also led him to theorize a whole new set of psychological principles, reworking ideas that had been in his head for some time and advancing his existing ideas into an almost spiritual philosophy.

His starting point was a process he called 'individuation'. Something, he realized, must have caused his mid-life crisis, as well as the mid-life crises he began to see in his patients. The normal life pattern was to grow to adulthood, gain independence from parents, find a sexual identity and gain fulfilment through work. This pattern, when followed correctly, should lead to total fulfilment in life, particularly in the rich and influential, who could achieve their full potential. So why should such people have a mid-life crisis?

Jung realized that there must be something more, above the material living we assume to be our goal, and that missing factor, decided Jung, was psychic integration. Advancing his idea of finding meaning in life, individuation thus becomes a developmental journey we should all take within ourselves to achieve psychological wholeness.

By this time, Jung had also begun to study Hermetic philosophy, and he saw a similar process to individuation at work in the alchemical transmutation of the soul. Both alchemy and individuation could be seen as a process of advancement towards perfection. Could alchemy therefore be important to psychology? Jung obviously thought it was, and as alchemy extended through many diverse cultures, he wondered if other factors could be found to be universal throughout different cultures. He began to read widely upon anthropology, religion and mythology, supplementing his reading by travelling the world and studying ancient cultures.

Over and over again, Jung found the same principles at work throughout the world. Mythology and folklore, it seemed, had universal elements which seemed to drive culture along, but being universal, they appeared to be above culture. What could this universal property be? The answer came from analysis of both his patients and himself, for within dream imagery he began to notice the existence of universal symbols.

Typical was the circular design known as the 'mandala'. The word is Sanskrit for 'circle', and it appears throughout ancient cultures, identified as the 'spiral' in stone age times. Throughout the world, it is said to represent the union of the microcosm, or man, to the macrocosm, or Divine. It symbolizes the mystical path through various layers of consciousness, until one meet, and joins with, the Divine. In other words, it is the symbol of the alchemical death and rebirth of consciousness.

The mandala began to rise within Jung's dream images, and he found himself being compelled to draw it over and over again. He saw it as symbolic of the self – the totality of the conscious and unconscious elements of the mind. This can be seen as the 'wholeness' of the mind, and it was now rising inside Jung's mind because, through illness, his mind was threatening disintegration.

It was therefore a symbol guiding him to make himself 'whole' once more.

Jung saw the appearance of the mandala as coming from 'outside' the totality of his own mind, yet playing an important role in his process of individuation. Hence, although he saw each person as a unique individual in their own right, he began to believe that there was a universal 'wholeness' from which all consciousness came. This 'wholeness' guided and transformed all societies and all individuals through repeating symbolic patterns identified in myths, folklore and dreams. On the one hand, this could be seen as psychological individuation rising from a universal centre, and on the other it was both spiritual and alchemical, guiding us towards meaning and destiny.

Such ideas led Jung to identify the universal centre of consciousness in his idea of the 'collective unconscious'. The natural spread of culture could not, he argued, account for the universality of myth and symbolism. Similarly, such myth and symbolism could not be universal in unrelated cultures without a psychic centre connecting them. In dreams, too, he noted the same universal symbolism rising in patients of low intellectual capacity. It was ridiculous to see such universal and meaningful images as rising from their personal minds. All minds, too, must rise from some connecting psychic centre.

We can now rationalize the central ideas of Carl Jung. Everyone is an individual, and in this sense each of us has our own life pattern, manifesting from a personal consciousness. Underneath this mind level, we all have an individual unconscious, a repository for our own forgotten and repressed memories and psychological idiosyncrasies. Dreams of a personal nature can rise from this unconscious to guide our process of individuation. However, beneath the personal unconscious, we are all psychically connected to a universal 'collective unconscious', where our psychology ceases to be personal.

The universal 'collective unconscious' can be seen on two levels. At the highest level of psychology, it connects psychically the whole of humanity. At a base level, this higher psychology is composed of instincts which guide our base functions. Yet the 'collective unconscious' can also be seen to exist at a lower level, and individual to each specific culture. All cultures – all societies – are formed by its connectedness. This is what makes specific cultures different. But in terms of the universality of mythology, the higher universal impulses and symbols go on to infect all those distinct cultures in the same way that the higher, universal impulses filter into the personal mind of the individual to assist individuation. Within this process, dreams and mythologies become the same impulse – the former guiding the individual, the latter guiding cultural development – rising from a universal 'wholeness'. As Jung pointed out in his autobiographical *Memories, Dreams, Reflections* (see Bibliography):

The collective unconscious is common to us all; it is the foundation of what the ancients called 'the sympathy of all things'.

Within the 'collective unconscious' Jung identified two further impulses, described in his theories of 'archetypes' and the 'shadow'.

Archetypes are essentially an extension of instinctual behaviour. Indeed, some archetypes *are* instinctual behaviour. These not being part of conscious thought as such, Jung proposed universal predispositions towards certain behaviour. Typical is the maternal instinct, or fear of the dark, which can be seen as universal guiding principles. Such predispositional archetypes are created, Jung thought, by repetition of situations and experiences. In this way, personal experiences of the individual can eventually engrave themselves upon the universal centre, causing behavioural idiosyncrasies to rise throughout humanity. Hence, much of our behaviour becomes, not personal, but collective – in this way, we seem to do things 'instinctually' and without thought.

However, other archetypes are much more defined. Such archetypes were depicted by Jung as almost living figures and take the form of character types such as the Hero, and Sage, the Judge, the Child, the Trickster or the Earth Mother. In an individual sense, these are psychological idiosyncrasies seen respectively as our courageous side, our developing wisdom, the conscience, our infancy, the villain within us, and, in the female, the maternal drive. On the cultural level, they are invested with the personal images of all mythological gods. Regardless of culture, these are the guiding representations of all deities throughout humanity, from Hero forms such as Hercules, to the Trickster Christians call the devil, to the Earth Mother who is the primeval Goddess, as well as Aphrodite or the Virgin Mary.

In this cultural sense, we can see these archetypal images still guiding us today, as we saw earlier with our continual creation of guiding stereotypes (see page 81), which again take on these specific forms. It is little wonder that mythologist Joseph Campbell found much inspiration in the works of Jung. However, Jung also felt that we could unconsciously communicate with these archetypes – this is the inner search through which individuation occurs. But, he thought, if these personality types were not in balance, their imbalance led to neurosis and psychosis. Such rogue personality traits can also be seen in schizophrenia and multiple personality; and we can even see them as the 'spirit guides' of shamans and mediums, guiding culture along. Again, the psychological and spiritual are coming together to form the same thing.

A similar process can be seen in Jung's concept of the 'shadow'. The shadow, he thought, is the dark side of the personality. It represents a conflict within the mind between the ego, or 'self', and unfavourable aspects of the personality. To Jung, it could rise through rage, and is symbolized by the battle between the Hero and the Monster in such myths as the battle between George and the Dragon, but it can also be seen as the inner turmoil between good and evil. In addition to lying as an impulse within the individual, it also had a cultural expression, for through the shadow collective infections could rise, instigating mindless mob activity. World War II, Jung thought, was an expression of the collective German shadow.

In this sense, the shadow can be seen as a form of psychical invasion, infecting many minds towards a single impulse. This impulse can be seen in mob activities such as riots, where rage takes over a crowd, leading to destructive and essentially mindless activity, where people are compelled to join in. In a real sense, a riot is leaderless, a collective 'thing' in its own right.

This leads us towards an intriguing possibility within Jung's shadow: is it really 'dark', or is it simply that collective action always seems to be destructive? In other words, as Jung suspected, could the shadow have a goodness about it too? If we are prepared to countenance this possibility, we can identify the shadow in all forms of hysteria, which seems to cause communal but spontaneous action – and as we must recall, such hysterical mechanisms were the process through which shamanic tribal ritual worked. In other words, we can see the shadow as the means through which paranormality manifests, rising from a superconscious, which, of course, the 'collective unconscious' is.

Carl Jung's speculations upon a 'collective unconscious' can be seen as a great general theory of paranormality rising from a superconscious. His insights were so exact because although Jung was an intellectual, he was also a shaman, and as with the shaman, his insights were passed on to society in general. Jung's insights led inexorably to the rise of spirituality in the 1960s, now symbolized as the New Age; Jung defined his own name for the revival, dubbing it the 'Age of Aquarius'.

In 1955, Jung's wife died. This caused another crisis in his life, and a deeper search for meaning. As well as having further visionary and symbolic dreams, he approached the next stage of shamanic practice. In the grounds of his new home in Bollingen, Switzerland, he began to build a stone castle, complete with mystical and alchemical symbols. Jung the shaman had become Jung the sacred geometrer, the magical builder of the doorway between the physical and the spiritual.

He also began to fear for the future of mankind, for if we did not become more conscious – more in tune with our psychic self – we would be lost. By ignoring his work, humanity as a whole was fragmented, lost in its own cultural identities, unable to achieve the form of global individuation he thought was essential, for in realizing such individuation, we could find the pattern of God that exists deep within us all.

Carl Jung died on 6 June 1961. In his final years, his search for unity of mankind had taken him above cultural expression. In a letter, he wrote:

> I had to wrench myself free of God, so to speak, in order to find that unity in myself which God seeks through man. It is rather like that vision of Symeon, the Theologian, who sought God in vain everywhere in the world, until God rose like a little sun in his own heart.

Why was Symeon's search for God in vain 'everywhere in the world'? Because the world of man was the world of defining God through cultural expression. A cultural expression of God contains the essential character of God, but the image is polluted into a man-based, cultural concept of God specific to a particular culture. By expressing the essential whole, culture creates religions that fragment the whole of humanity.

The true God was elsewhere, above culture, existing in a universal 'wholeness' that no culture could grasp. In being whole, it was above individuality, it was above cultural expression, it was above fragmentation. This true universal God was everything, and could never be understood in any other sense but the holistic. Jung identified this point in the final paragraph of his final book:

> The more uncertain I have felt about myself, the more there has grown up in me a feeling of kinship with all things. In fact, it seems to me as if that alienation which so long separated me from the world has become transferred into my own inner world, and has revealed to me an unexpected unfamiliarity with myself.

These words have been thought of as meaning that Jung had lost any sense of having definite convictions. His certainties, it seemed, had disappeared. But this explanation applies to Jung the intellectual: Jung the shaman was saying something quite different. His process of individuation had become complete, he had reached the universal God-head, and in reaching it, his individual identity, and all forms of cultural expression, had deserted him. His mind had risen above identity and above culture, and become part of the universal 'whole'. In the ultimate death and rebirth, he had psychologically annihilated himself in order to reach the wholeness of alchemical perfection. In order to understand exactly what this process means, we must move on to discuss the mystical philosophies of the East.

· MYSTICISM ·

Hinduism

■ The world today is brimming with religions, but remarkably few of them can be classed as great religions that have motivated millions and survived down the centuries. Of those great religions, we can actually define just two central traditions. The first – the tradition of the West – is known as the 'prophetic' tradition, and evolved into the Judaeo-Christian religions, which also birthed Islam. Based on the concept of 'monotheism', or the belief in one God, they give humanity a special place in creation, and provided the motive power that propelled man to his unique position in the world today. Alongside this western tradition is the eastern, or 'wisdom' tradition. Of these, the main movements are Hinduism and Buddhism, the latter being a natural offshoot of the former in the same way that Christianity and Islam can find their roots and mythology in the Judaic tradition.

The main reason for the evolution of these two distinct traditions can be found in geography. Formulated in the arid Middle East, the western tradition was born from the requirement of man to be ingenious. Living in a harsh land, people had to use technology and cunning to survive. This birthed the ego and the feeling that man could conquer nature. Hence, man-images replaced the more nature-based deities. Similarly, with the ego becoming divine, there was a huge spread of land for the god-kings to conquer.

Such impulses birthed the idea of advancement through man's endeavour. Prophets aided this advancement by passing on the message of God, who Himself had taken on a man-image, above nature. Such an evolving philosophy led to an understanding of reality as linear, in that life advanced from a beginning, and in advancing, required man to advance in kind. The modern, western world, with its technologies and sciences, is thus a direct descendant of this linear, prophetic tradition.

163

The eastern tradition was very different. Beginning in a more tropical environment, survival was still harsh, but did not require the same degree of technology as in the Middle East. Hence, early societies could remain far more in tune, and as one, with nature. The ego still surfaced, but not as the overall impulse it became in the West. Similarly, India – home of the tradition – was very much insulated from the outside world, surrounded by either oceans, mountains or jungle. Hence, the early Indians never birthed the same need to conquer as in the West.

Due to these factors, a more cyclical world view came into being. In this way, religions came from the wisdom of the ancients rather than the direct-voice communications of God through chosen men. Life itself went on to echo the cycles of nature, remaining much more in tune with all prehistoric religions. This is why in the modern world the West has gone on to become more technologically competent, the East only beginning to rise technologically today through abandoning their traditions and adopting the more aggressive nature of the West.

The actual roots of Hinduism are hard to define. An Aryan invasion into India from the West beginning around 1750 BC had a great effect on the existing Indian religious form. A definite warrior race, they brought with them their ego-based deities, and the plethora of Hindu gods seem to be based very much on this Aryan influence. However, as the Aryans settled the area, they eventually lost much of their conquering ways and adopted the cyclical nature of the indigenous peoples. Hence, it is impossible to tell how much of Hinduism is endemic, and how much came from outside India, but that the eventual form was cyclical there is no doubt.

The earliest Hindu religious text, a collection of hymns known as the 'Vedas', are thought of as Aryan in influence, and were followed by the philosophical 'Upanishads', based on the traditions of the priestly Brahmins. In addition, Hindus have two sacred epics in the 'Ramayana' and 'Mahabharata'. Among their many hundreds of gods, the principal deities are Brahma, Vishnu and Shiva, who represent the creator, preserver and destroyer respectively.

Many westerners criticize Hinduism as too complicated and so full of contradictory gods that the whole tradition becomes a farce, but this is to fail to understand the religion, which can be seen as more a philosophy of life than a religion in a western sense. Whereas the one God of the western tradition is seen as a literal reality, no such definite nature is given to Hindu gods. Rather, they are cultural expressions – archetypes, if you like – of forces within nature. They are simply a means to define those forces and pay homage to them. Indeed, the vast majority of gods are local cultural representations of the various societies within overall Hindu culture. Once this reality is grasped, we can immediately see that Hinduism manipulates cultural expression into a code of life and understanding of reality. Hence, going beyond the deities, the Hindu system becomes simple and straightforward.

In line with the cycles of nature, the individual goes through three distinct stages of life. The first is the life of a student, and comprises the youth and teenage years. During this time, individuals are required to learn their culture and morals so that they can grow into good and productive adults.

The early part of that adulthood comprises the second stage of life, which can best be defined as being a householder. In the West, such a stage would be classified as that of the worker, and although this is the stage of the worker, the most important element in Hindu culture is the individual's role in the family environment. Work is not done to better oneself, but to provide for a stable family. In this way, cultural tradition is maintained in an unending cycle of family values as the bedrock of society.

The third stage in life is retirement, and begins upon the birth of the first grandchild. During this stage, the individual's social obligations are thought of as being complete. But this does not mean that the individual can relax – far from it, for this is the time in life when individuals must turn to total meditation in order to discover themselves and the reality of the universe, thus maintaining the wisdom of the ages.

We can see here how Hinduism is geared to maintaining a form of cultural integrity based on long-established traditions, and this impulse permeates the whole of society, particularly in the caste system, or class identification.

Principal to the caste system is the idea that people are different. Some are reflective and highly spiritual, others are natural administrators or organizers, still others are natural producers and technologists, while others are of such low intellectual capacity that unskilled labour is all they are capable of.

These classifications are behind the caste system itself, which says that it is pointless trying to train someone for something they are incapable of doing. Hence, from the highest Brahmin caste to the lowest Untouchables, Hindu society is strictly regulated. As to the form of regulation, birth is the best indicator. A person must therefore remain in the caste to which they are born throughout their life.

If Hinduism has a dogmatic character, it is here that it manifests, for the caste system can be seen as a form of social control. While it fits ideally into the cyclical nature of the tradition, it can be abusive and allows no form of meritocracy to rise.

Above this strict and cyclical cultural order, there is God. But while God will be represented in the identifying deities of Hinduism, the actual nature of God is undefined. This is because life is finite, whereas God is infinite, and as such above finite understanding. In order to grasp such a concept, one is required to look at everything that can exist in the universe and say 'this is not God'. Once this process has been done, what remains *is* God.

Of course, nothing remains – in a finite sense, at least. In this way, the ultimate essence of God is ethereal and above understanding, thus preventing anyone identifying themselves in a God-form. Such a concept guarantees the cyclical nature of culture, with prophets unable to have the authority of God, which was essential to western religious forms.

Of vital importance to Hinduism is the 'jiva', or individual soul. Where jivas come from is unknown, but when they first exist, they inhabit the lowest form of life. At the death of that life form, they continue to exist and move on to inhabit a new, more complex life form. After an unknown number of incarnations, they eventually go on to inhabit a human life form.

Here, the nature of the jiva changes, and for the first time it is self-aware and knows itself. Its process of reincarnation is far from complete, but now it is responsible for its own advancement. Such advancement is achieved by 'karma', which is a moral law of cause and effect. Here, every action of life is seen as having consequences, and those consequences define the next incarnation. If good, the jiva will move up the caste system in future lives. If bad, the jiva will descend back down the life forms. As for the eventual destination of the jiva, it is involved in a process of purification, and once this is achieved, it is believed to leave the cycle of successive incarnations and achieve identification with God, where it loses existence in a finite sense.

Much of this basic social code of Hinduism has echoes of the alchemical quest and western mystical traditions. For instance, in the cabbala, God has many faces, which are simply cultural expressions of the Divine; this same concept exists with Hindu gods. Again, the process through which the jiva travels can be seen as a search for alchemical perfection. The philosophy behind the Hindu social order also contains other remarkable similarities to western occult tradition.

Hinduism identifies man has having four 'wants'. The first two are 'pleasure' and 'worldly success', and constitute the 'Path of Desire'. While Hinduism is basically a non-ego religion, it does in fact allow these egoistic wants to thrive. Indeed, it positively encourages the individual to pursue any form of pleasure or worldly success they wish, within, of course, the moral code. It does so because pleasure and worldly success can never be fulfilling. As Carl Jung noted through mid-life crisis, there is significantly more to life than this, and the sooner a person realizes this, the sooner they can move on to their higher wants, which constitute the 'Path of Renunciation'.

The first of these wants comprises obligations to the community and is known as 'duty'. Such a concept reinforces Hindu society as an interwoven cultural expression. Through it comes the self-respect of doing one's share. However, the time again comes when even duty cannot fulfil the individual. This is because the soul is infinite, and the finite life of the individual can never be ultimately satisfying to the soul. Hence, the ultimate want is 'liberation' from this finite existence. In other words, the individual eventually seeks out union with God.

Hinduism says that we are held to the finite world by three imperfections, which are 'joy', 'ignorance' and our 'restricted being'. To gain liberation, the individual must realize and overcome these obstacles through one, or a variation of, the 'Four Paths' of 'yoga'.

Yoga derives from the English word 'yoke', and means a process of uniting through discipline – but uniting with what? Answer: God, through which the finite is broken. Hence, yoga is a disciplined form of training required to form ultimate oneness with God.

As to the Four Paths of yoga, the first is juana yoga, or the path to God through 'knowledge'. Knowledge is approached through reflection in order to realize the infinite self of the soul. Alternatively, the individual can use bhakti yoga, which is the path to God through 'love'. Here, the process is to learn to adore God, and through this, finite love dissolves in order to allow a love of the infinite.

Karma yoga is the third of the four paths to God, and is the way through 'work'. Here, work constitutes a cause in the world and, as karma tells us, causes from work are good and result in good effects, which bring you closer to God. However, the fourth path to God is substantially different to the other three. Whereas knowledge, love and work can be seen as paths to God within the finite world, the fourth path, or raja yoga ('raja' meaning 'royal'), deals directly with the infinite and requires personal experience of it through 'psychological experimentation'.

There are eight steps to raja yoga. Step one requires abstention from injury, lying, stealing, sensuality and greed. In other words, the person must learn to be pure within the finite world. Step two involves observances, which are essentially cleanliness, contentment, self-control, studiousness, and the ability to contemplate the divine.

Step three moves on from essentially social requirements to the human body, for once the person is pure in a social sense, he must learn to stop the body from distracting the mind, in order to allow contemplation. This is achieved by learning the 'lotus position', perhaps the most famous element of yoga.

Once adopted, step four requires control of the breath, for this bodily function can distract the mind. Breathing exercises thus regulate breath in order to allow greater concentration, which allows the experiencer – now known as a 'yogi' – to turn completely to his mind.

Step five involves an even greater form of concentration in order to liberate the mind from the external senses. Hence, the yogi must learn not to see, not to hear, not to touch, not to smell, and not to taste. Once this is achieved, the yogi is left alone with his mind. But as step six identifies, the mind itself is chaotic.

To overcome this chaos, the yogi must learn to ignore the repressed thoughts of his own unconscious mind. Having already come to terms with himself in his physical existence, he must now self-analyse himself in a psychological sense, exorcizing all his inner turmoil and inner emotion. We know this process today as psychoanalysis. Sadly, in the West, even when it is attempted, we still require an outside 'analyst'. Yogis have been carrying out a more refined form of analysis for millennia – a process, you may recall, that Carl Jung strove to do continually throughout his life.

Once personal and unconscious idiosyncrasies have been sorted out, step seven requires a totally empty mind to concentrate totally upon an object. It does not matter what this object is. It does not even have to exist, but can be imagined. But whatever it is, it must totally and absolutely fill the mind, thus guaranteeing complete concentration, with no stray personal thoughts whatsoever.

Once this is achieved, step eight, known as 'samadhi', can be attempted. Here, the object must also vanish, leaving the mind empty and withdrawn from the finite world. In this state, the formless world of the infinite floods in, and the yogi becomes a 'knower' of the total being of God.

What has actually happened within this process? First of all, the yogi has achieved a trance state – he has achieved, through practice, shamanic abilities. Above all else, he has achieved the state by, first, annihilating the outside world, and second, annihilating himself. He has sought out God through moving outside his personal mind and entering an infinite realm of psychological existence, suggesting that the God-force of Hinduism is a deeper, more communal mind-level.

Here we can see almost exact parallels with Carl Jung. By spending a lifetime in a psychological search for the divine, he found it in his own deeper mind, finally achieving it by annihilating his psychological self. He identified this deeper mind as the 'collective unconscious', an infinite mind state that filters down to create culture and society, and regulates the actual psychological idio-syncrasies of the individual.

Is this the superconscious through which the paranormal manifests? We can gain a greater understanding of the process by looking to the religion that was birthed out of Hindu culture: the religion of Buddhism.

The Buddha

■ Buddhism is very much the philo-sophy of one man, known as the Buddha. The name actually means to be 'awake', and that is how Buddha described himself. He was awake, while all other people were not. He had gained knowledge of the absolute, infinite reality, while all others lived in a drab, finite world.

Buddha – born Siddhartha Gautama – was a prince of a small Indian king-dom, believed to have been born around 560 BC. At the age of 16 he married a neighbouring princess, who bore him a son called Rahula. However, his father had been aware for years that he was no ordinary prince. Soon after his birth, prophets had been called to offer his future, but their prophecies contained a crossroads in his life. If he succeeded his father, he would unify India. However, if he did not, he would become a world redeemer.

His father thus vowed that nothing would distract Siddhartha from court life, guaranteeing that he would succeed him. Palaces and women were therefore thrust upon him, and his father decreed that no nastiness would ever enter his life. Even when he travelled away from his palaces, guards would ride ahead of him, clearing any sight that might disrupt the path of destiny his father had chosen.

As might be expected, not everything went according to plan, and one day Siddhartha was troubled when, for the first time in his life, he saw an old, gaunt and gnarled man. Some time later he saw a diseased person lying at the road-side, and on another occasion he saw a corpse. Wondering what to make of ageing, disease and death, on a fourth occasion he met a shaven-headed monk, who told Siddhartha that he had seen how the effects of the body meant fulfil-ment could never come on the physical plane of existence but only by renounc-ing the world.

Suddenly physical pleasures became unimportant to Siddhartha, and one night, when he was 29 years old, he crept out of the palace and left his family to seek the truth of existence. Shaving his head and donning rags, he went into the forest and started his search. It lasted six years, beginning when he sought out two Hindu masters, in order to learn. Leaving them, he joined a band of ascetics, who thought the body hindered absolute truth. Subsequently, he nearly starved himself to death. However, the experience taught him that asceticism hindered the search for truth as much as his previous indulgences had, and this led him to adopt what became known as the 'middle way', searching for truth by way of deep thought and mystical concentration.

One evening, sensing that his search was nearing completion, he sat down by a bo tree and vowed that he would not get up until he had realized his goal. As the night progressed, Mara, the 'evil one', attempted to break his concentration by first offering him dancing girls, and then showering him with flaming rocks. But Siddhartha was not to be distracted, and as the sun rose the following morning, he achieved the 'great awakening'. His mind descended totally into itself, and the outside world disappeared, leaving the essence of the true being within. At this point, Siddhartha psychologically annihilated himself as 'enlightenment' was achieved, and henceforth he was Buddha, the awakened one.

For the rest of his life he worked and preached to form Buddhism. In a social sense, it was a natural progression from Hinduism, for Buddha spoke out against the corruptions of the caste system, but it also refined Hinduism, offering a new and refreshing philosophy.

Buddha spoke of the Four Noble Truths. First of all, he identified suffering. People suffered in life, and this caused their troubles. But why did people suffer? They suffered because, in not realizing the reality of the world, people 'miss the mark' and live life out of joint with how it should be lived.

Why do people miss the mark? Because of the Second Noble Truth, which is desire. Desire is egotistic, in that it involves personal fulfilment. This locks us into our own identities, making individualism of prime importance and ignoring the wider world of interaction with others and our surroundings. Such an attitude leads to dislocation, with each individual trapped and imprisoned by their own body and ego.

The Third Noble Truth is a natural extension of the second, in that desire is caused by our selfish cravings. By wanting only the things that fulfil us individually, we seek only what we desire, thus locking us into suffering.

As for the Fourth Noble Truth, this is the way out of suffering, desire and craving, and requires us to release ourselves from the narrow, myopic ways of self-interest and realize the infinity of universal life. This is achieved by following the 'Eightfold Path', which constitutes right views, right intention, right speech, right action, right livelihood, right effort, right mindfulness and right concentration.

In essence, this is a restatement of the Path of Renunciation of Hinduism, but without the cultural clutter. Based upon the eradication of suffering, desire and craving, it takes the person through social codes – live morally, and do not kill, steal, lie or be unchaste – approaches an understanding of a beneficent psychological state and, in right concentration, repeats the requirements of raja yoga. However, when it comes to the state achievable through meditation, Buddha offered quite a few surprises.

Of particular importance was the way Buddha described it exactly by using ambiguity. The state is known as 'nirvana', which means 'to extinguish'. This suggests that nirvana is, in actual fact, nothing, but while it can be seen as nothing in an atheistic sense, it is also 'eternal and incomprehensible peace', the 'real Truth and the supreme Reality'. Yet if it is truth and reality, how can it be nothing? This paradox extends to Buddha's understanding of the soul, which, while bowing to the requirements of reincarnation, does not, to Buddha, exist. What is going on here?

The best way to understand the Buddhist form of continuance – that is, the 'soul' – is to see it as a wave. A wave rises and exists for a moment, then on coming into the shore, it breaks up and annihilates itself. The wave no longer exists, but has become part of the sea once more, no longer identifiable as a wave. As the tide comes again, that wave will again become identifiable, but it won't be the same wave made of the same water molecules.

The notion of reincarnation can be seen as the sea which gives rise to the wave. Reincarnation exists and produces a life lived as a wave. When a wave, it has identity and purpose, but in the wave crashing ashore, or the person dying, that identity and purpose extinguishes itself. Hence, when the wave, or life, rises again, it is different, having none of the idiosyncrasies of the previous wave, or life.

This idea was socially significant. Unlike in Hinduism, redemption could not come in a future life, for that future incarnation bore no personal resemblance to the previous one. There was no moral cop-out in Buddhism. Here, the individual was responsible *in the present life* for everything he did, and could only approach nirvana in the present life, too. There was no wheel of rebirth in a personal sense.

Most theorizers leave an understanding of the Buddhist non-personal soul here, but this is a mistake, for what was Buddha really saying? In essence, he was taking away the cultural supernatural. In this sense, Buddhism *was* atheistic, for Buddha realized that to really get to know reality, you had to take away the cultural idiosyncrasies that polluted it. Hence, Buddhism was formulated as being devoid of authority, devoid of ritual, held no speculations, shunned traditions, relied solely on self-effort, and had no supernatural qualities whatsoever. If Buddha was to come back today and see the statues that were later erected in his image, he would be dismayed, for they prove that his message was misunderstood.

Buddha aimed to remove culture from the world, for he realized that the ultimate reality was *above* culture, and that all supernatural expressions were pollutions of that reality, based on the societal and psychological idiosyncrasies of the people. This is why Buddha's explanation of nirvana was exact in its ambiguity, for if he had described it, he would have given licence for cultural interpretation, and that is exactly what he didn't want.

But what can we identify of nirvana from the Buddha's teachings? In its meaning 'to extinguish', we can see both nirvana and, indeed, the ultimate destination of the 'soul' as a state devoid of historical or personal expression, a place beyond culture. But in its being 'truth' and 'ultimate reality', we can see an obvious existence, but of a significantly different order to the finite reality of the world in which we live. Some class it as 'total realization', which gives a valuable hint, for while Buddha rightly kept his mouth shut concerning what he experienced, others have spoken quite openly about the amazing world lying deep down inside the mind.

Mystical Experience

■ The final destination of the deep, meditative state associated with raja yoga is the mystical experience. No experience, it is said, is more profound than this. Generally understood as an experience that transcends normal consciousness, it provides the experiencer with an insight beyond time, space and that which is classed as physical. To physicist Raynor Johnson, normal consciousness is an appreciation of the world seen through five narrow slits in a tower, whereas a mystical experience allows us to view the landscape through a gaping hole in the roof.

Sometimes occurring spontaneously, at others brought on by various forms of meditation, drugs or sensory deprivation, the experience offers amazing insights into the true nature of the world. As R. M. Bucke wrote in 1901 in his book *Cosmic Consciousness* (see Bibliography), describing his first experience in 1872:

> ... there came upon me a sense of exultation, of immense joyousness accompanied or immediately followed by an intellectual illumination impossible to describe. Among other things, I did not merely come to believe, but I saw that the universe is not composed of dead matter but is, on the contrary, a living Presence; I became conscious in myself of eternal life ...

We can immediately see the separation here between the finite and the infinite. Yet we can also see the obvious religious implications of the experience. Indeed, it has been sought and incorrectly understood throughout all religions, and is believed to transport the person to a spiritual realm. To Zen Buddhists the state is known as 'satori', to Sufis it is 'fana', and as we have seen, yogis describe it as 'samadhi'.

Even in a less mystical religion such as Christianity, mystics such as St Teresa of Avila went in search of the state. She wrote of the 'orison' of union, where the soul awakes to the presence of God, a state St Paul described as 'the peace that passeth understanding'. Yet the experience is far more common than we might at first assume.

British polls carried out in 1978 and 1979, and published in the *Journal for the Scientific Study of Religion*, showed that 56 per cent of churchgoers could identify a mystical experience in their lives. Later, in 1987, the National Opinion Research Centre in Chicago showed that 43 per cent of adult Americans had also experienced this ecstatic state. Indeed, in 1969 the biologist Sir Alister Hardy founded the Religious Experience Research Unit at Oxford University, and they have collected over 4,000 case studies which transcend age, education, sex, geography and cultural background. The state, it seems, is universal.

Not all experiences are as profound as R. M. Bucke's, however. Indeed, most spontaneous experiences are mild, if nonetheless intuitive. Usually occurring when the individual is in a relaxed state of mind, they have been described by writer G. K. Chesterton as 'absurd good news', and the American psychologist William James referred to a feeling of 'aha' – the feeling when we suddenly see something in a new light.

Humanistic psychologist Abraham Maslow named these mild states 'peak experiences'. They are a sudden intuitive joyousness, a realization of new possibilities. He gave several examples of the state. Typically, a soldier returning from a theatre of war sees some women for the first time in many months and suddenly realizes that women are different from men. Similarly, a wife and mother is providing breakfast for her family just as she has done countless times, but suddenly, watching them, she realizes how lucky she is.

Such cases give a hint as to what lies behind the experience. Clearly women did not change in any physical way after the soldier's insight, and the family experienced by the wife and mother behaved just as they had done in the past. Rather, the experience is fuelled by a personal emotional awareness. A little piece of the experiencer's inner self explodes upon reality, offering a glimpse of a new emotional outlook, and a part of the inner self that is not part of the physical world.

For instance, we experience the physical world through our five physical senses, but these do not *fully* describe the world. The beauty of a rose cannot be experienced – we can see it and we can smell it, but these provide no aesthetic quality. The *feeling* of beauty comes from within, from an emotional centre that does not belong to the physical world, and it is this emotional centre that lies at the heart of the mystical experience, placing emotion above the limited vistas of the senses. But of course, in its full splendour, the experience is much more than this, as R. M. Bucke makes clear. Indeed, such a state can be seen as far removed from normal, waking consciousness, and with the English chemist Humphrey Davy's discovery of nitrous oxide, or laughing gas, in 1800, investigation of the state began.

Davy can be classed as the first of a number of experimental mystics who purposely induced the mystical experience with the use of such drugs. He wrote: 'I existed in a world of newly connected and newly modified ideas. I theorized. I imagined. I made discoveries.' In the mystical experience, it seems, we have access to a greater intellect. Yet, as Peter Roget, author of the famous thesaurus, soon realized: 'My ideas succeeded one another with extreme rapidity, thoughts rushed like a torrent through the mind, as if their velocity had been suddenly accelerated by the bursting of a barrier.'

Experimental mystic P. D. Ouspensky highlighted this factor – this problem – with great effect in his book *A New Model of the Universe* (see Bibliography). His insights came so fast that 'I could not find words . . . which would enable me to remember what had occurred even for myself, still less to convey it to somebody else.' He realized that everything was linked together, that everything is connected to something else: 'in order to describe the first impressions, the first sensations, it is necessary to describe *all* at once.' Such was the flood of impressions, of intuitions, of meaning, that in the state 'A man can go mad from one ash tray.'

Experimental mystic R. H. Ward came upon a similar problem, described in his book *A Drug Taker's Notes* (see Bibliography): 'I knew, I understood, I actually was, far more than I normally knew, understood and was.' Existing in a 'region of ideas', he wrote: 'I saw the meaning; the meaning, that is, of the universe, of life on earth, and of man.' But when he came to place this meaning in words, he found himself writing: 'Within and within and within and within'. The sheer flood of meaning was so much that it was beyond expression, the essence lost within that previously mentioned emotional centre.

How do we account for such an emotional and intuitive experience? First of all, we should rationalize the state, which William James attempted to do. For him, the experience held intuition and knowledge beyond mere intellect as

presently understood. They are states of 'feeling', in which time becomes imma-
terial. The experience can last a mere few seconds in linear time, yet it appears
eternal. And finally, thought James, the state swept the individual away, to
become aware of the presence of a superior power.

Is this the 'nirvana' that Buddha realized? Does the insinuation of infinity, of
absolute knowledge, of annihilation of the self, of intuition regarding a superi-
or being suggest it is the same thing? Carl Jung felt the mystical experience
involved a liberation of the unconscious. Alternatively, many scientists feel the
experience is more physical, induced by electrical stimulation of the temporal
lobes. For instance, in the 1930s neurosurgeon Wilder Penfield stimulated
mystical-like experiences in this way in epileptics.

The psychiatrist Eugene d'Aquili looks for explanation within the split-brain
concept. We know that the left and right cerebral hemispheres of the brain have
different functions – the left is essentially logical in nature, while the right is
seen as the seat of emotion (see page 41). We look upon the physical world
through the left brain. Thus, argues d'Aquili, the mystical experience is a transition to looking at the world through the more emotional right brain.

However, while such an idea explains the emotional element of the experience, it fails to tackle the 'wholeness' of the state – the literal invasion of ideas,
and the way they swamp the experiencer, as if they really have tuned in to the
very essence of the universe. This feeling of 'wholeness' does, however, bear an
uncanny similarity to the nature of the universe theorized by physicist David
Bohm.

In his *Wholeness and the Implicate Order* (see Bibliography), Bohm tells us of
an interconnected universe – a holographic universe – where everything within
it is linked together, where every particle within it is an expression of the whole;
a universe in which the part and the whole are one and the same, with the
universe bending in upon itself, annihilating space as we know it and becoming
a single entity. Could this universe be what is appreciated in the mystical
experience?

Material science would say no. Consciousness is a product of the individual
brain – a firing of physical neurones that have no connection with a wider reality outside the individual. However, some scientists are beginning to challenge
this reductionist idea. Principal among them is mathematician Roger Penrose,
who offers intriguing possibilities. For instance, it has been noted that an individual cell has a distinct cytoskeleton within it made up of tiny microtubules. It
is argued that these microtubules can act as minute on/off switches, forming a
circuit similar to that found in a computer. But of most significance is the fact
that these microtubules are so small that they could interact with, and amplify,

quantum effects. If this is proved to be so, then a real universal property could indeed invade the mind, thus explaining the wholeness of the mystical experience. In a real sense, we could well have access to the essence of the universe, transforming experience and allowing oneness with the supreme power of our enigmatic cosmos.

The theories of David Bohm and Roger Penrose are not generally acceptable to the scientific community as a whole. The central reason for this is that their acceptance would require a complete rethink of the current scientific world view. Such a change requires a new theory within which to relate the existing world view to a more holistic concept.

As with all ground-breaking new theories, this is unlikely to come from the scientific establishment. Epoch-making new theories have always come from rebels outside the establishment, and usually from a train of thought totally removed from the established view. Studies of the paranormal can be seen here as offering a glimmer of hope for that new theory.

In the above we can see ideas beginning to shape up of a real holistic universe – an information universe – where the totality of everything within the universe is expressed in every individual part of it. Hence, each particle *is* the universe – on an information level at least. Through the cytoskeleton of the neurone we have an additional indicator. For it allows that total information of the universe, at a quantum level, to invade the mind and thus bring quantum effects into the real world of human experience. Could this be the 'mechanism' through which my suggested superconscious works? Let us compare such an idea with the idiosyncrasies of the superconscious I have highlighted so far.

If this is the superconscious, then it would have to be above culture. Invading us through microtubules, this quantum effect is not only above culture, but above the totality of humanity.

If this is the superconscious, then it would have to exist deep down in the mind. Microtubules are an inner component of cellular constructions such as neurones. As such, they would be accessed through the deep mind.

If this is the superconscious, then it would have to affect the mind unconsciously, resulting in instincts and archetypal images. It is valid to say that, being a 'mechanism', this outside invasion *would* be a continual unconscious process. Hence, instincts and archetypal controls could unconsciously direct us from some deep, universal centre.

If this is the superconscious, then it must allow for information to invade the mind from outside that individual mind, thus allowing for possessions and information input suggestive of telepathy or clairvoyance. According to Bohm, this quantum reality would allow for all properties of the universe to exist in every part of the universe. We, as individuals, are part of the universe, and would thus have access to this totality, as best expressed in the total knowledge capacity of the mystical experience.

If this is the superconscious, then it would have to allow for psychokinetic abilities to change the nature of reality. We have already noted the importance of consciousness in ordering the reality we experience. While this is, at the moment, an idiosyncrasy locked in the quantum world, the possibility of quantum effects breaking out into the world of experience through microtubules would allow consciousness a role in changing probabilities in our world.

The above is highly suggestive that a superconscious could well be a reality. In moving on now to a study of paranormal phenomena concerned with divination, we can advance our understanding of its effects in the real world, and move closer to an overall theory that would explain the superconscious in terms of the existing scientific world view.

· DIVINATION ·

Forms of Divination

■ Divination is the occult science of foretelling the future or discerning a fact by supernatural means. There are many variations on the technique, including fortune telling, contacting spirits for direct communication, knowledge through various oracles, or character analysis.

Fortune telling, or scrying, is perhaps the most popular form of divination, involving concentration on an object to bring about a trance state through which information fills the mind. The object is often a crystal ball, and the technique involves many of the principles of raja yoga.

Where scrying can be seen to be genuine, we can imagine the diviner connecting with the superconscious and thus gaining information based on the hopes and wishes of the client rather than an exact future. However, in most cases basic psychology can offer a better explanation for the ability. Today, we know that the individual constantly gives out signals known as 'body language', and rather than being a supernatural talent, we can see the scryer as a natural reader of such signals.

Character analysis can equally be grounded in human psychology. The most popular method today is 'graphology', and is based upon an analysis of handwriting in order to divine the personal characteristics of the writer. Again, rather than having any supernatural air, we can see graphologists as people who can intuit character from writing styles. The practice is a marvellous indicator of subliminal forms of psychoanalysis, but devoid of any supernatural quality.

Similarly, divination through communication with spirits presents little problem for analysis. We have already seen (see pages 86–7), with the Delphic Oracle, how such divination in times past can better be seen as a form of political analysis, where the diviner uses psychological possession to give authority to the practice. Where any form of 'supernatural' is involved, we can refer to scrying, and suggest that the superconscious is accessed in trance states in order to intuit the hopes and fears of the client.

Oracles do, however, present a problem. There are two general forms of oracle divination. The first seeks out the future through the reading of signs upon the body. Here, the most popular form is palmistry, where the lines of the hand give indications of your path through life. One personal anecdote will provide an indication of how easily people can become hooked on it. In my early years, several amateur palmists read my palm and told me that I would live long but would have a particularly long illness in mid-life. I belong to a long-lived family, but at the age of 27 I came down with that enigmatic condition ME, now known as CFS or chronic fatigue syndrome. I'm 42 as I write, and still afflicted with it. If this is coincidence, it is a remarkable one.

The second oracle form presents even greater difficulties. The most common forms are the I Ching and the Tarot pack, and practitioners claim to be able to offer indications of the future through the chance tossing of objects or the turn of a card.

An ancient Chinese form of divination, the I Ching is based on the principles of Taoism. Tao, which means 'way', is an holistic philosophy which sees everything in the world as connected, and constantly subject to change. In this respect, time and space do not exist as understood in western terms. There is no definite past, present and future as distinctly separate things. In this sense, the future can be part of the present. Hence, with the I Ching the diviner offers 'possibilities' to guide the individual and allow them to have a real effect on the future.

Within this holistic and timeless world are two contradictory forces, which must be placed in balance. The first is 'yin', a passive, essentially female force; the second is 'yang', a more fiery, essentially male force.

To gain indications of the future, the diviner tosses 50 yarrow sticks, or three coins three times. Their fall produces a 'hexagram', which can be read by consulting the *Book of Changes*, which contains philosophical writings. The hexagram itself constitutes a pattern of solid and broken lines. The broken lines represent 'yin' and the solid lines 'yang'.

The system of the I Ching is believed to have been first devised by the Chinese emperor Fu Shi around 2850 BC. Lao-tzu was inspired by it in the sixth century BC when he formulated the central text of Taoism, and the I Ching was also important to Confucius soon after when he formulated Confucianism, adding commentaries of his own to the divinatory practice. The system was relatively unknown in the West until the nineteenth century, when practitioners

James Legge and Richard Wilhelm translated it into German, and eventually English. The I Ching continues to gain adherents in the West year by year.

The Tarot is much younger than the I Ching. The word is a French derivative of the Italian *tarocchi*, meaning 'triumphs', or 'trumps'. The actual pack consists of 78 cards divided into two parts. The Major Arcana, or trumps, has 22 cards, representing elements such as fortune, death, wisdom and so on. The Minor Arcana has 56 cards, representing a standard card playing deck with an additional picture card – the page – in each suit. The Tarot suits are wands, swords, cups and pentacles.

Tarot cards are read by shuffling them and laying them out in chance order. An enquirer asks a question, and the dealer will turn a card and intuit a possible answer, usually by consulting one of the dozens of books written to aid interpretation. Each card has a distinct meaning in its own right, but in addition the final layout can also be used for overall indications of the future direction the enquirer should take.

The early history of the Tarot is unknown, but one school of thought believes it was brought to Europe by gypsies. The earliest known deck, which contains just 17 cards, is kept in the Bibliothèque Nationale in Paris. They were created in 1392 by the painter Jacquemin Gringonneur for Charles VI of France. A full deck was known to be in existence 30 years later, painted by the Italian artist Bonifacio Bembo.

By the late fifteenth century, the Tarot was scorned, becoming known as the 'devil's picturebook'. By this time it was very much an 'occult' system, and popular recognition did not come until 1910. In that year, English occultist Arthur Edward Waite published his version of the Tarot, with images designed by occultist Pamela Colman Smith. While many variations of the Tarot exist today, the Rider-Waite deck, as it has become known, is still the most popular.

Where do the Tarot images come from? An exact answer is not known, but while the Tarot deck is relatively new – having been around only for about 500 years – the images are thought of as very ancient indeed. For instance, the eighteenth-century French Egyptologist Antoine Court de Gebelin thought the images came from the ancient Egyptian *Book of Thoth*. Nineteenth-century French occultist Eliphas Levi traced the images to the Hebrew alphabet, while Waite himself saw them as a blend of images from both the cabbala and Hermetic philosophy, tracing them back to Hermes Trismegistos. However, many Jungian psychologists regard the images as representing archetypal figures from the collective unconscious; in this way, the images invade the card reader's mind in such a way that the life pattern of the enquirer becomes known.

Such an idea fits in with scrying, in that the images cause access to the superconscious in order to intuit the hopes and dreams of the enquirer. In this way, the images assist the unconscious mind of the reader to open up to the collective unconscious. The Tarot reading thus becomes a form of 'supernatural' psychoanalysis. However, it is difficult to see such a system at work in the random tossing of yarrow sticks in the I Ching.

Another problem with all forms of divination is that even if we accept that such systems tap into the hopes and dreams of the enquirer, how does this relate to the future reality? The way we progress in life can, indeed, be due to our own wishes, but all too often, fate – whether controlled or chaotic – intervenes from outside the individual's control to offer direction. If the I Ching and Tarot are to be taken at face value, then the suggestion is that these 'outside' interventions can be realized before they happen.

Such an idea breaks the 'law of causality', which states that a cause must come before an effect of the cause. If divination is to be accepted, then we have also to accept that knowledge of an effect can be gleaned before the cause. However, some theorists negate this problem by putting the future effects of divination down to the puzzling intervention of coincidence.

Coincidence

■ 'Coincidence' is a magic word. It is invoked with absolute authority and conviction by the most unmagical people imaginable, yet when they use the word it offers a degree of stability and comfort that echoes the absolute conviction of a religious fundamentalist. The word speaks 'truth', in all its inescapable clarity.

Who are the people who use – and believe in – this magic word? They are known as sceptics, and whenever a paranormal event takes place they cling to their materialist safety by explaining the event with its use. 'This event,' they herald with all the authority in the world, 'was a coincidence.' Subject closed. Subject explained. Subject swept under the threadbare carpet.

The problem with this simple, reductionist view is easy to highlight. No one knows what a coincidence is, and having no explanation, its use turns a sceptic into a believer in the paranormal. For in essence, that person has explained a mystery with a paradox.

The *Oxford Dictionary* defines coincidence as a 'notable concurrence of events or circumstances without apparent causal connection'. And they can be quite bizarre. Here are a couple of examples.

The scientist Camille Flammarion was busy working on a manuscript when a gust of wind caught the pages and blew them out of the open window. At that point it began to rain. He realized that the pages would be ruined, so he left them. A few days later, the chapter that had blown out of the window arrived through the post from the printers. It seems that a worker from the printers was passing the window as the pages landed on the ground, picked them up, assuming that *he* had dropped them, and took them to work. The subject of the chapter was the wind.

In 1967 a London police station received a new telephone number: 40116. A constable asked a friend to call him during duty hours the following evening, but he got the number wrong. He said 40166. That evening, while on patrol, the constable observed a light on in a factory and went to investigate. As he arrived, the phone rang. He picked it up and found it was his friend ringing as requested. The ex-directory number of the factory was 40166.

Sometimes coincidental events can build up to almost cataclysmic proportions. For instance, on 24 August 1983, the Amtrak Silver Meteor train began its normal journey from Miami to New York. At 7.40 p.m. the train struck and killed a woman fishing from a bridge. Sixteen miles further on it destroyed a truck parked too close to the track. At 1.10 a.m. it hit a tractor-trailer on a crossing, derailing two passenger cars and injuring 21 people. Continuing its journey an hour later, at 2.37 a.m. it ran headlong into a car that had ignored warning lights on another crossing. At this point the rest of the journey was cancelled.

That irascible collector of anomalies Charles Fort suggested that a 'cosmic joker' was behind such coincidences. The ancient Greek father of medicine, Hippocrates, argued that 'sympathetic elements' had a tendency to seek each other out. English writer Arthur Koestler considered them 'puns of destiny'. The world answerable to mathematics has a predilection to throw up coincidences from time to time. Grounded in the laws of chance, a coincidental event is bound to happen, and has the same probability of happening as any other event, but Koestler felt that some coincidences were so 'meaningful' that something more had to be going on.

Science would class this attitude as nothing more than wishful thinking, for if chance allows for coincidence, then there is no need to 'invent' other factors to explain it. Which is all very well except for the awkward fact that, as with coincidence, 'chance' is beyond understanding by science.

It is here that coincidence meets divination. Chance, in its literal sense, means the way in which a fortuitous circumstance occurs. The process is accidental, in that no overall system exists or can be deduced from the chaotic nature of the universe. In this sense, universal forces are blind, and beyond understanding, for no pattern can be gleaned from chaos.

Such an understanding of chance began to rise some 400 years ago, with our growing scientific world view. Prior to this, the universe had no place for chance, for everything was ordered by God. In this sense, the universe was meaningful, but with the scientific banishing of God, His meaning had also to be banished. This left a huge intellectual black hole which had to be filled, and it was filled by chaos and the principle of non-understanding. Delete 'God', insert 'chance' – and no matter which you choose, both are articles of faith, for both are considered beyond ultimate understanding.

However, if you are not prepared to accept articles of faith, then you cannot accept the 'accidental' nature of chance. This leaves you with the puzzling possibility of order in the universe, and it is this order that divination is thought to tap, somehow offering understanding of how coincidental events will fall.

Austrian biologist Paul Kammerer had a long-term fascination with the 'ordered' possibilities of coincidence and chance. He would spend his spare time in public places recording, and later classifying, the events he saw. He grouped people into categories and noted how 'patterns' developed in 'clusters' of almost repeatable activity. He decided that such clusters were natural, but not necessarily causal, at least not in a meaningful sense understandable in terms of human interaction. Rather, they bowed, he thought, to some as-yet-unknown mathematical law, which constituted a 'law of seriality'.

Zoologist Sir Alister Hardy saw a similar process at work in the natural world. In particular, he noted the adaptive colours of many life forms which held survival value, in that they allowed perfect camouflage. Such colourings and markings could not have been produced by the individual life form itself, but had to be geared to some form of outside influence which could be seen as both meaningful and coincidental.

Famed ufologist Jacques Vallée was also aware of a form of underlying reality that organized the world through coincidental action. He thought of it as analogous to a form of computer retrieval system. In a library, we tend to store information, or books, in alphabetical order. A computer, however, works differently. Information is stored in a randomized database; to extract it, we input a 'keyword', and all information suggested by the word is retrieved. Vallée saw coincidental action in a similar way. A seemingly chance event occurs, and the underlying reality of the world throws up similarities to the event, thus causing a coincidence, or cluster of coincidental actions.

Of course, none of these speculations offer the slightest hint of an actual reality to coincidence as an ordered, or meaningful, event. No theory is offered here that can fit a definite scientific reality. But what they do tell us is that a feeling of unease is abroad in the world when we approach the unfathomable reality of chance, and such a feeling can only truly exist when the established explanation is shot full of holes. Indeed, established ideas on chance fall far short of a 'theory' in themselves. But is a theory of coincidence actually achievable?

Possibly. And in order to approach understanding, we need to look at the most popular, and apparently inexplicable, form of divination of all. This, of course, is astrology – the belief that the movements of celestial objects coincidentally reflect the movement through life of the individual.

Astrology

■ Few occult systems have caused as much controversy as astrology. For many, it rules their life, the person having complete faith in its machinations, while others are convinced that the whole thing is bunkum. Yet, as with many occult systems, the truth of the matter most likely rests in the middle ground, within the strange, magnificent limbo land between belief and incredulity.

The word 'astrology' can have many interpretations, but the basic Greek meaning of 'the study of heavenly bodies' seems to sum it up best. In a nutshell, astrology is governed by the belief that events in the heavens can reflect events upon Earth; or, as coined by the ancient magician, Hermes Trismegistos: 'As above, so below'.

It has been pointed out that God could well have been the first great astrologer. Genesis 1:14 makes it clear that astrology is fundamental to the universe: 'Let there be lights in the firmament of the heavens . . . and let them be for *signs* and for the seasons' (my italics). From then until now, astrology has fascinated millions. For instance, in 1976 the subject was thought to be of sufficient importance for 186 scientists, including 18 Nobel Laureates, to issue a statement declaring astrology to be totally without scientific merit.

However, such scientists are fighting a losing battle. A year earlier, a Roper Poll commissioned by the *National Enquirer* newspaper in the United States showed that 45 per cent of Americans polled believed in astrology. By the time of a Gallup poll in 1978, this had dropped to 29 per cent, but polls before and since have made it clear that the belief will simply not go away, no matter how hard scientists try to make it. Indeed, a bit of investigative journalism on job discrimination by the *Washington Post* newspaper in 1974 showed that at least two US Congressmen were prejudiced against 'water signs': Scorpios, Pisceans and Cancerians stood no chance of a job here.

My own wife, who is otherwise non-discriminatory and even a practising

Christian, has an aversion to Scorpios. When we first met, she asked for my star sign. 'Aries,' I replied. 'Oh, that's all right, then.' We have seven children, who were all born between 19 January and 20 June, so giving no possibility of them being born Scorpios. Three of them have their birthdays in the same week – 25, 27 and 30 April – which is exactly the opposite time of year from Scorpio. This, however, was not fortuitous coincidence, but planning.

Perhaps the most remarkable point concerning the success of astrology is the fact that it has survived for millennia without any form of overall organizational body. Religions such as Christianity have survived only because of huge and all-powerful organizational structures thrusting the system into the heart of national culture. Many religions with less power and influence simply fizzle out. Yet throughout its history astrology has had to fight national culture and has never achieved a large organizational structure. Even today it survives as little more than a ragtag cottage industry, with astrologers maintaining their independence from each other. In fact, so successful has it been in its chaotic state that in 1978 a full 1,200 of America's 1,750 major newspapers carried horoscopes.

There are many misconceptions concerning astrology. Foremost among these is the idea that astrological systems can predict a definite future. This is not so. Rather, astrology can be seen as a form of guide for life, offering indications but not definites. As many astrologers point out: 'The stars impel; they do not compel.'

There are, in fact, two major systems within astrology, known as 'natural' and 'judicial' astrology. Natural astrology was concerned with the charting of the heavens and devising numerical tables in order to predict the future positions of heavenly bodies. In days gone by, this system was the jealously guarded domain of priests. The forerunner of astronomy, its astrological secrets offered great influence, allowing the priests to predict such things as when spring would arrive, allowing farmers to sow their seed. As agriculture was vital to such early civilizations, foreknowledge of the yearly cycles gave priests power and influence equal to that of kings.

As our knowledge of the cycles of heavenly bodies increased, judicial astrology came into being. Dependent upon natural astrology, judicial astrology was concerned with more than simple seasonal cycles. Instead of just observing, priests began to relate the movement of heavenly bodies to the lives, hopes and ambitions of human beings. By asking questions concerning birth, the positions of heavenly bodies at that time could be noted, and as a life continued, the ongoing movement of heavenly bodies could perhaps offer indications of where a particular life was heading. First used to further a priest's power by offering indications of a king's future, it was not long before the idea grew that the heavenly bodies actually linked up with a person's ongoing life pattern, and once this system was in place, astrology as a form of divination was formed.

To provide indications of a person's life, astrology offers a hugely complicated astrological system which dates back 4,000 years to the ancient Babylonians. We know this because astrology is based upon how the stars looked then – which was totally different from how they look now.

As the Earth moves around the sun, it leans its axis of rotation by just over 23 degrees. Because of this, when the northern pole is leaning towards the sun it is summer in the northern hemisphere, and when the southern pole is towards the sun it is winter. This is why we have longer periods of daylight in summer than in winter. However, for two days a year, the poles are balanced, being neither closer to, nor further from the sun. These two 24-hour periods – 20/21 March and 22/23 September – are known as the spring and autumn equinoxes respectively.

Four thousand years ago the sun was in the area of sky known as Aries on the spring equinox. However, the Earth also wobbles, giving the phenomenon known as the 'precession of the equinoxes'. Stated simply, this means that the Earth is always shifting position in relation to the constellations, thus changing the position of the sun at the spring equinox. Thus, 2,000 years after the Babylonians, the sun was in Pisces at the spring equinox, and 2,000 years later still – today – it is moving into Aquarius on the spring equinox. This is what is meant by 'the dawning of the Age of Aquarius', and, as 2,000 years ago we were entering Pisces, explains why the earliest Christian symbol was the fish. In 20,000 year's time the cycle will be complete and the spring equinox sun will again rise in Aries.

The fact that most astrologers continue to see the stars as they were 4,000 years ago and not as they are today has brought a great deal of ridicule upon astrology. The argument goes like this: how can the stars possibly give indications of a person's life today when the star positions being charted are those of 4,000 years ago, thus bearing no similarity to the stars today? However, as soon as you hear this argument, I suggest you groan. The person asking the question has absolutely no knowledge whatsoever of astrology, and is asking the question from a position of ignorance. The simple fact is that, regardless of the fact that we are told we read our 'stars', astrology has nothing to do with the stars at all.

Astrology has to do with the planets – 'planet' being a Greek term meaning 'wanderer'. Initially seven planets were known, these being Mercury, Venus, Mars, Saturn and Jupiter, and – now known not to be planets – the sun and moon. The astrological argument is that these bodies are predictable and unchanging and can be seen as a huge celestial clock. It is the position of these planets in the sky that offers indications of a person's life. The closer the body to Earth, the greater its influence upon the person; the further from the Earth, the more general the influence. In this way, the discovery of further planets such as Pluto, Uranus and Neptune has little influence on the predictions of the astrological clock.

Astrologers soon noticed that the movements of the planets confined themselves to a narrow band of sky, never moving far from the path of the sun, known as the ecliptic. Hence, in order to identify the exact position of the planets at any one moment in time, this narrow band was split into 12 houses, each of which was given the name of the predominant constellation. This system not only gave us the Zodiac with our 12 star signs, but also the 12 months of the year. This is the only purpose of the 'stars' in astrology: they are simply markers to ease the task of the astrologer, and have no bearing at all upon prediction.

Once the correct system of astrology is identified, we can see how the recent mischief-making by the Royal Astronomical Society and their 'discovery' of a thirteenth sign, Ophiuchus, was irrelevant. Astrologers have always known of this constellation in the narrow astrological band, but 360 degrees divided by 13 is 27.692307. If it had been included in the astrological system, we would have had 13 months in the year and the last day of each month would have ended at about three o'clock in the afternoon.

Once adopted, the astrological system can be seen as a well-balanced astronomical system, with planets orbiting clockwise through a narrow band of sky through 12 exact houses of 30 degrees each. This then becomes an exact map, as though all the stars were fixed upon a single transparent sphere, with Earth and man in the centre. The horoscope of the astrologer reflects this heavenly system. Cast to represent a moment in time – usually birth – the horoscope is a circle split into 12 equal sections to represent the Zodiac. A horizontal line drawn through the centre is known as the 'ascendant' and the top of the circle is the 'mid-heaven'. The position of the planets within the horoscope thus becomes known.

However, it is here that scientific credibility leaves the subject, with astrologers offering their own subjective interpretations of the planets, based loosely upon the personality traits said to be existent in each house of the Zodiac.

As far as a definite scientific analysis is concerned, the reasoning behind such interpretations is impossible to fathom. Suffice it to say, however, that no true astrologer would claim to be able to make the sort of detailed general predictions that you will read in the newspapers. The subject is quite simply far more complicated than that, as we shall see.

Astrology has quite a history. Since mankind learned how to think, they built myths upon the 'supernatural' moon and sun. The stars they worshipped as omnipotent gods, investing them with animate attributes. These heavenly forces conspired to dictate the destiny of man, so it was obvious that the early shamans would attempt to wrest a little control over these awesome forces and influences.

Recent anthropological evidence suggests that as early as 32,000 years ago, Cro-Magnon man had begun the process by carving notches in bones to mark the seasons by reading the sky, and it is known that by 2872 BC Sargon of Agade used astrologer-priests to predict the future.

The Babylonians are generally accepted to be the first people in the West to use astrology as a formulated system, although some researchers argue that they were preceded by the earlier Mesopotamian peoples, the Sumerians. Sargon himself was Sumerian, but the question is, was he the exception of the time, or the norm? Clearly the Sumerian successors, the Chaldeans, practised a form of astrology. Installing themselves at the top of ziggurats such as the Biblical Tower of Babel, Chaldean astrologer-priests read the skies and made predictions for their kings. However, it is to the Babylonians we owe the astrological systems used today.

From as early as 700 BC, the Babylonians produced calendars including maps of the Zodiac complete with symbolic animal representations. It was they, too, who split the year into 12 months and the cycle of night and day into 24 hours. And finally, they gave us the all-important 360-degree circle, without which astrology and, indeed, calculation of any sort would be inexact.

However, it was not until 280 BC that the first known school of astrology was set up on the island of Kos by the ancient Greek, Berosos. In fact, without the input of the Greeks, astrology would most probably not have survived. The first to banish the gods through reason, the Greeks were also the first to replace kings with a form of democracy. And, moving with the spirit of the times, it was the Greeks who first opened astrology to the people. Prior to this, only kings could benefit from astrological predictions, but now they became available to all. With the devising of the *horoscopos*, meaning 'I watch that which is rising', astrology became very popular. Then, in the second century AD the Greek scientist Ptolemy gave us the *Tetrabiblos*, cataloguing the heavens for both astronomers and astrologers alike, whom he deemed to be of equal importance.

Of course, astrology was much wider than this. The ancient Egyptians, the Chinese, the Mayans and the Arabic world all practised it. One of the earliest known astrological predictions was that of the Magi, who followed a 'star' to be present at Christ's birth, and in the ninth century AD it was the Arab astrologer

Albumasur who wrote the influential *Introductorium in Astronomiam*, which became the cornerstone of the European revival of astronomy and astrology in the Middle Ages.

As the Middle Ages began, astrology was an accepted element of learning. In 1125 the University of Bologna founded a chair of Astrology, while the subject was taught at Cambridge from 1250. However, as the Scholastic philosophers began to frown upon the subject, and the Inquisition gained in strength, astrology became regarded as generally un-Godly and heretical. This state of affairs was to continue until after the Reformation, when astrologers such as Nostradamus appeared and Queen Elizabeth I began to consult her astrologer-magician, Dr John Dee.

The subject was to take a severe beating once more with the rise of science following Galileo. Reason and experimentation replaced belief and astrology was removed from academe. However, this was more of a conspiracy than a reality, for as scientists such as Kepler and, as we have seen, Newton (see page 106) – devised the modern mechanical view of the universe, both secretly delved into astrology.

The modern explosion of popular astrology began in the late nineteenth century when Richard James Morrison and Robert Cross Smith – known by the pseudonyms 'Zadkiel' and 'Raphael' respectively – began the Astrological Press. A further boost was given when medium Madame Blavatsky founded the Theosophical Society. However, if a defining moment can be offered for its spectacular rise then we must refer to an August 1930 edition of the *Sunday Express*. It was here that, to celebrate the birth of the future queen's younger sister, Princess Margaret, the first printed horoscope appeared in a newspaper – and the rest, as they say, is history. Today, anyone can learn the secrets of the stars simply by picking up the telephone.

Does astrology work? In 1939, a statistical study of astrology was compiled by the Swiss astrologer Karl Ernst Krafft. Examining the birth certificates of thousands of professional men – in particular musicians – he attempted to prove that the positions of the planets at the moment of birth affected temperament, and thus the kind of career an individual would take up. He claimed a high degree of success.

Krafft had followed in the tradition of an earlier astrologer, the Frenchman Paul Choisnard. Choisnard had highlighted what he saw as proof of astrology in a number of planetary relationships. For instance, he found a relationship between the sun and Mars in cases of premature death; the sun and moon seemed to offer relationships to celebrities; and the aspect of Mars was often noted in the natal horoscopes of soldiers. However, in 1950 the young French mathematician Michel Gauquelin decided to attempt the most rigorous statistical analysis yet, principally in order to prove astrology a load of bunkum. France was the ideal place for such an analysis, as it is one of the few countries that requires the time of birth – essential for an exact natal horoscope – to appear on a birth certificate. And his final results converted him.

Comparing some 25,000 horoscopes of professional men from doctors to soldiers, politicians to writers, sportsmen to clerics, he came across significant statistics. Widening his search to include Germany, Italy, the Netherlands and Belgium, statistical proof of astrology continued to rise. For instance, of 3,305 scientists, Mars was found in a significant position on 666 occasions. Chance would dictate only 551. Of 3,142 senior military men, Mars was evident 634 times, against a chance result of 524. And for 1,485 athletes, Mars appeared 327 times against a chance result of just 248.

Gauquelin's results were checked out by the psychologist Professor Hans Eysenck, who was equally shocked by the mounting evidence. Eysenck did some research of his own – noting, for instance, that statistically higher numbers of schizophrenics and manic depressives were born in the first three months of the year – and other researchers echoed Gauquelin's results in the United States and Britain. One particular quirk of the statistics was the fact that the more successful an individual was, the greater the chance of a planetary relationship, suggesting a strong 'fate' element binding the successful individual to the planets.

However, while this mass of statistical evidence seemed conclusive, cracks soon began to appear, coming to a head in 1975 when sceptic Lawrence E. Jerome showed that Gauquelin had misapplied certain probability statistics. When these are applied properly, Gauquelin's evidence is shifted to within chance levels, showing no planetary influences whatsoever.

So is the statistical evidence disproved? This is the greatest debate in astrology. Statistical evidence is always open to interpretation. The system has no exact rules, and while a certain methodology may be 'correct' for Gauquelin, it is 'incorrect' for others. As is usually the case with statistics, the particular statisticians picked the methodology they felt would be most appropriate to 'prove' their own stance. Statistics are without doubt the province of lies, damned lies and politics. In the final analysis, however, for as long as such analyses are open to attack by sceptics, they can never be conclusively valid. Hence, in a logical enquiry, the sceptics have guaranteed that Gauquelin and his ilk must simply be ignored. So is there evidence of planetary influences in other areas of research?

It has long been known that the gravitational pull of the moon and sun affects the tides. Similarly, such gravitational effects are known to exert influences upon the human body. However, these effects are so slight as to be almost unrecordable.

The phases of the moon have been shown to affect emotional tensions within the person – this is where the term 'lunatic' comes from – but it is difficult to see how short-term moon phases can affect a person's entire life from birth.

The sun has been shown to have several specific effects upon the human body. During high sunspot activity, the rate at which albumen curdles in the blood increases, while most magnetic storms, causing radio interference, seem to occur when two or more planets are in line with the sun and Earth.

The electric fields produced by all living organisms have been shown to shift with sunspot activity and moon cycles, and most recently it has been shown that the gravitational effects of moving planets can cause tides within the sun, triggering disturbances that affect Earth's magnetic field. It is tentatively argued that this magnetic influence can affect the highly delicate nervous systems of unborn children, and thus affect personality. This final idea, suggested by astrophysicist Dr Percy Seymour from Plymouth University, offers the best possibility yet for proving a link between the planets and life. Indeed, because of its implications it has been ill received by the scientific community as a whole. However, while seeming to offer evidence, it also highlights a fatal flaw with astrological systems.

Life begins at conception, and Dr Seymour correctly identifies a possible *pre*-natal influence. This is logical: conception is the time at which the life-cycle begins. Birth, on the other hand, is a random event unconnected with conception, yet it is the random birth which seems of most importance in casting a horoscope. This is a serious anomaly that does not bode well for astrology. It is conception, not birth which constitutes the beginning of life, and until astrologers can offer a valid reason why birth should be seen as more important than conception, the subject perhaps deserves the suspicions it receives.

However, there is another explanation to account for the apparent success of astrological systems. The horoscope takes a map of the heavens and places the individual at the centre of it. It elevates us from an insignificant cog in the cosmic creation to the centre of all things, and provides meaning in an otherwise meaningless universe. In providing the horoscope, the celestial plan becomes a map of our own psyche, and with our psyche laid bare, we are open to psychological analysis.

This is the reality of the horoscope. The planets are no longer planets, but Jungian symbols of our own future. They offer a vision of our hopes, our fears, our wants, our dreams. With these laid bare before us, we can analyse our own psyche, plan what we wish to achieve; and in this analysis, we realize where our future direction should be.

However, such a realization can be frightening. To face the future alone is a fearsome thing; hence, the planets offer a path within a universal meaning, so that we are not alone. We take destiny with us, and from the mish-mash of options before us, the path becomes clear. We cling to a fact – an indication in the 'stars' – and plan a course through life, and because of the 'stars', that course opens up and we advance. We thank the 'stars', but all they have really done is given us the confidence to make the future so ourselves. For it *is* we who are the centre of the universe, and perhaps in a greater way than we think.

Life is a process of optimism and pessimism. We advance in line with our mood. Reality is a peculiar thing: imbued with pessimism, it closes before us, offering dead ends to keep us down; yet imbued with optimism, opportunity seems to rule and we advance by fortuitous accident as if the gods had meant it to be. This is fate. Yet it is our fate, not the province of some cosmic master. Astrology is simply the tool which allows us to achieve, ourselves, what we really want to achieve. But perhaps something more.

The universe is laid bare within the quantum field. A world of particles, it is a strange world for us to live in. Principal within quantum theory is the role of human consciousness. Put simply, no quantum event can be seen unless there is consciousness there to observe it. Even stranger is the probability of a quantum event. It is fundamental to the mathematics of the quantum field that until an event is observed, there is a probability of every possible outcome taking place. It seems, therefore, that we may well be 'gods' ourselves, observing the outcome we want there to be – for in observing a quantum event, in a real sense, we *choose* how that event will unfold.

Bearing in mind the quantum effects within microtubules, perhaps this is also true in the greater reality of our world. Maybe astrology realizes this magical link between ourselves and the reality we inhabit, but the ancients misunderstood the influences of the particles within and around us, and symbolically placed emphasis on the larger heaven that they could see. Perhaps it is not the heavens that affect personality, but the personality that affects the heavens – or at least, the smallest interactions, the particles, within it. As Hermes Trismegistos was supposed to have said: 'As above, so below' – but we got it the wrong way round. For it could be *us* 'above', affecting the quantum world of probability 'below'.

We are, of course, revisiting old ground in this suggestion, for we are saying that optimism or pessimism can open up the world to become sympathetic with what we really want to achieve. We are saying that psychical manifestations can order the world by some subtle form of mind power akin to psychokinesis. In a real sense, we are arguing that the reality of the world is dependent upon our own paranormal powers.

On the other hand, we are also saying that this ordering of the world – for good or for bad – is a product of our own attitudes; and those attitudes manipulate the world to produce, for want of a better word, fortuitous and meaningful 'coincidence'. Perhaps we need to return to this subject once again.

Synchronicity

■ Dame Rebecca West had visited the archives of the Nuremberg war crimes trials in order to look up facts concerning one of the accused. To her annoyance, she found that the trials were published under arbitrary headings and were of little use to a researcher, as it was almost impossible to go straight to a particular episode. Approaching a librarian, she said: 'I can't find it . . .' and as she did so, her hand unconsciously reached out and took a volume off the shelf. She opened it at the exact page she required.

Many researchers have attempted to place an extra-sensory explanation on this popular anecdote. It is, of course, feasible that such a mechanism was involved, but it is equally viable to invoke the sceptic's answer – that it was pure coincidence. I opt for the latter. Except, of course, that I would class it as a 'meaningful' coincidence, in which the world had somehow been ordered by the requirements of the individual.

Perhaps the most amazing coincidence of this order happened to British actor Anthony Hopkins. Early in his film career, he was asked to star in the film *The Girl from Petrovka*. To prepare for the role, he attempted to find a copy of the original novel. His search proved totally fruitless – no one, it seemed, could help him. Then one day he wandered into a London underground station – and found a copy of the novel on a bench. Hopkins eventually flew abroad to make the film. He met the author of the novel, who told him of his annoyance at losing a copy with notes inside, which he had lent to a friend in London. It soon transpired that this was the very copy that Hopkins had found.

Such an incident could not have been formed by any known level of extra-sensory ability. In a real sense, events had somehow conspired to assist Anthony Hopkins in his endeavours, and such a conspiring of events, I argue, could well be the mechanism through which astrology works.

Seen in such a meaningful way, coincidences such as this will be experienced by most people at some time in their life. If the person is generally pessimistic, reality conspires to present insurmountable hurdles; if optimistic, opportunity seems to open up. Horace Walpole invented the word 'serendipity' to describe a similar process, where fortuitous and unexpected discoveries are made, apparently by chance.

Once we get into such a serendipitous frame of mind we feel we can walk on air, for the world seems to open up and become benevolent. We can be carried along by a wave of chance, which leaves us elated. Lucky gamblers will know the feeling all too well, a feeling that they cannot go wrong – and when it is working to their ultimate advantage, they can't.

The frame of mind behind such experiences has already been identified in Maslow's 'peak experience' (see page 173). Maslow actually found that if he could get his subjects to talk about these moments of elation, they could reproduce the feeling at will, maintaining the absolute meaningfulness and elation of the moment. Allying this psychological state to serendipity can be most illuminating, for as noted earlier , the peak experience seems to be at the lower end of a psychological scale that escalates to the mystical experience, where the world seems to become not only meaningful, but 'whole'. Perhaps, when serendipity strikes, we are tapping into this 'wholeness' of reality, producing a magical series of events through a state of mind that can clearly be seen as shamanic.

Carl Jung became fascinated with fortuitous, meaningful coincidence, and felt that the process could well be behind divinatory forms such as the I Ching and astrology. He first realized the process in the mid-1920s when he was researching the 'collective unconscious'. In particular, he noted that the archetypal and symbolic dreams of his patients could often be reflected in the outside world through coincidental events – events that were, he realized, statistically incomprehensible.

Referring to a phrase used by French psychologist Pierre Janet – 'lowering of the mental threshold' – Jung began to see the collective unconscious as conspiring with the unconscious mind of the patient to produce such events. He named this phenomenon 'synchronicity', and described the reality of such events through an 'acausal connecting principle'. He first used this term in an address in 1930 for Richard Wilhelm, who had translated the I Ching and popularized it in the West. To Jung, synchronicity was the process through which the psychic world connected to the physical, and it was to lead to a unique collaboration.

In 1928, Viennese physicist Wolfgang Pauli visited Jung for psychotherapy. Pauli had created a folklore all his own within the scientific community, for he was a bit of a jinx. Whenever he was about, you could guarantee that any scientific experiment would go wrong. Eventually collaborating with Jung, Pauli felt that the perfect balance of forces within nature and the universe, in both the macrocosm of cosmology and the microcosm of quantum mechanics, suggested a similar coincidental force at work. It was to be the first, brave, attempt to unify consciousness with the laws of physics. However, as no definite 'mechanism' could be identified to account for the connection, it could easily be ignored by science.

The most obvious manifestation in the real world of such synchronistic events has come to be known as 'luck'. As in the days of superstition, this is a meaningless word that, through cultural interpretation, is seen as a definite force in the psychology of the individual. A lucky person is seen as one who manifests a real ability upon the world, yet this accepted word is even more meaningless than the unaccepted word 'synchronicity'.

'Luck' is, of course, accepted because it fits in with the chaotic world view of 'chance', itself a meaningless word, decreed meaningless because it fits in with a meaningless universe. 'Synchronicity', on the other hand, attempts to place meaning on chaos, and so cannot fit into our present world view. Hence, the meaningless nature of luck, combined with its total acceptance within the world, becomes a form of superstition equally as omnipotent as the superstitions described earlier You should ponder this point every timesomeone tells you that we have advanced out of our superstitious ways – for in reality, we have not.

Dr Richard Wiseman, a psychologist at the University of Hertfordshire, has recently attempted to come to terms with luck. Dr Wiseman is the ultimate sceptic of the paranormal, and during 1996 he could often be seen on the BBC paranormal series *Out of This World*, performing what I would call 'psychological acrobatics' in his attempts to place rational and material explanations upon phenomena. Indeed, his attempts were heroic, if nonetheless misplaced.

I point out Dr Wiseman's sceptical nature for a very good reason. Stated simply, if his research can be seen to offer signs of synchronicity at work, then the fact that he would so obviously be trying to disprove such an influence would be strong evidence that such an influence actually exists.

Dr Wiseman and his colleagues performed a series of psychological tests on 150 subjects evenly divided between those who considered themselves lucky and those who did not. The central finding of the study was that lucky people were more successful at working out probability (calculating the odds) in mathematical problems: 46 per cent of lucky people got the answers right, compared to 32 per cent of those who considered themselves unlucky. Such results go a long way to demonstrating that lucky people do, indeed, have a superior ability to calculate odds, but perhaps we need to look deeper into them.

In 1995, an infamous book called *The Bell Curve*, written by Harvard psychologist Richard Hernstein and political scientist Charles Murray, was published (see Bibliography). Decreed racist propaganda by most commentators, the book claimed that IQ (Intelligence Quotient) was the deciding factor in the progress of the individual. In an attempt at social engineering, the claim was made that those with low IQ bred faster than those with high IQ, eventually leading to a lower IQ in the population at large. The result of this is that a growing 'underclass' – in particular in black ghettos – would result in a need to halt welfare benefits in order to cut down on the breeding among people of low IQ.

This right-wing nonsense caused a huge debate in the British broadsheet press, particularly upon the nature of IQ. One school of thought suggested that IQ was, in fact, a cultural phenomenon, in that an IQ test tested only those cognitive abilities of use to a particular cultural expression. Because blacks were open to different cultural expressions than the accepted 'white' culture, this could account for their apparently lower IQ. Such an idea suggests that blacks are just as intelligent as 'whites', but the cultural expression of intelligence is different. Their 'lower' IQ has nothing to do with cognitive ability, but more to do with their psychological refusal to toe the line of white culture.

This was later reflected when statistical evidence emerged that black children under five had an equal IQ to white children, but as schooling began, their academic abilities declined slightly. In a nutshell, the educational process of a predominantly white culture did not take into account the psychological needs of blacks. And what kind of overall psychology would this manifest in the black community? It would inevitably lead to a feeling of disenfranchisement, in that the blacks would appear not to belong to the predominant culture in which they lived.

This seems to be what is happening in the growing 'underclass' that exists in all western capitalist cultures. Comprised of whites as well as blacks, this underclass forms the bottom 10 per cent of the population in economic terms, and is more likely to comprise of single-parent families with no hope of bettering themselves. And this underclass has a most particular psychology: in the main, they are totally pessimistic in nature. Often classed as 'idle', they are known as the 'scourge of the welfare state'. Their usual answer to such attacks is that there are no opportunities for them. The world, it seems, somehow conspires to keep them down.

We can now begin to see what is happening here. In the main, they are not 'idle', but totally suppressed by their own minds. In an almost synchronistic way, the world *does* conspire against them, but a large degree of this 'unlucky' state is the result of their own pessimism. I am not in any way saying that if they snapped out of it their chances would improve – our culture classes them incorrectly as failures, and would not offer them much of a helping hand – but I am saying that their pessimism is a contributory factor in their feeling of desolation.

At the opposite end of the social scale there is, of course, the new 'meritocracy'. Here, people from all social backgrounds have 'made it big', and many of them, while exhibiting high IQs, will contend that they were lucky: they just happened to be in the right place at the right time. Of course, the process also involved great determination – for instance, stage magician Paul Daniels classes luck as years of dedication meeting a moment of opportunity – but events somehow conspired to produce serendipity. Uppermost in the psycho- . logy of such 'success stories' is optimism. Unlike the pessimistic 'underclass', the new 'meritocrat' is optimistic. Does this suggest synchronicity at work in the real world, dependent upon the degree of optimism or pessimism displayed by the individual?

Such a suggestion brings us back to Dr Wiseman's study of luck – for a full 37 per cent of the lucky subjects believed that they could control their luck, whereas only 5 per cent of unlucky people thought so. Dr Wiseman did point out that some of this could be explained by the fact that lucky people tended to remember the good times rather than the bad. Even so, he noted the difference in mental attitude, with the lucky subjects being more optimistic, which in turn increased their overall self-esteem.

Further indications of synchronicity come out of the life histories of some of the lucky subjects. Consider the 'lucky' woman who managed to escape the Japanese in Burma, had avoided both train disasters and car crashes by minutes, and had been twice 'rescued' by passers-by after being confronted by rapists. If we take this last point in particular, most people would consider it unlucky to be confronted by rapists in the first place. However, an optimistic person full of self-esteem is more likely to take risks, and thus place themselves in a position where dangers can lurk. However, luck then breaks out, and passers-by appear on the scene. Such fortuitous coincidence cannot, in any way, be explained by the woman's ability to calculate odds, for the passers-by behaved coincidentally from 'outside' her own mind.

The above interpretation of Dr Wiseman's results are, of course, my own. I feel the results can show synchronicity at work through the psychological states of optimism and pessimism; others may see no such indication. When faced with a glass containing 50 per cent fresh air and 50 per cent water, a pessimist would say it is half empty and I would say it is half full. Both interpretations are correct, and perhaps this is equally true with Dr Wiseman's results. But the point is that if his results can offer a synchronistic interpretation, then they cannot be discounted as not – unless, of course, we enjoy psychological acrobatics.

We can see here that optimism and pessimism can be regarded as regulating the world about us. Just as we can experience 'wholeness' in the mystical experience, we may also be able to use the 'wholeness' of the universe to bend reality to echo our hopes, fears and dreams, as suggested by astrology.

Such ideas speak volumes for the existence of a superconscious at large in the world, and a superconscious that we can input to order the world to reflect our outlook. It is now time to attempt to pin down the superconscious in logical terms.

· WHOLENESS ·

In Search of God

■ As this book progresses it becomes obvious that, rather than simply attempting to understand the supernatural, I am going in search of God. This is the cultural tag that western society places upon the superconscious, and for millennia the search has been a religious one.

The search begins with questions: who are we, what are we, how did we get here, where do we fit in the scheme of things, and how should we behave within this scheme? The answers have usually constituted 'belief', in that there was no way to validate the answers in terms of the facts of the observable world.

Such beliefs offered unified visions, in that they saw the world as a complete system, with everything that was in the world being part of the unified picture. However, as science gained primacy over religious belief, the observable facts of the world bit deep into religious certainty. Concepts such as an Earth-centred universe, the Virgin birth and the Resurrection all became fallacy, understood as nothing more than allegories.

This situation had to come, for religious beliefs held no authority outside their particular culture. The reason for this was obvious, for a religious interpretation of God was, in the main, a cultural interpretation of the world as a particular society saw it. However, being seen as fundamental truth as opposed to cultural philosophy, the various cultural interpretations led to aggressions throughout the world as religious certainty was upheld.

Science broke the mould of such aggressions. It split the world into its constituent parts and collected data concerning the facts of the world in order to formulate theory. Such a process was the antithesis of religion, for where religious belief could be seen as a unified process, fundamental to science was the idea of separateness, with the world cut up into intellectually manageable bits. This had a great effect on society. Whereas religion held society together in a

199

unified, moral whole, science gave licence for disintegration and moral apathy. Whereas religion saw society as groupings of people under an overall supernatural Lordship, science gave birth to the primacy of the individual, free to take from the world whatever they chose.

During the twentieth century, however, science has been slowly and reluctantly taking another path. Through relativity and quantum theory, the mechanistic view of the universe, composed of its separate parts, has taken a battering. Today, 'whole' field theories are discussed. The universe is not a single reality, but a reality based upon probabilities. Such probabilities can change based upon the 'relative' frame of reference of the observer. If the observer sees the universe from a different frame of reference, then the universe which is observed is different. As to the process of observation, consciousness itself plays a part in the universe so created.

These intuitive 'facts' of the universe are at odds with the still existent attitudes of most scientists, who cling to a mechanistic interpretation that is outdated and redundant according to the evidence they have accumulated. The separate disciplines of science are still as important, and are still required, but the time when science alone could build the data into a satisfactory world view has gone – for the separateness of science is as wrong as the cultural interpretations of religion. They are the great thesis and antithesis of history, and it is time for synthesis.

The truth of Sir Isaac Newton does, of course, tell us that we should never have lost the overall vision of 'wholeness'. It was central to his work that the universe was unified. Indeed, the idea is implicit in the word 'universe' itself, 'uni' meaning 'one'.

The father of the modern world, the French philosopher René Descartes, understood this too. Working in the seventeenth century, he devised duality – separating body from mind and passions from reason. Dividing the world into elements for logical deduction, he took us out of creation in order to allow science to rise, turning everything, from the universe to the human body, into material machines.

This laid the universe open for study in a materialistic sense, and as science advanced it clung to this material concept, going on to separate the 'machine' into its constituent parts. But in doing so, scientists ignored the mind and the passions of Descartes; they took his philosophy in part, for the other end of his duality formed a bridgehead to God and the soul. He separated them from the 'machine' for they appeared beyond logical study, but were existent in the world nonetheless. As with Newton, Descartes too was intellectually raped, thereby stripping him of his soul, and God of his emotional independence.

Today, we see science as the ultimate form of atheistic intellect. Stripped of superstition, it studies Descartes's 'soulless' machine. Or at least, this is what science would have us believe. In reality, Descartes's soul still exists in the scientific world.

Edward Larson of the University of Georgia and his colleague Larry Witham recently demonstrated this. They sent questionnaires to 1,000 scientists listed in the 1995 edition of *American Men and Women of Science*, and showed that 40 per cent of those polled still believed in God. Even immortality was believed by 38 per cent. It seems that the unease of philosopher Ludwig Wittgenstein is still felt. As he wrote in 1951, in his *Tractatus Logico-Philosophicus* (see Bibliography): 'We feel that even when all possible scientific questions have been answered, the problems of life remain completely untouched.'

Descartes understood life. He split it into the logical and the emotional. We can see that religion catered for the emotional, and science caters for the logical, but they are simply relativistic frames of reference from which to view the same universe in different ways. Hence, whether a truly existent Being, or merely a wishful fallacy, God has His place in the scheme of things, and cannot be ignored.

Of late, several scientists have realized that the soul and God have their place in the universe. Typical is Paul Davies, a popular writer on science and a physicist at the University of Adelaide. In *The Accidental Universe* (see Bibliography), he wrote:

It is hard to resist the impression of something – some influence capable of transcending space–time and the confinements of relativistic causality – possessing an overview of the entire cosmos at the instant of its creation, and manipulating all the causally disconnected parts to go bang with almost exactly the same vigour at the same time, and yet not so exactly co-ordinated as to preclude the small-scale, slight irregularities that eventually formed the galaxies, and us.

Davies – who recently won the Templeton Prize for Progress in Religion – is not talking here about a God in religious clothes. He finds the possibility of God as some form of cosmic magician doing miracles, or moving the physical elements of the universe about to satisfy His whims, both repugnant and childish. Rather, he has the courage to see, within the universe, a process of complexity.

To him, the ability of the universe to self-organize itself to the point of allowing the emergence of consciousness and life seems to hold within it a form of meaning – or, at least, a form of 'rationality' – rather than blind, chaotic meaninglessness. He sees 'God' as an 'abstract principle' implying a form of purpose behind physical existence.

Physicist David Bohm, who, as we saw on page 175, offers the greatest modern vision of the 'wholeness' of the universe, argues that we must see overall reality through a unification of Descartes's duality. To him, quantum theory offers a view of the universe alien to science's separate disciplines, and to the idea that 'mind' is distinctly different to the universe. Bohm saw the 'non-locality' of the quantum world in holistic terms, with everything being part of a co-ordinated 'whole'. To understand such a concept, we must step back from the scientific way of observing the world as 'separate' and see it from a view of connectedness, with concepts such as consciousness as much a part of the universe as a particle. To Bohm, the universe is indivisible from any of its parts.

Such views must, among other things, place life as central to the cosmos – a view which is, of course, religious as opposed to scientific. Nowhere was this attempted more persuasively than in the scientific theories surrounding the 'anthropic principles'.

The anthropic principles arose as a logical deduction from the simple fact that the universe appears so ordered as to suggest 'purpose'. The forces that bind the universe together are so mathematically perfect that just a minor alteration in their ratios would have meant that the universe could not have come into being. The word 'coincidence' has often been used as the only viable explanation of this perfect order.

However, if purpose is implied within this coincidental order, how do we decide what that purpose is? Physicist Robert Dicke offered a logical answer to this in 1964, arguing that no 'coincidence' was involved, as such. Rather, the universe was how it was because that was the way it had to be to create conscious observers. The 'weak anthropic principle' states that the universe is there because we are here, and we are here because it is there. This fact of our existence within the universe allows us to view the universe, and in viewing it, we determine the 'truths' of the universe due mainly to our existence within it, and our ability to observe it through our own perspective. Such a view places our existence in the universe as fundamental to the universe itself. To reiterate: it is there because we are here, and we are here because it is there. The two are one and the same.

The weak anthropic principle led on to a 'strong' and a 'final' anthropic principle. The strong principle states that the universe must be such as to admit the creation of observers within it at some stage. The final principle states that intelligent information-processing must come into existence in the universe, and, once it comes into existence, it will never die out. This final anthropic principle, suggested by physicists John Barrow and Frank Tipler, went too far for most scientists. It suggests an absolute primacy for humankind within the universe, with our self-awareness being the only purpose of the cosmos. In an earlier time, such a suggestion was made in the 'creation myth', and it is just as fatuous and egoistic now as it was then.

Such a view did great damage to the anthropic principles, whereas if we stay with the 'weak' principle, a great deal of logic is involved with its implications. Its message is simple, for it clearly hints that consciousness is part of the universe. It is consciousness that allows the universe to exist. Indeed, the same thing is implied in the role of the observer in a quantum event. Here, a definite reality is created from probability by the act of observation.

However, there is one severe problem with the weak anthropic principle, for it indicates that without the observer, the universe cannot exist. As the universe has a 'history' stretching back to the Big Bang, and *prior* to the evolution of self-aware humanity, how could it have existed before we appeared to observe it? As physicist John Wheeler said in 1975, in his 'participatory anthropic principle': observers are necessary to bring the universe into being.

There is, of course, a simple answer to this problem, and that answer is God. God would be conscious, and thus able to observe, and in His being able to observe, the universe could exist. However, rather than being a God invested with cultural clutter and interpretation, that God could be the 'abstract principle' indicated by Paul Davies.

Such an idea is as old as reason itself. The ancient Greek philosopher Plato conceived of a cosmology where a relationship had to exist between the 'mentality' of the universe and its 'physicality'. Realizing a symmetry within the physical structure of the cosmos, he hypothesized 'ideal forms', where the 'idea' for the physical symmetry existed in some ethereal perfection (see page 79). Between this mentality and physicality was 'intelligence', which he called the *anima mundi*, which can be translated as the 'soul of the world'.

Such a concept places 'perfection' as a universal theme. This is, of course, alchemical, giving the universe a requirement to become more perfect. Indeed, the *anima mundi* is central to western occult traditions, organizing the universe and connecting it to the minds of men.

Of course, Paul Davies would be as appalled at my attempt to identify his 'abstract principle' with the *anima mundi* as he is at the thought of a magical God. But this is to miss the point. Davies offers an understanding in terms of science, and science alone. The *anima mundi*, on the other hand, belongs more to the esoteric world of religious mysticism. And here, never the twain shall meet. However, free of such cultural clutter, they do meet. Forget the cultural

203

interpretation of the two meanings and look, instead, at what each is saying, for both indicate the existence of a universal organizing principle, shaping the cosmos and shaping ourselves.

In this sense, science and religion can be seen as having a similar job. One may offer an overview of belief, while the other offers a specialized approach through observation and reason, but they are essentially the same thing – a process of placing mentality within the world. While religious mysticism has always expressed itself in the form of superconsciousness – or God – scientists such as David Bohm and Paul Davies are realizing that the fragmented scientific search is approaching the same concept. We can advance our understanding of such a concept by looking to one area of science that refuses to accept superconsciousness in any form – and that area of science is evolution.

A New Theory of Evolution

■ The days have long gone when biologists accepted a divine plan for the existence of life on planet Earth. Evolution has toppled creation, and blind forces have replaced an ordered God, sculpting life from no other drives than accident and chance. The complexities of life have been reduced to simple laws, governed by Richard Dawkins's metaphor of the 'selfish gene', where the only purpose of evolutionary life is gene replication. The myriad species that exist are simply 'vehicles' to allow our genes to thrive.

Prior to this new view of life taking hold, species had been created by God. Such a divine plan held no intellectual authority other than faith. However, as the eighteenth-century Enlightenment progressed, faith could no longer be used by the intelligentsia to uphold the truths of the universe. Man's increasingly rational mind, combined with observations of nature, demanded a new, mechanistic model of life to echo the increasingly mechanistic nature of the new industrial society. In other words, a new 'cultural' explanation was required.

Principal to God's creation was the idea that species were created in their exact form and have remained unchanged throughout natural history. The biologist the Compte de Buffon was the first to challenge this view, setting the scene for evolutionary theory. Spending most of his life observing nature, he argued that species were not fixed, but changed. He even went so far as to suggest that apes, quadrupeds and man had evolved from a common ancestor.

This was, of course, supposition. The first attempt to lay down theory came from the physician Erasmus Darwin. He argued that an animal's structure determined the way it acted. Hence, if for some reason its behaviour had to change – due to changes in environment, for example – then its structure would have to change to allow for its new behaviour.

Darwin had proposed a definite idea of how species could change, and to echo this hypothesis, physical evidence began to arise to offer further proof. Much of this evidence came from geology. Foremost was the observable fact that fossilized creatures appeared distinctly different from existing life forms, suggesting a reality to evolution. Of even more importance, however, was our growing understanding of erosion and deposition, which demonstrated how, over the millennia, our environment had changed, offering a stimulus for change in animal species.

This evidence had a great effect on French naturalist Jean Lamarck, who made the first definite connection between the structure of an animal and its environment. Life forms not only changed in line with changes in their environment, but their form was a definite result of it, too. For instance, a giraffe has a long neck because of its diet of leaves. By having a long neck it can reach higher up a tree, thus providing a more extensive source of food. However, Lamarck did not leave it there, for he tentatively proposed that a new generation of a life form inherited its characteristics from its parent.

As there was no real mechanism for understanding this form of inheritance, following Lamarck evolutionary theory became unpopular. Clearly something was wrong with such ideas, and if they were to be worked upon, evolution theory would have to be advanced in a way that only a genius could work out. That genius came in the form of Erasmus Darwin's grandson, Charles Darwin.

Like most geniuses, young Charles led an early life that suggested he would waste his life away. Sent to Edinburgh University to study medicine, he dropped out and instead went to Cambridge to study theology. However, he seemed to spend most of his time studying beetles, often popping one in his mouth for lack of a third hand. Hence, when, in 1831, he learned of a vacancy for a naturalist on the *Beagle*, charged with surveying the coastline of South America, he jumped at the chance.

Darwin spent five years on the *Beagle*, studying nature in remote places such as the Galapagos Islands. The voyage convinced him of the gradual change of species. Opting for selective breeding as an evolutionary mechanism, he decided that species not only changed in line with their environment, but they *had* to change, or die out. Furthermore, only those species that adapted successfully would survive; those that didn't would inevitably become extinct, because they could not compete with successfully adapted species. Evolution was, in a real sense, a case of the survival of the fittest.

Following his voyage, Darwin settled down to work out the principles of his developing theory. His work was helped significantly when he read *An Essay on the Principles of Population* by the Reverend Thomas Malthus. Malthus argued that, if left unchecked, a population will double every 25 years, thus outstripping the natural resources available to feed it and bringing famine. This acute pressure on resources was aimed only at human populations, but Darwin realized that the process would be endemic throughout nature. In his epoch-making *On the Origin of Species* of 1859 (see Bibliography), he applied it to the whole natural world, arguing that environmental pressures caused a process of 'natural selection', where adaptation of species became an absolute requirement of survival.

Darwin enshrined the theory of evolution through natural selection in the popular psyche, causing an intellectual rift between science and religion that survives to this day. However, solutions to the deeper problems of how inheritance of characteristics down the generations worked had to wait until 1953 and the discovery of deoxyribonucleic acid, or DNA, by biologists Francis Crick and James Watson.

DNA molecules contain the blueprint of a species in a four-letter digital code. Existing in all cells, the DNA molecule takes the form of a double helix, or two identical chains wound around each other. Containing all the genetic information required for a new generation, when reproduction occurs, each molecule reproduces itself by uncoiling one of the identical chains, thus providing the information for the new molecule, and guaranteeing inheritance of characteristics from the parent.

The increasing evidence from genetics, as well as archaeology, gives the impression that evolution is, of course, a truth, and not simply a theory. This was inevitable. Newton told us that every action has an equal and opposite reaction, and this seems to work equally well with society. Following Darwin, the hysteria involved in the religious condemnation of evolution would inevitably lead to an intransigent stance being taken by evolutionists. Over the years, this has led to Darwinian evolution becoming more of a belief than a scientific and rationalized system of thought. The end result of this is to attach to evolution theory ideals that cannot be proved within the confines of evolution theory; ideals that, when analysed, dissolve into notions with no substance.

To explain what I mean, consider the case of Darwinian evolutionist Dr Richard Dawkins. Holding the post of Professor of Public Understanding of Science at Oxford, he is famed for ridiculing all forms of argument that conflict with the absolute correctness of evolution. Yet we can so easily use Dr Dawkins' own words to destroy the certainty of the system he maintains.

Darwinian evolution is built, as we have seen, on the idea of natural selection.

The defining point of natural selection – a process I accept to be essentially correct, yet flawed in many areas – is the idea that evolution is slow and is the product of aeons of time. Dr Dawkins makes this point in his *River out of Eden* (see Bibliography): 'A key feature of evolution is its gradualness.' Simple and straightforward, and to most evolutionists an absolute truth, proved by theory and observation. But he then goes on to say: 'This is a matter of principle rather than fact.'

Dr Dawkins's scientific certainty is beginning to crack. But why does natural selection have to be slow? Well, after being overwhelmed by a barrage of contrary theory, he now accepts that *some* episodes of evolution *could* be rapid, but only the general principle of gradualness can explain such things as the human eye. 'For,' he makes clear, 'if it is not gradual in these cases, it ceases to have any explanatory power at all. Without gradualness in these cases, we are back to miracle, which is simply a synonym for the total absence of explanation.'

I will not delve into the supposed impossibility of evolution producing the human eye. The argument has been used often and is fatuous. Natural selection *does* offer an explanation of the human eye, as it explains the central processes of life. Natural selection works – as a theory. But a theory is all it is, and for as long as Dr Dawkins and his kind turn it into a belief system through fear of miracles, the possibility of building upon the theory will not happen. If we relate this form of scientific certainty to Newtonian gravity, relativity would never have been proposed.

Having said that natural selection explains life, I must qualify the statement by showing where the theory breaks down.

A gene is an autonomous byte of life. It is, therefore, the fundamental root of life – what Dr Dawkins calls the 'selfish gene', totally divorced from anything else in the universe. But with it being an autonomous entity, for natural selection to be totally valid it must offer an undeniable process whereby genes cease to be autonomous and produce biological systems such as the human being. In other words, an overall design function is required to allow genes to co-operate to form life larger than their own autonomy.

Of course, such a facility would decree natural selection to be only one process of evolution, offering the tantalizing prospect of an overall guiding intelligence. This is anathema to evolutionists, and lies at the heart of the insistence of Dr Dawkins and his kind that gene replication is all that is needed.

The usual argument against the idea that a design function is needed to complete evolution is to say that I am talking about a God, or, alternatively, such a design function could only exist if life knew its final form at the beginning. But neither of these need necessarily be so.

French philosopher and evolutionist Henri Bergson suggested something similar to a design function in the early years of the twentieth century. Rather than evolution being a process of blind forces, he suggested that nature could have an urge to create. This creative force he called the '*élan vital*', giving nature a motive power to advance life in a more ordered form.

French theologian and philosopher Pierre Teilhard de Chardin was greatly impressed by Bergson, as well as the more esoteric, eastern philosophies – he spent much of his life in China. He saw evolution in a cosmic perspective, requiring four central stages – galactic, Earth, life and human.

Such a process tells a continuing story, placing humankind as a natural progression from the Big Bang and echoing the 'anthropic principles' identified earlier. Evolution here implies 'complexification', with both physical matter and consciousness being at large in the universe, and going on to evolve into more complex forms. Such a process implies planning by intelligence, but does not require an absolute plan. Teilhard devised the 'omega point', a point in universal evolution that evolution 'aspires' to attain. Once it has done so, the omega point moves on, beginning a new stage of evolution. In a process of 'cosmogenesis', the Earth is presently evolving into an intelligent concept with humankind at its centre. Invested with consciousness, we are presently evolving the 'noosphere', a collective human consciousness within the biosphere of the Earth.

While highly mystical, such a view does, however, act as a bridgehead between religion and science, placing consciousness within evolution and suggesting a form of superconscious to which all individuals connect.

Maverick biologist Rupert Sheldrake offered a similar evolutionary system in his *A New Science of Life*, published in 1981 (see Bibliography). Sheldrake argued that the 'formative' causes of chemical, biological, social and mental organization are due to non-physical fields within such systems. Calling them 'morphic fields' – *morphe* being Greek for 'form' – the idea echoes Plato's *anima mundi*, with 'ideal forms' existing within consciousness to produce ordered physicality.

Such fields were not around at the beginning of the universe as such, but evolve in line with physical evolution. Causing a process called 'morphic resonance', the fields contain 'memory' of the physical form, and with this existing outside of the physical form, the memory is retained in the universe and passed on to all similar future biological organisms. This produces a 'morphic system' that allows order within species.

Such an idea is similar to my suggested design function, allowing evolution through a form of repetition, where the system becomes easier to produce the more times it is produced. However, morphic fields are also connecting systems, working on society and the mind as well as on the biological. Hence, the concept allows for Jung's collective unconscious to formulate culture, and allows the individual's mind to connect with the outside world, validating paranormal abilities such as past life memories and extra-sensory perception.

Sheldrake – who has been virtually ostracized by the scientific community for his ideas – has skilfully encapsulated all the requirements of a superconscious, allowing paranormal abilities and tying them to the universe as a whole, but without the requirement of a definite God, nor an exact 'form' being inherent in the beginning of the universe. But his theories fail in that he does not identify a 'mechanism' that can fall in line with scientific procedure.

Cyberneticist David Foster makes a simple observation, however. Cybernetics is the science of making machines behave intelligently. However, as he is well aware, intelligence can only be programmed into a system by an entity of higher intelligence than the system being programmed. Moving away from cybernetics to the universe at large, Foster argues that this same requirement could exist in nature. For him, an acorn can be seen as the 'program' of an oak tree; or, at least, the device through which the 'program' is inputed. Seeing nature in this way implies that a more intelligent entity would be required to devise the acorn in the first place.

Again, we have the insinuation of a higher intelligence within the universe, an overall superconscious. However, the process need not be quite as esoteric as we might at first assume.

Computing has recently come up with the concept of 'genetic algorithm', based on the principles of evolution. The idea that Darwinian natural selection could be applied to the formulation of 'programs' was proposed in the 1960s by computer expert John Holland. The idea is that various simple programs interact and alter each other in a similar way to mutation through natural selection in order, over many generations, to evolve a better program to fulfil a predetermined task. Such processes are proving their worth in fields as varied as the money market and missile guidance systems, but the central point of the process is that only general rules need to be built into the software to allow evolution.

In the above we can see a real, working evolutionary process that requires neither God, nor knowledge of a final form at the beginning of the process. Put simply, if the form of the final program was known, there would be no need for the process. And this concept – the need for a basic design function – could apply equally well to evolution proper. The only stumbling block to theorizing is to decide what the original design function could be.

In losing its autonomy to co-operate in the building of a biological life form, a gene indulges in the creation of a 'system'. Human society apes this process.

Man is predisposed to organize into a society. Like most other life forms, social living seems to be not only a fundamental process, but an evolutionary principle. For instance, man has evolved the motive power for society through family, village, town, city, city-state, nation, empire and, today, multinational. So could it be that, up to the point where living with the environment becomes static (the goal of natural selection), life is predisposed to evolve 'systems'? Could the original design function be nothing more than a rudimentary form of systems management?

This is, of course, supposition. Without some form of mathematical evidence in favour of the idea, it remains of little importance. Yet could it be that the mathematical principle required to prove this basic design function has been available for over 200 years?

The eighteenth-century Swiss mathematician Daniel Bernoulli devised what has come to be known as the 'law of large numbers'. F. N. David explained the law thus in his *Games, Gods and Gambling* (see Bibliography): 'Probability tends towards certainty as the number of events involved approaches infinity.' The law appears to be a universal principle, and tells us that order evolves out of disorder as the number of events involved increases. This 'coincidental' order can be found in the decay of a radioactive substance. The decay of an atom cannot be predicted; no matter how long it exists, it has a probability of disintegrating in the next second. Yet a radioactive substance – a collection of atoms – has an exact half-life that can be predicted with absolute accuracy. Known as the half-life of an isotope, it validates the law of large numbers, with the isotope grasping order from apparent chaos.

The process can be seen, too, in something as innocuous as a pile of sand. Pour sand on to the ground and it will form a pile. Initially it is a small pile, and sand will fall from top to bottom in a chaotic fashion. However, as the pile grows, increasing the number of grains of sand, the falling sand will form into ordered waves, creating a 'system'.

Atoms and grains of sand are seen to be as autonomous as our selfish gene. Yet, if enough numbers are involved, autonomy disappears to be replaced by order, and in co-operating to produce such order, a 'system' has come into being. Evolution, I suggest, could work in a similar way. As enough genes congregate to produce a specific life form, their autonomy disappears and the basic design function impels them to form an ordered system above the requirements of their natural autonomy, and perfectly in line with Bernoulli's law of large numbers. Dr Dawkins, it appears, is wrong. We should really be talking about the 'selfless' gene.

However, the half-life of a radioactive isotope tells us that the principle is not just evolutionary in a biological sense, but universal. Consider. Our sun is said to have been formed by the clustering of gases into a 'solid' mass. This involved a continual growth to an optimum size, increasing the number of clustered atoms and, in line with the law of large numbers, increasing the bias towards order. The same principle, of course, can be applied to the planets. Life began with single-cell micro-organisms. As more cells clustered around them, the mathematical bias increased towards order. Primitive man lived in tribes. As physical communication with other tribes swelled the numbers, the mathematical bias increased towards order. A baby, at the point of conception, is a dual-celled organism. As more cells cluster around it, the mathematical bias increases towards order.

I would therefore suggest that the clustering of things – of atoms, of cells, of people, of events – is the driving force, indeed, the intelligence, of the universe, and that the process is both alchemical – in that higher perfection becomes an evolutionary principle – and synchronistic. And that, in being 'intelligent', the process forms a universal higher consciousness by implication.

Higher consciousness thus becomes a congregation of particles forming more than the sum of their parts, and this concept of 'wholeness' filters down throughout existence. Hence, living organisms also become a congregation of cells forming more than the sum of their parts. Life becomes a congregation of events forming more than the sum of its parts. But most importantly to this study, culture becomes a higher conscious mechanism of collective individuals forming more than the sum of their parts. Thus, human beings, human culture and human life as lived exist collectively in the 'wholeness' of an ordered and intelligent universe.

Of course, the above does not offer an exact mechanism for an existent super-conscious within the universe, but it does offer a degree of mathematical credibility that can be observed in the world. In this sense, it holds as much proof as relativity theory, quantum mechanics and the Big Bang. Further, it does not upset any fundamental element of any of these theories, nor the existing theory of evolution. All the concept requires for acceptance is a shift in the scientific world view, which leaves scientists with a simple question to ask themselves: are they unbiased enquirers open to logical theory, or are they religionists, upholding dogma?

· CONCLUSION ·

■ We have been on a journey throughout the universe and throughout history. The story I have told has been about the 'supernatural', but it has left us with conclusions that strike at the heart of humankind, our knowledge, and the life we live based upon that knowledge. And it leaves us living in a most enigmatic universe.

As we have seen, 'possessions' are personal, psychological fragments, but they are also outside, cultural entities. In this sense, their true reality is neither psychological nor spiritual, but communal. Hallucinations, also, are personal mind creations, but they are also outside, cultural forms. Thus, they too are neither psychological nor spiritual, but communal.

In order to understand such concepts, we need to change our compartmentalized way of thinking. We need to cease observing the world in terms of two schools of thought – the psychological or the spiritual – but see it instead in terms of a unified ideal of psycho-sociological phenomena, where the cultural expression is as one with, and as important as, the inner psychological state of the individual.

Within this new world view, the most surprising concepts can exist. For instance, it tells us that God can be real within a culture – cultural expression is truth, but only within a particular culture. Religion can thus become both good and evil at the same time. Where it is the cultural expression of voluntary believers, it is the most absolute form of good, but when it is forced upon others of a different cultural expression, it denies their culture and thus becomes evil. The good or bad of a book such as the Bible lies not in the book, but in the intent of those who read it.

Seeing God as a cultural expression of the superconscious answers many theological problems, not least the unease expressed in the age-old question: if

God is so powerful, why is there evil in the world? Because, as a cultural entity, He is invested with our ways, and while He is an expression of a universal force, He is also an expression of ourselves. Just as, in a universal sense, we are created in his image, in that we are formed due to universal order, His cultural expression tells us that He was also formed in our image. And therefore for as long as there is bad in humanity, there will be bad in our cultural expression of the supernatural.

The implications of this psycho-sociological approach to culture extend way beyond religion. Consider our health. We have seen how healing can be a real force of a superconscious, but through culture the superconscious defines what our reality will be. Hence, to a culture that denies healing as a property of the universe, healing is less likely to work. While healing should never be seen as an alternative to medical science – these ideas could well be wrong – the growth of alternative medicines can here be seen to be causing a possible cultural change in our reality. This allows us to offer a real test of my theories, for while we are becoming more in tune with healing, countries such as China are beginning to adopt the materialist approach of the West. Hence, if my ideas are correct, soon alternative therapies such as acupuncture will be more likely to work in Los Angeles than Shanghai.

Equally, such theories have implications for politics and society. The defining moment of the late twentieth century was an image of German youth atop the Berlin Wall, smashing it to pieces. We see this as a politico-social moment – but let us see it, instead, as a cultural 'magical' ritual. What form of 'magic' did it cause? A psychic wave of peace that was above the local politics of the world's regions. As well as freeing eastern Europe, the wave went as far as the Middle East, South Africa and Northern Ireland. It was as if a world optimism had broken out to produce a synchronistic cluster of events of global proportions.

Many would say such an idea is ridiculous. Rather, world leaders took the initiative and achieved the impossible by their skills as statesmen. They could well be right, but following the election of Tony Blair as Prime Minister of the UK on 1 May 1997 another brief psychic wave surfaced. Prior to this, the UK was experiencing the pessimism of the dying years of the Thatcher revolution, where a 'feel-good factor' was impossible to achieve. This pessimism infected everything that the UK attempted to do in a cultural sense, from continual failure in the Eurovision Song Contest, to years of deplorable sporting failures, particularly in cricket. Within days of Blair's success the UK won the Eurovision Song Contest decisively, and there was an enhancement of our sporting powers from rugby through tennis to cricket, with a marvellous First Test result.

Such synchronicity speaks volumes for the existence of an overall, cultural wave of optimism that is more than the sum of the individuals involved. Then, as Blair's 100 day honeymoon came to an end and fears grew of a recession on the horizon, these achievements waned, hinting that there could be a cultural force involved, above the skill of the sportsmen concerned.

I do not know whether the ideas in this book are truths or absolute bunkum. What I have done is to look at the subject and devise ideas that could account for phenomena within an overall psychological, sociological and historical world view. The truth or otherwise of these ideas depends upon whether they fit and whether they can be seen as rational.

Personally, I am generally sceptical of much of the paranormal, particularly in regard to some of the personalities who claim paranormal powers. But I am also open-minded enough to look at such claims in a logical light, and follow them to a natural, and hopefully logical, conclusion with theory. For instance, if we take Count Saint Germain (see pages 96–100), it is said that the logical answer is to automatically dismiss him as a charlatan. I disagree. Science and logic is a dual discipline. On the one hand, it is inquisitive to the point of defining rational theory, but on the other, it is dogmatic, in that it denies that which does not fit neatly into its world view. Taking this second factor into account, it is the heart that dismisses Saint Germain, not the logical mind, for it is illogical to ignore anything, whether it fits into the existing world view or not.

This duality of heart and mind is a definite aspect of culture, and it brings us to the core of the science/religion debate. Which train of thought is correct? Is either of them correct? The theories in this book could well provide the definitive answer, for it is correct to have a religious overview, as it is here that we find meaning and identity to satisfy the heart, but it is also correct to split the world into specialized bits in order to observe, experiment, and devise theory. This is how we advance, but neither view has an overall, philosophical credibility within culture.

Science and religion have battled for primacy for nearly five centuries now, and it is this battle that is erroneous, not either of the systems. Rather, we should see them as the new cultural yin and yang. Religion is cohesive and conservative, offering societal and moral stability, reminding us of our spirituality, which can be seen here as our overall cultural community. Science, on the other hand, is more anarchic, pulling society apart into compartments, but thrusting us forward towards advancement. They are the new mystical forces of cohesion and chaos and, as eastern mysticism has known throughout time, both forces are needed, for through their interaction we find balance.

To validate such concepts, both science and religion must come together to study the supernatural in an unbiased way. While maintaining their individual integrity, a bridgehead is required in order to analyse phenomena presently regarded as paranormal to see if their cultural power really is an existent force. For if it is, only by understanding the paranormal can mankind, our world and the universe be 'whole'.

· BIBLIOGRAPHY ·

Barrow, John, *The World Within the World* (Oxford University Press, 1988).

Bauval, Robert, *The Orion Mystery* (Heinemann, 1994).

Bohm, David, *Wholeness and the Implicate Order* (Routledge & Kegan Paul, 1980).

Bucke, R.M., *Cosmic Consciousness* (University Books, NY, 1961).

Campbell, Joseph, *The Hero with a Thousand Faces* (Paladin, 1968).

Darwin, Charles, *On The Origin of Species* (John Murray, 1859).

David, F.N., *Games, Gods and Gambling* (Collins, 1962).

Davies, Paul, *The Accidental Universe* (Cambridge University Press, 1982).

Dawkins, Richard, *The Selfish Gene* (Oxford, 1976).

– *River out of Eden* (Weidenfeld & Nicolson, 1995).

Eliade, Mircea, *Shamanism* (Pantheon, 1964).

Ellenberger, H. F., *The Discovery of the Unconscious* (Fontana, 1994, orig: 1970).

Fairley, John, and Welfare, Simon, *Arthur C. Clarke's World of Strange Powers* (Collins, 1984).

Foster, David, *The Intelligent Universe* (Abelard, 1975).

Freud, Sigmund, *The Interpretation of Dreams* (The Modern Library, 1950).

Gauquelin, Michel, *The Scientific Basis of Astrology – Myth or Reality?* (Stein and Day, 1969).

Guiley, Rosemary Ellen, *Harper's Encyclopedia of Mystical and Paranormal Experience* (Harper Collins, 1991).

Haining, Peter, *Ghosts* (Macmillan, 1975).

Hancock, Graham, *Fingerprints of the Gods* (Heinemann, 1995).

Hernstein, Richard, and Murray, Charles, *The Bell Curve* (Free Press, 1994).

Hough, Peter, *Supernatural Britain* (Piatkus, 1995).

James, William, *Varieties of Religious Experience* (New English Library, 1958).

Jerome, Lawrence E., *Astrology Disproved* (Prometheus, 1977).

Jung, C.G., *Memories, Dreams, Reflections* (Routledge & Kegan Paul, 1963).

– *Synchronicity* (Routledge & Kegan Paul, 1972).

Kardec, Allan, *The Spirits' Book* (Lake Livraria Allan Kardec Editions Ltd, 1972).

Keeton, Joe, and Petherick, Simon, *Powers of the Mind* (Robert Hale, 1987).

Koestler, Arthur, *The Roots of Coincidence* (Heinemann, 1972).

Leakey, Richard, *The Origin of Humankind* (Weidenfeld & Nicolson, 1994).

Lindbergh, Charles, *The Spirit of St Louis* (Charles Scribner's Sons, 1953).

Manning, Matthew, *The Link* (Colin Smythe, 1974).

Maslow, Abraham, *Religious Values and Peak Experiences* (State University Press, Ohio, 1962).

McLynn, Frank, *Carl Gustav Jung* (Bantam, 1996).

Neihardt, John G., *Black Elk Speaks* (Pocket Books, 1972).

North, Anthony, *The Paranormal: A Guide to the Unexplained* (Blandford, 1996).

Ouspensky, P.D., *A New Model of the Universe* (Routledge & Kegan Paul, 1931).

Penrose, Roger, *Shadows of the Mind* (Oxford University Press, 1994).

Picknett, Lynn (ed.), *Encyclopedia of the Paranormal* (Macmillan, 1990).

Playfair, Guy Lyon, *The Flying Cow* (Souvenir Press, 1975).

Price, Harry, *Fifty Years of Psychical Research* (Longman's, Green & Co, 1939).

Randles, Jenny, *Sixth Sense* (Robert Hale, 1987).

– *The Paranormal Source Book* (Piatkus, 1996).

Rhine, J.B., *Extra-Sensory Perception* (Society for Psychical Research, Boston, 1934).

Richardson, Alan, *Priestess: The Life and Magic of Dion Fortune* (The Aquarian Press, 1987).

Schmeidler, Gertrude, *ESP and Personality Patterns* (Yale, 1958).

Sheldrake, Rupert, *A New Science of Life* (Blond & Briggs, 1981).

Targ, Russell, and Puthof, Harold, *Mindreach* (Delacorte, 1977).

Thom, A., *Megalithic Lunar Observations* (Oxford University Press, 1971).

Unexplained, The (part work, Orbis, 1980–83).

Urmson, J.O., and Rée, Jonathan (eds.), *The Concise Encyclopedia of Western Philosophy and Philosophers* (Routledge, 1991).

Ward, R.H., *A Drug Taker's Notes* (Gollancz, 1957).

Watkins, Alfred, *The Old Straight Track* (Abacus, 1974, orig: 1925).

Watson, Lyall, *Beyond Supernature* (Hodder & Stoughton, 1986).

Wilson, Colin, *Mysteries* (Hodder & Stoughton, 1978).

– *Beyond the Occult* (Bantam, 1988).

Wilson, Ian, *Mind Out of Time* (Gollancz, 1981).

Wittgenstein, Ludwig, *Tractatus Logico-Philosophicus* (Routledge & Kegan Paul, 1951).

· INDEX ·